Greek Tragedies as Plays for Performance

Greek Tragedies as Plays for Performance

David Raeburn

WILEY Blackwell

This edition first published 2017
© 2017 John Wiley & Sons, Inc.

Registered Office
John Wiley & Sons, Ltd, The Atrium, Southern Gate, Chichester, West Sussex, PO19 8SQ, UK

Editorial Offices
350 Main Street, Malden, MA 02148-5020, USA
9600 Garsington Road, Oxford, OX4 2DQ, UK
The Atrium, Southern Gate, Chichester, West Sussex, PO19 8SQ, UK

For details of our global editorial offices, for customer services, and for information about how to apply for permission to reuse the copyright material in this book please see our website at www.wiley.com/wiley-blackwell.

Library of Congress Cataloging-in-Publication Data

Names: Raeburn, D. A., author.
Title: Greek tragedies as plays for performance / David Raeburn.
Description: Chicester, West Sussex; Malden, MA: John Wiley & Sons, Inc., 2016. |
    Includes bibliographical references and index.
Identifiers: LCCN 2016032959 (print) | LCCN 2016036064 (ebook) | ISBN 9781119089858 (cloth) |
    ISBN 9781119089896 (paperback) | ISBN 9781119089889 (pdf) | ISBN 9781119089933 (epub)
Subjects: LCSH: Greek drama (Tragedy)–History and criticism. | Theater–Greece–History–To 500.
Classification: LCC PA3131 .R28 2016 (print) | LCC PA3131 (ebook) | DDC 882/.0109–dc23
LC record available at https://lccn.loc.gov/2016032959

A catalogue record for this book is available from the British Library.

Cover image: Red-figure volute krater with an actor holding his mask, from Ruvo, c.410 BC (ceramic), Pronomos Painter (c.420-390 BC) / Museo Archeologico Nazionale, Naples, Italy / Bridgeman Images

Set in 10/12pt Warnock by SPi Global, Pondicherry, India
Printed in Singapore by C.O.S. Printers Pte Ltd

10 9 8 7 6 5 4 3 2 1

Figure 0.1 *Bacchae*, Cloisters, New College, Oxford 2013. Source: Reproduced by permission of the Archive of Performances of Greek & Roman Drama.

Contents

Preface   *ix*
About the Companion Website   *xi*

1   Introduction   *1*

2   Aeschylus   *15*

3   *Persae*   *21*

4   The *Oresteia*   *33*

5   Sophocles   *81*

6   *Antigone*   *87*

7   *Oedipus Tyrannus*   *105*

8   *Electra* (Sophocles)   *123*

9   Euripides   *137*

10   *Medea*   *143*

11   *Electra* (Euripides)   *157*

12   *Bacchae*   *173*

   Appendix A: Glossary of Greek Tragic Terms   *189*
   Appendix B: Rhythm and Meter   *191*

   Index   *195*

Preface

It is a remarkable fact that many of the tragedies which have survived from ancient Athens still have the power to move an audience in the theater today nearly two thousand millennia after their original performance. This is true although they were composed in a form and under conditions largely alien to the modern theater and entirely so if compared with our experience of drama in the cinema or on the television screen. One important reason for this strange phenomenon must be the universality of their themes which makes them relevant today as they were in the fifth-century BC. These plays are also powerful dramatic constructs and it greatly aids our appreciation to explore how the three great Attic tragedians set about the task of engaging and sustaining their own audience's attention, exciting emotion and stimulating thought.

For its proper understanding an ancient Greek vase demands to be viewed not only as an artefact in its own right but also as an object of its own time. Similarly, a Greek tragedy should be regarded as a play for performance, with account also taken of the medium in which it was composed, the resources that the dramatist had at his disposal, the social and historical context in which it was first produced, the subject matter on which the poet drew and the ideas which may have inspired him as an individual artist.

In this book I attempt to give an account of 10 of the 33 extant tragedies that have survived from ancient Athens in more or less complete form. My aim is to demonstrate how these plays were contrived and operated as pieces essentially composed for theatrical performance. The ten – four by Aeschylus and three by each of Sophocles and Euripides – have been chosen as they are generally considered among the very finest Greek tragedies and, in almost all cases, frequently revived today. In particular, the *Oresteia* and the two *Electra* plays complement one another in being based on the same myth and so well illustrate the differences in artistic approach between the three dramatists. As a classical scholar I have studied all these plays from various academic standpoints and have taught them to students in the original Greek. I have also engaged with them in the many live productions that I have directed with students in schools and universities, whether in the original or in translation. Some of them have been mounted in open-air spaces in which it has been possible roughly to reproduce the spatial relationships between actors, chorus and audience which would have characterized a play's performance in the ancient theatre. These productions have never aspired to reconstruct a play's original performance. Too little is known of many aspects, such as music and choreography, to make that conceivable. Nevertheless, I believe that some features of the form and style of ancient tragedy are essential to the effective communication of a classical text in the modern theater.

I hope, therefore to blend some of the insights of scholarship into Greek tragedy with the practical artistry of the theater. The aim of bridging the study and the stage in this kind of way inspired the influential Prefaces to Shakespeare, published between 1927 and 1944, by Harley Granville Barker, an actor, playwright and director who broke new ground in the presentation of Shakespeare's plays for the audiences of his time. It is in a similar spirit that I have approached my task in the exploration of my chosen Greek tragedies.

My book is intended first of all for students who may be reading these plays, whether in the original or in translation. I would encourage them to view the texts as the script for a continuous and highly structured theatrical performance and to visualise them in action, as far as possible, as they might have been performed in the theater for which they were composed. In this latter regard, I have occasionally suggested stage directions of my own, where this has posed a major problem to scholars.

I also hope that my detailed discussions of individual plays will prove of interest to a wider readership. The last fifty years or so have seen a remarkable revival in the live performance of Greek tragedy not only in schools and universities but also in the professional theater, on the cinema screen and even on television. New translations have abounded and also "acting versions" or adaptations by distinguished poets which can be regarded as new plays in their own right. The unfamiliar form of the ancient texts, however, is often baffling to new audiences or readers. My book hopes to guide this broader group of aficionados towards an understanding and fuller appreciation of this kind of drama.

If my accounts of the plays can be of value to actors and directors, as Granville Barker's Prefaces have been, then so much the better. Actors may be particularly interested in the ancient tragedians' approach to characterization, while directors may find it useful to consider how intimately content and form are interconnected in these challenging dramas. If the question that concerns them is, "How do I use this text to create my own original piece of bold and exciting theatre?" they will probably not find this book very helpful. The approach needs to be more in the spirit of an orchestral conductor studying a score prior to rehearsal, such as: "How can I best engage with the creative mind that gave birth to this ancient text, in the light of the form in which he composed it, the conditions under which it was first performed and (maybe) its own political and historical background – in order to bring it to life for a modern audience in a clear, interesting and vibrant realization?" That question, indeed, is the one with which this book is primarily concerned.

There are several whom I need to thank for their help in this enterprise. Andreas Knab attended some lectures I gave on the subject matter of this book and encouraged me to write it by transcribing my notes. Ryan Kourakis Beadle and Kresimir Vukovic between them typed up my manuscript drafts. Ben Cartlidge, Lucy Jackson, Philomen Probert and Guy Westwood joined me in doing the readings for the recordings, expertly engineered by Jamie McIntyre and financed by the New College Ludwig Fund for Humanities Research. I am also indebted to my colleagues at New College, Oxford, Jane Lightfoot and Robin Lane Fox, especially for their encouragement of the productions I have mounted with their talented students in the College Cloisters during recent years. Several of the illustrations in this book are photographs taken by Jane Lightfoot.

I dedicate the book to the memory of my late wife, Mary Faith, and to the innumerable students in schools and universities and at the Greek Summer Schools sponsored by the Joint Association of Classical Teachers, who have taken part in the many productions of Greek tragedies that I have directed. It is thanks to them that I have been able to develop the approach that I have adopted in these pages.

1

Introduction

Greek tragedy was an art form initiated in ancient Athens towards the end of the sixth century BC and developed during the fifth century BC. Although tragedies continued to be acted and composed during the fourth century and later, all that survives to us in more or less complete, as opposed to fragmentary, form consists of 33 plays, said to date from 472 to 406 BC and traditionally attributed to Aeschylus, Sophocles and Euripides.[1]

These plays have been studied and valued in later times for a variety of reasons. Most of them survived in the first place because they were selected in late antiquity or the Middle Ages as 'set books" in schools for the purpose of teaching the grammar and syntax of the ancient Greek language. Although there were occasional performances from the Renaissance onwards, they were primarily regarded as materials for pedagogic purposes or textual criticism until the early twentieth century, when interest in them as major works of drama became established among a wider public. In due course this inspired a plethora of new translations or original plays based on them. Scholars have explored their stagecraft as well as their literary qualities. Much recent work has examined the plays as socio-historic documents which help to illuminate the period in which they were composed on general issues such as group identity, gender and class. Finally, the last century has seen an unprecedented rise of public interest in those ancient texts as plays for performance on stage by professional or amateur actors.

The aim of this book is to focus on four tragedies of Aeschylus, three of Sophocles and three of Euripides, exploring each play on its own in terms of its original status as a theatrical arte-fact. I try to show how these ten texts "work" as drama and, more specifically, how the three great poets used the characteristic *form* of the Greek tragic genre to create dramatic sequences that would engage and hold their audiences' attention and stir their emotions in the theater, while at the same time encouraging them to reflect on matters of profound importance. This introductory chapter attempts to define the ancient poet's task in terms of this form, the social context in which the plays were composed to be presented, and the human and other resources that were available at the time. All these factors dictated their composition and are important to their consideration as works of art.

Greek Tragedy as a Genre

"Greek tragedy is a hybrid form, and the different parts of the drama are differentiated in form and style" (Rutherford 2012, 29). All our surviving plays follow a standard pattern, a sequence of discrete sections akin to the "movements" of a classical symphony or the "numbers" of an

Greek Tragedies as Plays for Performance, First Edition. David Raeburn.
© 2017 John Wiley & Sons, Inc. Published 2017 by John Wiley & Sons, Inc.
Companion website: www.wiley.com/go/raeburn

eighteenth century oratorio and in modern music theater. Put as its simplest, these movements alternate between spoken "episodes" (scenes) for one to three solo actors and "odes" (songs) performed by a chorus. The normal meter for the former is the iambic trimeter, while the latter are delivered in a variety of so-called lyric meters. Variations on this pattern are mentioned later but it is enough at this point to note the hybrid character of Greek tragedy and the particular challenge that it presented to the ancient dramatist in creating a continuity in unfolding his story on stage to his audience in a compelling and satisfying way. To understand how these plays "work" as drama, we need to analyse the "structure of feeling," the controlled *sequence* of emotional responses implicit in this basic alternation of movements for chorus and solo actors and to observe how these two disparate elements are united in the individual texts.

This peculiar form calls for some explanation. Here we have European drama in its infancy and we need to ask how it came about. Unfortunately, the detailed evidence for the origins of Greek tragedy is difficult and obscure; we can never be entirely sure how or when it began, and this book is not the place to argue a problematic issue.[2] Tragedies were certainly being performed at Athens by the end of the sixth century and we have the firm date of 472 BC for our first surviving example of the genre, Aeschylus' *Persae.* An answer to the question, "How did Greek tragedy take the hybrid form that it did?" may be more easily sought if we briefly examine the performance genres which existed in Greece earlier in the sixth century.

The ancestor of the tragic chorus is surely to be found in the so-called genre of "choral lyric," that is the performance of cult poetry sung and danced by a choir to the accompaniment of the lyre or other musical instrument. These performances were originally "sacral," religious acts offered in honour of gods or heroes in the hope of blessings for the local community. Examples would include the "paean" performed in honour of Apollo, or the "dithyramb" which was associated particularly with Dionysus, the god of wine and (later) of the dramatic festivals at Athens. Subsequently, choral lyric could be essentially secular, as in the *epinikion*, a hymn celebrating the victory of an athlete in one of the great inter-state festivals like the Olympics, an art perfected in the fifth century by the poet Pindar. The whole genre evidently goes back to the seventh century and was mainly developed in the southern part of Greece, the Peloponnese, not so much in Athens itself, though an Attic vase dated to 560–50 BC[3] offers evidence for pre-dramatic performances by a chorus of satyrs, who were always associated with the worship of Dionysus. It is significant that the choral songs of Attic tragedy adopt certain features of the Doric dialect which was spoken in some cities of the Peloponnese.

The other performance art from which Greek tragedy fairly obviously derives was the public recitation of epic verse by professionals known as "rhapsodes." By 514 at the latest, and very possibly earlier, competitions in the recitation of Homeric verse were held in Athens at the Great Panathenaea, the quadrennial festival in honour of the city's patron goddess Athena, alongside contests in athletic and equestrian events. The *Iliad* and *Odyssey* themselves derive from a tradition of oral recitation in a preliterate culture and make perfect performance poetry in their combination of third-person narrative and speeches, often quite long, that are put into the mouths of the various characters. Epic poetry would doubtless have demanded the kind of projection of voice and personality that was associated with acting or any form of public speaking; it must also have included an element of impersonation in the delivery of the speeches. The rhapsodic contests can thus be seen as leading naturally into tragedy, in which a story was presented by masked actors individually impersonating a variety of characters, with the narrative element covered by more nondescript "messengers," through whom the audience could learn, by ear, of such events in the story as could not convincingly be enacted before their eyes.

If tragedy starts with a chorus and a messenger, it is not difficult to regard the tragic contests at Athens as entailing a marriage between two pre-existing art forms, choral lyric and epic recitation. These contests were an important feature of the City Dionysia, the annual festival in honour of Dionysus, which may have been inaugurated in its earliest form by the tyrant Pisistratus in about 534 – though scholars debate the dating of the various additions which led to the festival as it became in the Periclean age, during the second half of the fifth century, when the art of tragedy had grown to maturity. There was a tradition in ancient times that credited a certain Thespis with the idea of introducing a solo actor (himself), perhaps by detaching the leader of a lyric chorus and getting him to deliver long speeches in response to questions put to him by the chorus. This would fit the Greek word for an actor, *hypocrites*, usually understood as meaning "answerer." Thespis is also supposed to have disguised himself, a crucial innovation which leads to drama as we understand it, and to have worn stylized makeup or a linen mask.

For all these uncertainties, when it comes to our first surviving tragedy, the *Persae* of Aeschylus, we find a sequence of long movements for the Chorus of Persian Elders, punctuated by other movements, including a central Messenger scene, which involve one or two solo actors who make their entrances and exits at various points in the drama. That the chorus was initially thought of as the primary element is suggested by the term *epeisodion*, meaning "insertion," which was later used as the formal description of the intervening scenes for solo actors and gives us our own word "episode."

The Social Context

Before we can fully understand how the individual plays work as drama, it is important to consider the various external factors which will have shaped the poet's composition. First of all is the social context in which the plays were first performed at Athens.

Tragedies during the fifth century were designed for presentation at the City Dionysia, the festival of Dionysus at Athens, which was held over five or six days in late March when the seas were navigable and the city full of visitors after the winter.[4] A preliminary procession brought the image of Dionysus to his theater, which was situated on the south slope of the Acropolis; and this was followed on the next day by another, very grand, procession to the sacred precinct adjacent to the theater, where animals were sacrificed and bloodless offerings made. During the Peloponnesian war, at some point before the performance of tragedies, the sons of citizens killed in battle were paraded in full armor in the theater, as was the tribute brought by Athens' subject allies. Tragedies were also performed at another festival, the Lenaea, of which we know much less.

The dramatic performances took place over the next three or four days. Three tragedians competed, each with three tragedies and a satyr play, an altogether lighter affair, which involved a chorus of equine satyrs and so brought the poet's entry to a more specifically "Dionysiac" climax. Contests in comedy were added in about 486 and room in the program was found for five of these plays too. From the late sixth century each of the ten tribes had contributed choruses, one of men and another of boys, for contests in the dithyramb, a choral song in honour of Dionysus. With all this fitted into such a short spell of time, the days must have been extremely long and the demands on the audience's concentration phenomenal.

The three poets chosen to compete in the tragic contests were selected by a leading state official, the eponymous archon. Each poet was his own director, composer and choreographer;

he could also be the leading actor. Central to the festival organization was the *chorêgia*, a form of service performed for the city-state by a wealthy citizen. The chorêgos funded the chorus and was like a modern "producer" in that he was responsible for recruitment, training, maintenance and costuming of a chorus for one of the various competitions. Just as prizes were awarded to the competing poets and, later on, to the leading actors, the chorêgos stood to win an ivory crown and high prestige for what the judges decided had been the most successful production. The actors themselves were funded by the state.

We need to remember two important implications of this account. First, tragedies were, in principle, composed for a single performance at a festival that included elements of religious and civic activity besides work in other genres. There was no question of "taking tickets" for a convenient date during a run. Second, for many people, tragedy was art very much for glory's sake.

The Theatrical Space

When studying Greek tragedies it is important to visualize them as they might originally have been performed. A certain amount can be validly inferred from the text, though much of the detail is speculative.

Scholars debate the precise details of the theatrical space for which our surviving plays were composed. The Theater of Dionysus, which can be visited today, with its stone seating, reflects a late fourth-century reconstruction. However, we may fairly assume that earlier spectators sat on wooden benches rising up in a tiered horseshoe over the hillside at the foot of the Acropolis. This audience area, the *theatron*, surrounded a central performance area, probably circular,[5] of about 24 meters in diameter and known as the *orchêstra* or dancing-floor. Entrances and exits for the chorus and actors were initially down passages at each side of the *theatron*, called *eisodoi* and these could be used to suggest two different offstage locations (e.g. city and shore).

At some point a wooden stage-building, the *skênê*, was introduced, to back the *orchêstra* along the side that was unoccupied by the spectators. I believe that this was probably fronted by a slightly raised platform with perhaps three steps leading down from it, though some scholars dispute its existence.[6] The structure, once introduced, certainly provided a central upstage entrance through a double doorway and was normally used to represent a house, palace or other building, though other locations came to be indicated by painted panels applied to the building's façade.

We know of two stage devices: a low trolley on wheels, the *ekkyklêma*, which could be rolled out of the central doorway with a tableau usually understood to represent what was going on indoors; and some kind of crane, the *mêchanê*, which allowed actors, usually playing gods (the deus ex machina), to appear above the *skênê* roof.

Such was the spacious open-air setting, with a distance of over 100 meters from the central doorway to the furthest spectator, for which our tragedies were planned. It was very different from our smaller-scale indoor theaters with their proscenium arches, curtains and artificial lighting which can be skillfully used for emphasis and atmosphere.

The Audience

The Theater of Dionysus was able to accommodate an audience of perhaps 15,000, a size that reflected the character of the occasion and, in principle, involved the whole male citizen body of Athens. Whether women attended is another matter of scholarly debate. Some think they did, but in a separate area. Many roles and choruses in the plays were female, but all the performers were male and the plays themselves seem to be essentially oriented towards men, even where they suggest some sympathy with women's feelings and points of view. Men could well have attended the theater in a spirit of democratic participation, much as they attended political assemblies. Certainly there will have been a degree of partisanship in the audience in favor or otherwise of the poets, actors and chorêgoi involved. Given the festival context and the large theater, the atmosphere could well have been more akin to that of a modern football match than to an ordinary theater visit today.

Actors, Chorus and Others

We now move on to the human resources that the dramatist had at his disposal. By the middle of the fifth century, the single "actor," often the poet himself, had grown to three professionals who divided all the roles in the play between them. This was achieved by changes to the actors' costumes and masks, which could easily be effected inside the stage building. Actors were supplemented by an unlimited number of non-speaking extras, "dumb masks" as they were called.

The chorus in Aeschylus' time numbered twelve and Sophocles raised this to fifteen (*Vit. Soph.* 4) – why we can only guess. Perhaps the larger number offered greater choreographic possibilities; the poet was his own composer and choreographer as well as the script-writer. In the fifth century members of the chorus were representatives of the citizen body who needed to be trained, except, probably, for their leader, the *koryphaios* ("head man") who delivered short speeches of his own during the episodes and could engage in dialogue with a soloist.

Modern drama has no equivalent for the chorus and it is often seen by directors as a "problem" when it comes to revivals of Greek tragedy. The choral songs, however, are as integral to the tragic composition as the Hallelujah Chorus is to Handel's *Messiah*. Literary study of the ancient genre naturally encourages a wish to advance theories about the chorus as representing the "ideal spectator" or "the common man," but these are of limited value. The chorus in each play has its own collective identity as elders, local maidens or whatever, which comes in and out of focus as they are involved in the play's main action or detached from it. It is probably better to see the chorus as one instrument or resource which the playwrights used in different ways in the dramatic continuum. All one might usefully say in generalization is that the chorus, through its collective nature and its proximity to the audience in the *orchêstra*, serves as a kind of intermediary between actors and spectators. Often, though not always, it operates as a guide to the audience's responses and sympathies as the action proceeds. This applies not only to the choral songs but also to the iambic interventions of the coryphaeus during the episodes.

Properties, Costumes and Masks

Props abounded in Athenian comedy but in tragedy the texts suggest that they were used very economically, unless they were in effect part of a costume, such as staves carried by old men. They normally have a particular significance in the dramaturgy which goes beyond their immediate function (Taplin 1978, 77). Avoidance of the purely adventitious seems to be an important aspect of the Greek tragic aesthetic.

The iconography of costumes in vase painting suggests that the actors wore very richly decorated dresses with fitted sleeves in a stylization and formality appropriate to a grand occasion.[7] Euripides may have gone in for greater realism, to judge from a scene in

Aristophanes' *Acharnians*. The high-heeled boots, *kothurnoi* or buskins, which are sometimes associated with Greek tragedy, did not come in till a great deal later.

Masks and their implications demand slightly longer discussion. They were essentially the device which allowed multiple impersonation and clearly defined the face of a character within the large theatrical space. With the attachment of wigs, they enabled an actor to combine male and female, old and young, characters within a single performance. In the fifth century they do not seem to have used the standardized tragic mask with downturned mouth that featured in later theater. It looks rather as if they were essentially designed to identify the actor's character and, if made of linen, to fit the outline of his face.

How far the mask had, beyond this, a kind of religious mystique and whether the actor developed a kind of "relationship" with his mask that affected his performance are matters of speculation. It is clear that nothing like our modern notion of "casting" can have applied. Whatever illusions may be open to today's actor through makeup, we still take account of facial type along with other factors such as age, sex, height, physical build or other less definable personality traits in the allocation of roles.

Acting Style and Characterization

Masking obviously requires the actor to use his hands and body expressively. It is unlikely, however, that the acting style in the Greek theater involved the kind of sign language characteristic of Japanese classical acting. Greek poetry and art, despite the formal features that distinguish the different genres, retain a compelling naturalness, which suggests that actors, though performing expansively in a large public space, will not have followed a stereotyped body language, except in ritual actions like supplication or gestures of prayer. More likely, they will have taken their inspiration from the immediate requirements of impersonation within the specific dramatic context. Paramount for the actor would have been his skill in vocal projection and expressive delivery of the verses composed for him by the poet.

An actor attempting to interpret a Greek tragic role today will need to forget all he or she has learned about Stanislavsky and subtexts or Freud and the subconscious. That said, it is possible to overemphasize the "alienness" of Greek tragedy, as exemplified particularly in the mask convention. Some modern scholars have argued that the ancient poets were not interested in characterization as such. But stylization does not imply the absence or distortion of human truth. Homeric epic is highly stylized in its language and poetic rhythm, but what makes the *Odyssey* and the *Iliad* immortal is their basic humanity. Similarly the dramatis personae of Greek tragedy can still be seen as real people acting recognizably in recognizable human situations. I aim to show how the poets, while not attempting fully rounded portraits of their characters, did point up those details of characterization that were relevant to their specific artistic purposes.

The Sound and Rhythm of Greek Tragedy

Nothing differentiates the two elements of the hybrid art form more than the meters that give them their characteristic pulse and musical movement. The solo actors in the episodes spoke expressively, for the most part either in formal, often very long, speeches termed *rheseis* or in the line-for-line dialogue known as *stichomythia*. These were composed from the outset largely in iambic trimeters, less commonly in trochaic tetrameters, rather than the dactylic hexameter of the epic poems.[8] Iambs and trochees involve the separation of long syllables by single shorts, where dactyls consist essentially of one long followed by two shorts. The iambic meter had been used earlier, in the seventh century, by the Ionic poet Archilochus of Paros for verse of a satirical character and had been taken up in Athens in the sixth century by the statesman Solon for the poetic expression of more serious moral or political ideas. Aristotle (*Poetics* 1449a) considered it the meter best suited to normal speech. It is thus ideal for the colloquial verse found in Aristophanes' comedies, but the tragic poets also found it an excellent medium for more formal speeches and dialogue.

Choral passages, on the other hand, were *sung* to "lyric" meters and composed in more complex rhythmical phrases called *cola* (limbs) which involved the separation of long syllables by *either* one *or* two short syllables. Cola were formed into stanzas or *strophes* (turns) corresponding in principle to complete choreographic sequences. Strophes often end in cadences and it was normal for them to be replicated in *antistrophes* which repeated the syllable patterns of the different cola precisely or almost precisely. This symmetry was sometimes crowned in a triadic structure by a freestanding *epode* consisting usually of similar, but occasionally of contrasting, metrical phrases.

Apart from these two main types of delivery, in moments of particular pathos or excitement, solo actors could be called upon to sing either in exchange with the chorus in what was known as an *amoibaion* or *kommos*, lament, or else in freestanding monodies. The movements for soloist and chorus together were a special feature and are often high spots in the drama when performed. Another interesting exchange is also found, the *epirrhema* in which choral singing is contrasted with solo speaking or vice versa. It seems that the evidence is not there to describe what the vocal delivery of all the various sung sections was like; but the importance of singing in ancient Greek culture and the training which actors underwent (see Hall 2002, 22–3) suggest that it might have been a little like modern opera singing.

Common to both chorus and soloists was the use of the anapaestic meter, which serves as a kind of halfway house between the more heightened language and emotional registers of lyric and the less lofty one of iambic. Anapaests are often used to cover transitions, but Aeschylus used them importantly for choral entrance marches and other significant moments.

Music played a crucial part in the differentiation between these three "modes of utterance." The sung lyrics were accompanied onstage not, as originally, by the lyre but the *aulos*, an instrument described in the next section, which sounded rather like an oboe. Iambics were not accompanied, but anapaests probably were. The delivery of the latter was probably closer to speech than to song[9] as a rule, with the rhythm more sharply defined than in the more fluid spoken iambic verse. Sometimes, though, anapaests contain a patina of Doric vowels, like the choral lyrics, which suggest that such passages would have been *sung* in carefully defined rhythm.[10]

We can thus see an art form emerging in the hybrid which offered considerable scope for variety and contrast in the *sound* of its performance. The comparison with the classical symphony or eighteenth century opera or oratorio is useful; but the movements of Greek tragedy are more obviously discrete because of the three distinctive vocal and musical registers. (For access to an oral demonstration of these, see section "Recordings".) It was the dramatist's task to weld these disparate elements in their plays into a calculated and unified sequence and with a continuity which gave a good shape to their drama and so to its impact on the audience in the theater.

Music

Music was an essential ingredient in the tragic recipe and I have already indicated its importance in describing the three "modes of utterance." It is difficult to assess the part it would have played by itself in the drama's total impact. It would appear that, when it came to selecting poets to be allotted choruses for the tragic festivals, skill in music was a less important criterion than poetic, rhetorical and dramatic talent (West 1992, 351).

The chorus and the soloists in their lyric movements sang to the accompaniment of the *aulos*, an instrument consisting of a pair of pipes with finger holes and a double-reed mouthpiece strapped to the player's face. The performer, known as the *aulêtês*, was an important member of the artistic team, who is thought to have led the chorus into the *orchêstra* on its first entrance and out of it at the end of the play. He would have been important in conducting the chorus through their odes, probably providing introductions to get them into position and short interludes between the strophes. He would have helped the all-important leader in holding the weaker brethren together (Wilson 2002, 39–55).

The sound of the *aulos* was a penetrating one, more like that of an oboe than the flute with which it used to be commonly identified. It was widely used in a variety of other, non-theatrical contexts and noted for its ability to express and arouse a range of different emotions, from calmness to orgiastic frenzy, through the use of different "modes" or scales with a characteristic series of intervals. That instrument will certainly have contributed to the effect of the sung lyrics and spoken anapaests; and the audience will have expected it much, I imagine, as a modern church congregation expects hymns to be accompanied by an organ. Given the importance and poetic quality of the words in Greek tragic odes, one must suppose that it would have part of the aulete's art to ensure that his accompaniment reinforced rather than detracted from the audience's concentration on the poet's text and its meaning.

Though the *aulos* was tragedy's primary instrument, other instruments were evidently used for incidental purposes. Some kind of drum certainly features in Euripides *Bacchae*.

With regard to the singing itself, the melodic score, presumably replicated by the *aulos*, for the tragedies we possess is virtually lost to us.[11] It was evidently based on the "enharmonic" scale which had only a small range of notes (West 1992, 351). It seems likely, though far from certain, that the melodies sung by the chorus and solo singers were influenced by the natural pitch of the words as they were sounded with the "tonic" accents, which itself provides a kind of tune of its own.[12] If this was the case, we should have to assume that the strophic pairs corresponded metrically but melodically only within the limited range of notes in the adopted musical scale or "mode."[13]

We are able, however, by metrical analysis, to recover or at least to offer a reasonable interpretation of the rhythmical score of the lyrics in Greek tragedy. It is indeed its complexity and excitement that leads me to believe that rhythm counted for more than melody in the musical impact of the odes. When these are delivered aloud in the original Greek, there can be no questioning their emotive value. An important, very possibly, the chief dimension of Greek tragedy's music *does* survive in the lyric meters, and the poet's deployment of these is an essential aspect to consider in the examination of individual tragedies as plays. The recordings accompanying this volume attempt to illustrate the effect of these rhythms as deployed in particular dramatic contexts (see also Appendix B).

Choreography

We are even more in the dark when it comes to the "dancing" element in Greek tragedy. Dance was, of course, pervasive in ancient Greek culture, and there is some general evidence that the choreography of tragedy involved stylized mime in the form of rhythmical gestures and derived some inspiration from the poses adopted in sculpture (Pickard-Cambridge 1968, 246–7). Can we go further than this in determining what the movement and gesture of the tragic chorus was like and also how crucial it was?

There have been a number of theoretical attempts to describe "Greek Dancing" (Ley 2007, 150–65), but none seem to accommodate the variety of identities among the tragic choruses. We should surely *expect* the Elders of Argos with their staves in the *Agamemnon* to move in a very different way from the Furies in the *Eumenides*. This might be confirmed by the contrast between two vase-paintings which show groups standing with an aulete and so demonstrably members of a chorus: the one of bearded men in a stationary position, the other of dancing girls.[14] It certainly seems a reasonable supposition that dancing in the Greek theater was not always what we understand by ballet but could sometimes have simply amounted to stately, processional movement.

There are other questions to which we should like answers. Did choruses move and gesticulate throughout an ode, or could some (or even all) of a song be essentially static? Did the choreography of strophe and antistrophe always mirror one another, even when there was a marked change in the context or argument of the latter? We can only guess at the answers to these questions on the basis of a priori aesthetic assumptions. One criterion must surely be whether movement would have enhanced or detracted from the audience's attention to the poetic content of the text.

I base my own intuition on many attempts to realize the choruses of Greek tragedy in live production for modern audience in ancient-type spaces. This experience, for what it is worth, suggests to me the following: the Attic poets did not choreograph their plays to set rules or formulae but used movement, significant gesture and also stillness as was appropriate to the corporate identity of the chorus of a particular play, the function and mood of individual odes in the dramatic sequence and the content or imagery of the words being sung. I doubt whether particular steps were entailed in the different meters, but it would obviously be natural for conventional ritual gestures to be used in prayers, lamentations and so on, as they were normally formalized in non-theatrical contexts. My own view is that choreography, like the musical accompaniment, was essentially subordinate to the text, not dancing for dancing's sake.

Summary on Performance

What is certain is that the ancient experience of drama could not be more different from our own experience of it before our television screens today. In Greek tragedy we find plays composed in a strange form and a complex verse medium, designed for performance by daylight in a very large space and in a very public context, and acted by professionals whose faces were visible only in the single expression on their masks. By contrast we are regularly presented today with drama scripted in naturalistic prose dialogue, watched in the privacy of our homes with the aid of electricity. We are invited to observe and identify with fictitious people who are very highly characterized in appearance, personality and motivation, seen within the limited space of a screen, often in close-up, which allows the slightest movement of the actor's face to speak volumes.

What is a Tragedy?

Did the ancient tragedies entertain a clear concept of "the tragic"? The term "tragedy" is dear to literary theorists and great play is made with it. The Greek word *tragoidia* simply means a "goat-song," which may have originally meant a song sung in a competition where a goat is the prize, though nobody really knows. At Athens "tragedy" was distinguished from "comedy" as representing any play which qualified for performance in a tragic contest. Where comedy in the fifth century amounted to contemporary political or social satire of a boisterous and bawdy kind, tragedy was usually more solemn in its narration of exciting stories based on the heroic past. But this story did not *have* to end unhappily or even to inspire tears rather than laughter. Euripides' *Ion*, for example, though classified as a tragedy, is much closer to what we understand as comedy.

Aristotle's famous doctrine of *katharsis*, whether understood as "purgation" or "purification," is an important early attempt to explain tragedy's emotional impact and to consider why the spectacle of suffering should give pleasure. The doctrine must be, at least in part, a response to Plato's puritanical view of poetry as wicked and bad because it was removed from reality and encouraged people, particularly actors, to be hysterical and uncontrolled. As regards the subject matter of tragedy Aristotle simply says that it is a "representation of an action that is *serious*," and that for a definition fits most of the surviving dramas. The notion of the "tragic hero" who comes to grief through a "tragic flaw" of character is based on a misunderstanding of Aristotle and is not applicable to many Greek tragedies. It may, however, be useful to think of tragedy as involving a *pathos*, some kind of identifiable suffering, whether of individuals or humanity generally. The emotions which this is said to arouse are, typically, "pity" and "fear;" and these correspond well with our own notions of identification with the characters and sympathy with them in the thought that "this could happen to me." Even so, theory is not always helpful and it may be better, in the first instance, to examine and interpret the plays individually in their own terms.

Form, Content and Meaning

With these perspectives on the form of tragedy and the theatrical medium within which the ancient dramatist operated, we can briefly explore the subject matter of Greek tragedy and the general question of "meaning" or "artistic purpose," beyond mere entertainment, which lay behind the craftsmanship of the individual plays which we shall be examining.

Like the Homeric rhapsodes, the tragic poets based their plots on myths drawn from the heroic past. These myths would have been familiar in broad outline to their audiences, either from the *Iliad* and *Odyssey*, the so-called "epic cycle" or other sources such as choral lyric. The details, though, were never constant and the dramatist was free to elaborate or vary them as he wished, to accord with the line he was taking on the story and its meaning as he perceived it. The Greek mind liked to see the particular in relation to the general, a respect in which the tragedian would be following the tradition of choral lyric, which often included an appropriate myth and also contained a "gnomic" element, the statement of moral truth by way of warning or instruction. Similarly, the tragic poet was not simply a scriptwriter for popular entertainment. In the context of the religious and civic festival he was there to *teach* his fellow citizens and communicate some kind of "message," whether of contemporary or universal relevance. Aristophanes in his *Frogs* makes Dionysus bring back Aeschylus from the underworld as the best poet to save the city in a time of crisis. Though a flight of comic fancy, this must be based on the way in which poets, both tragic and comic, were conceived as existing to benefit society.

Some plays reinforce the values of the Athenian *polis*, the city-state, others may challenge them.[15] Others again may be felt to affirm the famous Delphic maxims of "Know yourself" and "Nothing in excess." In the development of empire and the flowering of civilized art of different kinds which characterized fifth century Athens, there was always the temptation for some to forget their limitations as human beings and to fly too high.

At this point we come to another dimension, essential to the context and understanding of Greek tragedy: the part played by the gods. Greek religion had no "church" or dogma enshrined in sacred texts, and so each of the three tragic poets with whom we are concerned approached and interpreted the gods in a different way. But the gods are always there in the plays, just as they were worshipped in the fifth century and later in the rituals that attended all the festivals and other events in the state or inter-state calendar and innumerable aspects of everyday life. The significance of the gods and their relationship with men in the plays become clearer in the dramatic analyses that are the main substance of this book.

Tragedy therefore contains a great deal of profound human, political, philosophical and even theological interest and it is proper to ask what the poets were trying to "say" or "put across" in their particular plays. "Authorial intention," though, is problematic for some who take the view that what an author first "meant" is neither recoverable or of any importance. I would myself maintain that the inherited text of a Greek tragedy remains a constant, as is the musical score of an opera or a symphony. Despite many centuries of transmission, it is still possible to feel that most of the tragic texts are coherent, satisfying and original unities which communicate a powerful impression of a clear artistic purpose. If we can locate them in the context of their historical period and of what we know about the society and poetic traditions in which they were composed, a reasonable stab can be made at establishing the preoccupations which inspired their authors. Modern performances may fairly be compared for their fidelity to those original preoccupations as for their theatrical effectiveness.

Play Analyses

The method followed, therefore, with the individual plays explored in this book is first to set the texts in the context of their own time and then to suggest a possible "meaning" which underlies the analysis of the drama's shaping in an effective sequence. I then attempt a blow-by-blow account of what "happens" in the play in terms of Greek tragedy's characteristic form and the resources at each poet's disposal. This is done poet by poet and in chronological order, as far as dates can be established. I aim to show the function of each movement within the dramatic sequence as a whole and would strongly encourage the reader to follow the play in the Greek text or a translation as the analysis proceeds. A brief synopsis of each play is given rather than a fully detailed account and the dramatic analysis is also preceded by notes on historical background, where needed, and on the play's dramaturgy generally. Analyses may include some discussion of problems relating to the staging of the plays in the ancient theater, but we can never reconstruct the original staging of any play in full detail. That said, I would re-emphasize the importance of visualising a play's action in imagination as far as it is possible. This will greatly enhance our understanding and appreciation of a text for what it is: the notes or "score" for a sequence of significant sounds and bodily movements which constitute the essential substance of a play.

The main substance of my discussions is very closely tied to the text of the plays and the best value will be obtained if they can be read in conjunction with a full text, whether in the original or in a translation. Line references are to the Loeb edition which prints the original Greek with a sound English translation in parallel. With the wide readership I have outlined in mind, all quotations are in English, usually my own. In the spelling of Greek names I have, as a rule, preferred the conventional latinized forms to direct transliterations, for example, Aegisthus and Bacchae rather than Aigisthos and Bakkhai.

Structural Terminology

The analysis of most plays in this book follows the traditional terminology derived from Aristotle (*Poetics* 1452b) in establishing a template for all tragedy. It has the merit of drawing attention to the primacy of the Chorus and applies well to most tragedies. Some modern scholars (e.g. Taplin), prefer to divide the plays into acts and act-dividing songs.

Aristotle called the opening scene a *prologos*, "before-word," that is what is said before the entry of the chorus, whose entrance song is termed *parodos*. The action after that consists essentially of scenes for solo actors alternating in regular succession with choral songs. We call the former "episodes," from the Greek *epeisodion*, meaning "insertion", that is. a movement which falls between two choral songs or *stasima*. A *stasimon* is understood as a movement for the chorus when they are in *stasis*, the station that they have taken up after the Parodos. This alternation continues until the closing scene called the *exodos*, which concludes with the exit of the chorus. For the terminology of movements for chorus with soloist together (*kommos, amoibaion, epirrhema*), see Appendix A.

Recordings

The recordings of selected extracts from the ten plays form an integral part of this publication and I hope that readers will wish to listen to these as their study of each play proceeds. Their purpose is to show how sound and rhythm contribute in an important way to the drama's movement and continuity, and the analyses regularly refer to the rhythms of the choral meters. Discussion here inevitably becomes rather technical and readers may wish to listen to Track 0 ◉ for a talk introducing the meters associated with the three different "modes of utterance" (p. 7), This is intended to complement Appendix B in which I attempt to offer a simple written elucidation of lyric structure and the various metrical patterns involved. Any who find themselves deterred by talk of "syncopated iambic trimeters" or "dactylo-epitrites" in the play analyses are urged to skip those parts of the book and to move on.

I would, nevertheless, encourage them to listen to the recordings, even if the language is "all Greek" to them, so that they can experience the musicality of the poetry for the emotional effect of the rhythm in its dramatic context. There is pleasure to be gained from the sound of ancient Greek in itself and, where tragedy is concerned, this is an important aspect of the drama which no translation can adequately reproduce.

Apart from the choral movements, some extracts have been included from the long iambic speeches, particularly messenger narratives, from stichomythic dialogue and also the fine exchanges between soloists and chorus. All passages are flagged up with a line reference and a serial number for listening to electronically at the appropriate point in the discussion of each play.

The pronunciation of ancient Greek follows the recommendations of Allen (1987). The readers have attempted, though not with total consistency, to follow the "tune" suggested by the "tonic" accentuation (see note 12) and to exploit the expressive power implicit in the music of the words. The text of the tracks generally follows that of the latest Loeb edition, so that they can be followed in the translation, but I have used my own discretion in the conjectural restoration of corrupt passages to preserve rhythm with some degree of sense.

Notes

1 *Prometheus Bound* is now widely thought not to be by Aeschylus but the work of an unknown dramatist of the next generation. *Rhesus* is very probably a product of the early fourth century rather than the work of Euripides.
2 A very good account is available in *The Cambridge History of Classical Literature*, Vol. 1, Part 2, Chapter 1.1.
3 Amsterdam, Allard Pearson Museum 3356.
4 The article on "Tragedy (Greek)" (by Richard Seaford) in *The Oxford Classical Dictionary* supplies the essential information.
5 Some other early theaters (e.g. at Thorikos), had an orchestra which was more rectangular, no doubt for topographical reasons. For a helpful discussion, see Wiles (1997, 46–52).
6 In favor of the platform Arnott (1965, 34–5); against Rehm (1992, 34–5). See also Taplin (1977, 441–2).
7 The evidence par excellence for this (and for masks too) is the famous Pronomos vase in the Museo Archaeologico Nazionale at Naples, H3240.
8 For the technical descriptions see Appendix B.
9 Scholars often use the terms "chanting" or "recitative" to describe this intermediary style of delivery, but these are more suggestive of singing than speaking. The German "sprachgesang" is possibly more useful.
10 The term used for them is "lyric anapaests."
11 All we possess in a papyrus fragment for a passage from Euripides *Orestes*, which derives from a period late in the fifth century when music was becoming more experimental and therefore atypical of the genre as we otherwise know it, certainly in Aeschylus and Sophocles.
12 Ancient Greek was radically different from modern in having no *stress* accent. The accent is one of *pitch*, on the basic principle that one syllable in a word is sounded higher than other syllables in the same word. The circumflex accent differs from the acute in having a double note (a higher and a lower) and often presents an actor with special expressive possibilities.

13 In this, as in other aspects of this section, I have profited greatly from discussions with Prof. Armand d'Angour.

14 National Museum of Denmark, Copenhagen 13817, dated 430–420 BC; and British Museum, London 11856, 1213.1 (E467), dated 475–450.

15 A tendency today is to see tragedy as serving an essential "function" within the Athenian polis. Some plays do indeed raise questions of political importance, but many do not.

References

Allen, W.S. 1987. *Vox Graeca*. 3rd edn, Cambridge: Cambridge University Press.

Arnott, Peter, D. 1965. *Introduction to Greek Theatre*. London: Macmillan.

Hall, Edith. 2002. "The Singing Actors of Antiquity," in *Greek and Roman Actors*, edited by Pat Easterling and Edith Hall. Cambridge: Cambridge University Press.

Ley, Graham. 2007. *The Theatricality of Greek Tragedy*. Chicago: Chicago University Press.

Pickard-Cambridge, A. 1968. *The Theatre of Dionysus at Athens*, 2nd edn, revised by J. Gould and D.M. Lewis. Oxford: Clarendon Press.

Rehm, Rush. 1992. *Greek Tragic Theatre*. London: Routledge.

Rutherford, R.B. 2012. *Greek Tragic Style*. Oxford: Oxford University Press.

Taplin, Oliver. 1978. *Greek Tragedy in Action*. London: Methuen.

Taplin, Oliver. 1977. *The Stagecraft of Aeschylus: the Dramatic Use of Entrances and Exits in Greek Tragedy*. Oxford: Clarendon Press.

West, M.L. 1992. *Greek Music*. Cambridge: Cambridge University Press.

Wiles, David. 1997. *Tragedy at Athens*. Cambridge: Cambridge University Press.

Wilson, Peter. 2002. "The Musicians Among the Actors," in *Greek and Roman Actors*, edited by Pat Easterling and Edith Hall. Cambridge: Cambridge University Press.

Further Reading

Hall, Edith. 2010. *Greek Tragedy: Suffering Under the Sun*. Oxford: Oxford University Press. A modern exploration of the genre with short accounts of all the plays and an extensive bibliography.

Pickard-Cambridge, A. 1968. *The Theatre of Dionysus at Athens*. 2nd edn, revised by J. Gould and D.M. Lewis. Oxford: Clarendon Press The standard work of reference with all the evidence documented.

Rehm, R. 1992. *Greek Tragic Theatre*. London: Routledge. A very good general introduction to the tragic genre, with accounts of some plays.

Rutherford, R.B. 2012. *Greek Tragic Style*. Oxford: Oxford University Press. An outstanding analysis of the genre in its component parts for the more advanced student who can read the texts in the original.

Storey, Ian, C. and Allen, Arlene. 2014. *A Guide to Ancient Greek Drama*, 2nd edn. Boston, MA: Wiley-Blackwell. Another very useful work for general reference.

Taplin, Oliver. 1978. *Greek Tragedy in Action*. London: Methuen. An illuminating study of the three tragedians' professional skills viewed thematically, with reference to particular plays.

2

Aeschylus

The Plays

Aeschylus may properly be regarded as the father of European drama. He is credited with almost eighty plays, some of which were satyr plays, and many of his tragic contributions to the festival took the form of "trilogies," that is sets of three plays connected in plot and overall theme. Six certainly authentic works of his survive: *Persians* (472 BC), *Seven Against Thebes* (467), *Suppliant Women* (about 463?), *Agamemnon, Libation-Bearers* and *Eumenides* (458). *Persians* is a complete play in itself, but *Seven Against Thebes* and *Suppliant Women* are single parts of trilogies (preceding a satyr play), the full meaning of which can only be a matter of speculation. The last three are the sole surviving examples of a connected trilogy, the *Oresteia*, which ranks as one of the very greatest works in our legacy from the ancient world.

One other play credited in ancient times to Aeschylus, *Prometheus Bound*, has also come down to us. Over the last century, its authenticity has been challenged and most scholars today would date it to a period some years after his death.

Life and Times

Aeschylus was born about 525 BC at Eleusis, a town in Attica which was famous for the mystery-cult of the goddesses Demeter and Persephone. He was very probably of aristocratic birth. After a successful career in Athens as a dramatic poet between, perhaps, 499 and 458, he died in Sicily. His life coincided with the years when Athens and most other Greek states were at war with Persia, after which Athens developed both as a democracy and as an imperial power in the Aegean area. Ancient evidence records that he fought in the battles of Marathon (490), Salamis (481) and Plataea (479), at all of which the Athenians played an important part in the defeat of the Persian invasion of Greece. His epitaph famously made no reference to his art but to his soldierly prowess at Marathon.

Achievement as Dramatist

Aeschylus won his first tragic victory in the festival of 484 and is said to have won the first prize on twelve other occasions. He is credited by Aristotle's (*Poetics 1449a*) with the intro-duction of the second actor, that is another "answerer" who could reply not only to the Chorus

Greek Tragedies as Plays for Performance, First Edition. David Raeburn.
© 2017 John Wiley & Sons, Inc. Published 2017 by John Wiley & Sons, Inc.
Companion website: www.wiley.com/go/raeburn

but to another solo character in the play. If that is right, he was responsible for an innovation of great importance: it brought the crucial element of personal conflict into the potential texture of drama. The *Oresteia* requires a third actor, but Aristotle attributed the innovation of this to Sophocles, who was competing alongside Aeschylus during his later years and won a victory over the older poet in 465.

Aeschylus' earlier plays could all have been mounted before the *skênê* or stage-building (see p. 4) became a feature in the ancient theatre, but it is certainly required for the *Oresteia*. Though we have no external evidence that this was a further innovation of Aeschylus, it could well have been and it certainly marked an important milestone in the development of Athenian drama. Though this poet's dramatic use of the spoken word was ultimately the paramount aspect of his art, he was far from blind to the value of spectacle and visual meaning in the theatrical experience. Some scholars, in structuralist mode, like to apply the polarities of "private" and "public," or even "female" and "male" to the contrasting locations of the *skênê* interior and the *orchêstra*, the choral dancing-floor surrounded by the citizen body of the audience; but semantics of this kind are not consistently observed or relevant. More mistaken was the outdated view that the *skênê* platform (if it existed) was the domain of the solo actors who never invaded the *orchêstra*, which belonged to the Chorus. It is clear from the *Oresteia* that Aeschylus regarded the two areas as a unified space and allowed for regular interchange.

Thought and Outlook

Aeschylus was deeply conscious of suffering and evil as basic to human life and held a complex view of their causes: men can come to grief through their own decisions but also as a result of past events beyond their control. Justice requires the punishment of the person who overreaches his mortal limits, but it must be an enlightened justice that accepts a complexity of determinants to human behavior. As an Athenian living in an age of developing democracy he seems optimistically to have believed in the importance of social institutions which favored persuasion rather than violence as the means of resolving civic conflict.

All this for Aeschylus needed to be expressed in terms of the divine as well as the human. The gods are a vital dimension in his conception of a world order in which human beings can develop in societies and also recognize their human limits. He predates the rationalism which swept over Athenian thought during the latter half of the fifth century and was evidently a profoundly religious man to whom the gods were transcendentally important. The *Oresteia* suggests a real theologian who was concerned to find a unity in the different strands of cult-worship that flourished in his day.

Some readers of Aeschylus may be puzzled by a view of human behavior which allows the characters to act freely and to make their own decisions, but always against a background of divine involvement. This "multiple causation" is fundamental to ancient Greek thinking and not so different from, for example, our modern approach to criminal behavior which insists that members of society are responsible for their actions but also allows that that there are factors of heredity, environment and circumstance that may well have contributed to the crime and help others to its understanding. The guilt of Agamemnon, Clytemnestra and Orestes needs to be seen in similar terms.

Dramatic Technique

If Aeschylus was a profound thinker, he was also a great storyteller, who knew just how to develop the public narration of the epic tales, familiar from the rhapsodic performances, within the growing hybrid form. The saying attributed to him that his tragedies were "slices of fish taken from the great banquets of Homer" (Athenaeus 8.347d) suggests a kind of *personal* indebtedness. He had a wealth of material at his fingertips to stimulate his imagination and to pose the challenge of a new kind of presentation within the young theatrical medium. The conflicts and dilemmas of the well-known heroes and others were a strong point of contact between him and his audience; and they offered exciting subject matter for vivid re-enactment through the developing art of impersonation by skilled performers of the individual characters.

We can see in Aeschylus a consummate artist with an unerring instinct for the developing medium. His use of the second and third actors, and his exploitation – if not the actual invention – of the *skênê* and its associated machinery have often been commented on. I would also want to emphasize his sense of structure and his feeling for continuity.

Clear structure can invariably be seen in the design both of whole plays (or a trilogy) and of their constituent movements. In each of the three parts of the *Oresteia* we find a triptych of preparation – central action – aftermath; but each movement within these main divisions has a corresponding strength and variety in its construction; for example, the elaborate Parodos of *Agamemnon*, the complex *kommos* in *Choephori* and the long closing scene between Athena and the Furies in *Eumenides*. (For technical terms see Appendix A.) Within scenes for solo actors too we may instance the three different speeches for Agamemnon's Herald, each ending on a different note; or the contrast between the lyric and iambic sections of the Cassandra scene. In most of these examples, the choice of different meters or "modes of utterance" (pp. 6–7) plays a sophisticated part. Beside formal contrast and variety, Aeschylus makes useful play with *similarity*, as in the parallel breakdowns of Clytemnestra and Orestes after their murderous acts towards the end of the first and second plays. Skillful transition is another crucial factor, often achieved by passages of anapaests or short runs of stichomythia between a soloist and the Coryphaeus. In such cases we can note an interaction between actors and chorus, so that the hybrid character of the genre never appears to obtrude or grate.

Structural transition within a play's individual divisions leads on to the essential continuity which runs through the whole sequence of discrete lyric and iambic (or epirrhematic) movements. In this Aeschylus shows the most extraordinary feeling for his theatrical medium and form. The drama does not stop when the Chorus has its turn and takes over from the soloists; it advances in an inexorable tide. In *Agamemnon*, particularly, we are conscious of the great successive waves of mounting foreboding, which culminates in the homecoming of Troy's conqueror and its inevitable outcome. Within the different movements momentum is sustained even when, as in the Cassandra scene, the main action is held in suspense. The drama of the Trilogy never, or hardly ever (see p. 73), seems to come to a standstill. Tension and the audience's interest are sustained throughout in what is, overall, an overwhelming experience.

Aeschylus' dramaturgy is rooted in his religious sense. This is apparent in the overriding prominence that he gives to the Chorus with its cultic roots and to his quasi-ritualistic use of words as the main engine that drives his tragedies. We are always conscious in his plays of the sacral origin of this fundamental element in the hybrid genre. It is particularly obvious in the constant use of prayer and incantatory language, deemed to be potentially efficacious, as in the cult-hymns sung and danced to the lyre's accompaniment in honour of gods or heroes. This kind of "word power" is crucial to Aeschylus' peculiar dramaturgy, which applies the primitive assumption that words sacrally delivered have the power to affect the future *within the context of the drama itself*. It is words more than acts which give the plays their dynamic impulse and tension; this needs to be understood if the drama is not to appear static and uneventful.

Words in Aeschylus are ominous: they operate like prayers or curses. Good news or hopes expressed for a desirable outcome are more likely to bring about that outcome; bad news or the voicing of fears will actively damage the future issue. Names can be regarded as omens in themselves, potential signs or even determinants of a person's destiny. The Greeks popularly used chance remarks (as we often superstitiously do today) as a form of divination; and a word conveying a positive or neutral sense might also bear a negative connotation. In all Aeschylus' authentic plays the risk that any utterance can affect events either favorably or adversely is a recurrent concern. The word *euphēmia*, meaning "well-omened speech" was essential to Greek ritual. Often it simply implied silence, saying nothing at all to avoid any sound which might impair the validity of a sacrifice or other ritual proceeding. In Aeschylus it includes actual speaking, but with reticence (euphemism in the modern sense) or careful avoidance of potentially damaging language.

These assumptions about the potency of words are cardinal to Aeschylus' technique in his use of the tragic medium. It is this that made the hybrid form of tragedy the ideal medium for him to express and develop his ideas and vision. The Chorus with its origin in various forms of religious ritual is for him the primary element in the hybrid. The assumed efficacy of language, for good or for evil, in the ritual context is natural to Aeschylus, not an artificial convention. The notion that words in themselves have power is what gives his dramas their particular dynamic.

It is possible, I think, to go a little further in this regard and to envisage, in Aeschylus' case, a potential ritual purpose in the performances of the tragedies he composed for the festivals of Dionysus. The *Oresteia*, with all its religious as well as its political overtones, might have aimed to promote civic peace and reconciliation at an important stage in the growth of Athenian democracy. However that may be, the least that can be said here is that Aeschylean tragedy exhibits an awesome solemnity which transcends the mere use of ritual forms for dramatic purposes.

Characterization

For a modern actor the realistic delineation and exploration of a role's detailed traits and inner life are all important. By contrast, Aeschylus' original performers will have been primarily concerned with the clear and expressive projection of the artificial language composed for them to deliver in a large theatrical space and to have supported this with appropriate movement and gesture. Here Aeschylus' skill as a dramatist is to be seen in his own artistic purposes. By way of illustration I briefly examine the dramatis personae in *Agamemnon*.

In this play the characters may be seen first of all at an allegorical level in relation to the problem posed by the kind of justice implicit in the law of retribution. Agamemnon himself is Man driven to wrongdoing for the sake of justice and paying the penalty accordingly. He is also Man suffering for the sins of his fathers, impelled by the gods through madness (*atê*) into slaying his own child. The *hybris*, insolent pride, inspired by his wealth and prosperity generates the *hybris* which, with the forceful aid of Persuasion (*Peitho*), prompts him to the final act (entering his house over the purple tapestries) that leads to his destruction. Clytemnestra is the agent of Persuasion who lures Agamemnon on to his ruin. She is also identified with the *daimon*, the evil genius of the house which exacts its victims from one generation to the next. The other four characters emphasize the tragic problem. The purpose of Cassandra is, at the moment when Agamemnon's death is finally assured, to reveal the catastrophe when it comes as one of a series and also typical of a wider issue than the individual event. The Watchman establishes and the Herald quickens the sense of impending disaster. At the play's end the evil usurper Aegisthus underlies the theme of inherited guilt and heightens the point that the justice done is an evil one which has only created a fresh situation of a similar kind.

Yet Aeschylus' characters are not made of cardboard. I consider them again in order of their appearance in the drama. The Watchman's weariness, anxiety, suspicion of Clytemnestra and loyalty to Agamemnon are all entirely to the point. Clytemnestra has to be an extremely powerful and dominating character if she is to fulfill her function in the total design: hence her "male-counselling heart" and her self-assertion as a woman in a man's world. Yet after the murder she can be presented as a frightened mother who has avenged her child but now realizes the fate that awaits her in turn. The Herald convinces as an individual through his personal joy in homecoming and subsequent consciousness of his terrible predicament in following good news with bad. Agamemnon has the kingly magnificence and authority to inspire the respect of the Elders, but he is accorded both the arrogance and the gullibility that will lead him to his demise over the trail of purple garments. Cassandra gains human reality in the weirdness of her clairvoyant utterances, then the realization of what Apollo has done to her and finally the nobility with which she advances to her death in the spirit of a willing victim to a sacrifice. Aegisthus is a foil to Agamemnon in that he is a luxurious rather than a warrior type and lacks the dignity to compel respect. He is nastily vindictive, a tyrannical coward, whose less subtle characterization fits the disturbing atmosphere of the act's dénouement.

Style

Aeschylus possessed an astonishing gift with words. His poetry is chiefly remarkable for his rich use of metaphor as his imagination made a unity of his experience and enlarged the significance of what he was communicating though the likenesses that he was able to perceive and explore in nature and human life. Furthermore, his musical ear knew how to exploit the beautiful sounds of ancient Greek and a wide range of poetic rhythms that had evolved in earlier forms of Greek composition. These are powerfully displayed, whether in the sonorous and flowing iambic speeches and dialogue or in the songs he wrote for his choruses in regular syllabic patterns of meter, used to express mood and even, through the force of repetition, his dramas' basic themes.

He employed a rich poetic vocabulary, often characterized by original compound adjectives. The sonorous music of his verse is perhaps unequalled in ancient Greek poetry and certainly impossible to do justice to in modern translation. Aristophanes made fun of his grandiloquence in his *Frogs* half a century after he died. His language is often dense and cannot have been easy to follow at first hearing, particularly in the choral lyrics which would have been sung to the accompaniment of the pipe and also have involved some "dancing," whatever that meant (see p. 9). His audience cannot have been wholly literate, but it was perhaps more used to *listening* than we are today and so better able to detect the poet's ambivalences and subtleties of meaning.

Spectacle

The *Oresteia* makes it clear that Aeschylus knew how to engage his audience's eyes as well as their ears in the public, festal setting of the Theater of Dionysus. It is not too difficult to picture the central scene of *Agamemnon* in terms of *orchêstra* and *skênê*, platform and facade, the tableaux in each act of the Trilogy with the *ekkyklêma*, the sudden entrance of the Furies or the layout for the trial of Orestes. We cannot know how the great lyric songs were choreographed, but we can have little doubt that they were interesting to watch and also contrived economically and appropriately to communicate the form and meaning of their impressive content. In spectacle, no less than in his richly layered characterization and extremely skillful manipulation of tragedy's dramatic form and essential resources, Aeschylus was evidently a master artist and craftsman who knew his business through and through.

Summary

Though Aeschylean drama comes at an early stage in the art's development, it would be very wrong to describe it as "primitive." It is too skillfully constructed, imaginatively conceived in terms of the theatre, clothed in the most beautiful and magnificent poetry and, finally, the mature fruit of a profound-thinking imagination.

Further Reading

Lloyd, Michael (ed.). 2007. *Oxford Readings in Classical Studies: Aeschylus*. Oxford: Oxford University Press. A collection of influential articles on the plays.

Owen E.T. 1952. *The Harmony of Aeschylus*. Toronto: Clarke, Irwin and Co. A rather forgotten but extremely important set of lectures which emphasize the power of words in Aeschylean dramaturgy.

Scott, William C. 1984. *Musical Design in Aeschylean Theater*. Hanover, NH: University Press of New England. A useful study of the relationship between meter and themes in Aeschylus.

Sommerstein, Alan H. 2010. *Aeschylean Tragedy*, 2nd edn. London: Duckworth. An excellent comprehensive work on the poet and his plays.

Taplin, Oliver. 1977. *The Stagecraft of Aeschylus: the Dramatic Use of Entrances and Exits in Greek Tragedy*. Oxford: Clarendon Press. A very interesting and thorough exploration of the practical "grammar" of Greek tragedy.

Winnington-Ingram, R.P. 1980. *Studies in Aeschylus*. Cambridge: Cambridge University Press. The outstanding critical study of the ideas in the plays.

3

Persae

Introduction

The Persians (or *Persae*, to call it by its conventional Latin title) is the earliest surviving Greek tragedy. It was composed for performance in 472 BC as the second in a group of four separate plays, only loosely related in theme (see Sommerstein 2010, 62–5). The chorêgos was the young Pericles who later became the leading politician at Athens, and the tetralogy won the first prize. The poet was now aged about 50 and, although tragedy was still at a comparatively early stage in its development as an art form, the dramaturgy is already confident and assured. The Chorus is heavily predominant and only two solo actors are required.

The play's subject matter is unique in extant tragedy in being set in recent events rather than the world of myth. The centrepiece of the drama is a narrative of the famous defeat of the Persians by the Athenian fleet at the battle of Salamis in 480. A precedent for this had been established by Aeschylus' predecessor Phrynichus, who is known to have composed two plays based on contemporary happenings. *Persae*, however, is a highly stylized poetic drama which mythologizes history for the purpose of the *tragoidia*. When analyzed as a whole, it can be seen to follow the pattern of choral lyric performance in the three elements of ritual utterance (invocation of deities, formal lamentation and so on), narrative and also the 'gnomic' element which points up the universal and suggests a moral conclusion. As in ritual hymns, word power is fundamental to the dramatic technique; viewed in that way, a play which has often been regarded as static and disjointed in construction can be seen as dynamic and satisfyingly continuous. The drama is also highly ritualistic in that some of its movements are based on typical ritual performances. The grand costumes of the Persian Elders and Queen Atossa must also have contributed to the hieratic effect. Despite the strangeness of its idiom, *Persae* has been revived quite often in modern times and found compellingly impressive.

Historical Background

A sketch is needed if the play's detail is to be understood. In 499 the Greek cities in western Asia, known as Ionians, rebelled against the domination of Persian rule. After the revolt was crushed in 494, the Persian king Darius was determined to punish the Athenians who had sent help to the Ionians. He made a raid on Attica, only to be defeated by the Athenians in the Battle of Marathon (490). Ten years later (480), his son and successor Xerxes launched a second invasion of Greece, conveying an enormous force from Asia into Europe on a bridge of

Greek Tragedies as Plays for Performance, First Edition. David Raeburn.
© 2017 John Wiley & Sons, Inc. Published 2017 by John Wiley & Sons, Inc.
Companion website: www.wiley.com/go/raeburn

boats across the Hellespont. Although he successfully fought his way through the pass of Thermopylae to enter Attica and burn Athens, he was tricked by the Athenian Themistocles into ordering his fleet into unfavorable waters at Salamis and suffered a crushing defeat. Greece was thus saved from Persian rule and Xerxes' remaining land army was beaten by Spartan infantry at the Battle of Plataea the following year (479). In the years that followed, Athens initiated a league of Greek states, now liberated from Persian rule, for common defence against Persia, and this resulted in the Greek seizure, under an Athenian general, Cimon, of Eion, a key Persian stronghold in Thrace to the west of the Hellespont. In 472, however, the date of our play, the Persians still remained a threat and it was not until 469 or 468 that Xerxes was finally defeated near the mouth of the River Eurymedon on the south coast of Asia Minor.

Synopsis

The Chorus of Persian Elders describes Xerxes' great expedition to Greece and voices anxiety for its return. Their foreboding is reinforced when the dowager Queen Atossa recounts a dream she has had and a sinister omen. A Messenger reports the Persian defeat at Salamis and the army's subsequent retreat through Greece. Atossa sees this as the fulfillment of her dream and the Chorus laments. Libations are offered to the spirit of the dead king Darius who is summoned for advice in a ritual incantation. The ghost appears, to interpret Xerxes' disaster at Salamis as the punishment of the gods for his presumption and to prophesy the final defeat at Plataea. Finally, Xerxes himself enters, unattended and in rags, and laments his humiliation.

Interpretation

The governing themes are the danger of excessive wealth and the punishment of Xerxes by the gods for his *hubris* in transgressing human limits through his defiance of nature in building the bridge of boats across the Hellespont. The idea that great wealth or prosperity induces an arrogance that plunges a man into injustice and then ruin (sometimes called the *hubris*-syndrome) was first articulated by the Athenian statesman Solon in the sixth century and is a recurring theme in Greek tragedy.

Edith Hall (1989), in an important study, sees Aeschylus' stereotypical depiction of the Persians, with its focus on tyranny and effeminacy, as an expression of the Athenians' self-image as democratic and manly. We may certainly note the play's double perspective: ostensibly, the Persian defeat at Salamis and the humiliation of Xerxes are movingly presented from the Persians' own point of view, but there is also a strong pro-Athenian undercurrent. Given that the play's form owes so much to the choral lyric hymn, it is tempting to regard its performance in 472 as, in itself, a kind of ritual act which was designed to help the Greeks finally to win a still continuing war. Lines 790–1 suggest the threat of a future invasion and the possibility of an even larger armament. In that case, the tragedy might be seen less as a belated thanksgiving for a past mercy than as an expression of gratitude betokening a lively sense of favors to come. The Athenian chorus and actors, dressed up as Persians, might thus be sharing in the humiliation of their enemies and so deprecating the danger that could come from too overt an expression of triumph.

The Dramaturgy in General

In formal plot terms, the play's action follows the pattern of a so-called *nostos* scenario, which relates to the homecoming of a hero, such as those of Odysseus and Agamemnon from Troy, both familiar from the *Odyssey* and contrasted in their outcome. The return of Xerxes from his expedition to Greece is thus the dramatic issue which the Chorus of Elders is aiming, in their ritual words and actions, to promote advantageously. The pathos of the tragedy consists in the destitution of Persian families through the loss of their younger menfolk and in the humbling of Xerxes himself, who appears in the closing scene with his garments in tatters.

Original Production

According to custom, Aeschylus himself would have been his own director, composer and choreographer. He would almost certainly have been one of the solo actors, combining either Atossa and Xerxes or the Messenger and Darius.

Aeschylus is said to have been a skillful choreographer, original in the *schemata*, poses and gestures, that he contrived for his choruses (Pickard-Cambridge 1968, 250). His 'dance' movements for the Chorus in *Persae* can never be recovered, though the text at line 1046 implies gestures like the movements of oars. The melody of the accompanying pipe-music is similarly lost, but the varied meters point to an elaborate rhythmical 'score' which must have been a major factor in the drama's impact and indeed makes this work (as others by Aeschylus) closer to music theater than what we understand by a normal play. The musical design and the effect suggested by the different rhythmical patterns are explored in the dramatic analysis, supported by the recordings.

No *skênê* is required for this play, though it is possible that a lowish structure was set at the back of the *orchêstra* to represent Darius' tomb at the moment when his ghost appears. Indeed, the chief technical problem is how the appearance of the ghost was managed (see section "Second Stasimon"). Spectacle would have played an important part in the ritual movements of the Chorus, dressed in gaudily magnificent costumes, as in the arrival of Atossa, similarly attired in her regal finery, on a splendid chariot.

Dramatic Analysis

Line numbers refer to the Greek text in the Loeb edition (see the end of this chapter), which has a parallel English translation. For the terminology of the discrete movements, see Appendix A; for the lyric structure and meters, see Appendix B or hear TRACK 0 ◉

Parodos (1–139)

Aeschylus launches his play without a prologue and establishes the public character of his tragedy from the very outset. This noble movement states the main themes or "subject" before these are developed and recapitulated, as in some kinds of musical composition.

Introductory Anapaests (1–64)

The grand, spectacular entrance song for the Persian Elders, richly costumed in their luxurious barbaric finery, begins (as often in Aeschylus) with a long passage of 'marching' anapaests, probably in spoken delivery to the accompaniment of the *aulos*. Whether Aeschylus intended the opening lines to be delivered on the march or after the twelve choreutes had reached their first position in the *orchêstra* is not clear. The latter could have been more impressive as the Elders introduce themselves in an address to the audience as the trusted guardians selected by Xerxes himself (5–7) to watch over the land in his absence. We cannot be sure either whether these lines were delivered by the full Chorus in unison, just by the Coryphaeus or divided between individual speakers.

The keynote of this opening passage is the power and magnificence of the Persian expedition: its wealth, variety of troops and weaponry, its formidableness. The long catalogue of names of the Persian chiefs who have gone reinforces the feeling of confidence that is communicated. All these utterances are words of good omen for the Persians. Yet the Elders' "evil-prophesying heart" (10–11) is already troubled over the king's *nostos*, his homecoming, established here at the very outset as the issue motivating their ritual performance, understood in choral lyric terms. The recurring gold imagery and the emphasis on wealth is, from a Greek point of view, an unconscious omen of danger. The participle *oichomenōn* used to refer in line 1 itself to the Persians who are "departed" derives from a verb which, can also mean "I am lost, ruined, dead." This verbal ambiguity strikes an immediate discord; it is twice repeated in this section with the same verb (13, 60), to very sinister effect. <TRACK A1, lines 1–20> ◉

Song in Lyric Metres (65–139)

This main section of the movement falls metrically into two parts: ionic and (largely) iambo-trochaic. The former has rhythmical associations with the oriental and is comparatively fast-moving. It describes the great host's crossing of the Hellespont from Asia to Europe over the bridge of boats and pictures the savage power of Xerxes in the pride of his onset. All this would have offered exciting scope for Aeschylus' choreographic skills. <TRACK A2, lines 65–80> ◉ The epode (93–100), which most authorities transpose to follow 114, is a transitional 'gnomic' passage which warns that mortals can be deceived by the god and lured into the nets of *Atê*, ruin. Perhaps this point marks a slowing down of the tempo, with the choreography coming to a halt before the second, iambic-trochaic, section, which is heavier in its measures and more sombre in atmosphere. The words presage lamentation, rending of clothes and Persian women bereaved of their husbands, images that anticipate many of the themes that will recur at the tragedy's climax. <TRACK A3, lines 116–37> ◉

In musical terms, then, the sequence has moved from a major to a minor key. Though there were sinister overtones very early on, by the end words of evil omen have prevailed over words of good in a passage that contains no formal invocations but has all the atmosphere of a ritual performance designed to promote Xerxes' *nostos*.

Transitional Anapaests (140–54)

These lines form a bridge to the entrance of Atossa and the scene which follows. They must be delivered by the Coryphaeus, who invites the other Elders to sit down and take counsel and so provides a belated motive for their presence. The passage is so brief that there is no need to suppose that "sitting down in this ancient building" (140–1) refers to a structure which is visible onstage or that there were actually twelve beautifully arranged chairs there for the Elders to sit on.[1] The rest of the play demands no such obtrusive properties, and the proposal to take counsel is immediately (150) interrupted by the dowager queen's arrival. That is the point: the moment establishes a pattern of "frustrated intentions, with increasing dramatic significance."[2]

The Leader's suggestion is at once invalidated and dramatically overshadowed by the dowager queen's majestic arrival in a chariot, attended by extras. This is probably followed by the Elders' prostration before her in a large gesture of obeisance which characterizes them as barbaric. This and the elaborate compliment paid to Atossa as "a light equal to the eyes of the gods" (150–1) will have struck the Athenian audience as dangerously excessive and hence ominous.

First Episode (155–531)

This long formal division of the play can better be considered as two submovements or sections:

a) Atossa and Coryphaeus (155–248)
b) Messenger, Chorus and Atossa (249–531).

Atossa and Coryphaeus (155–248)

This consists of two runs of trochaic tetrameters separated by an iambic rhesis. The use of the two different non-lyric meters is interesting and interpreted in different ways (see Garvie 2009, 105). I doubt myself whether the trochaic tetrameters were accompanied by the *aulos*, but the marked rhythm of these long verses fits well the Coryphaeus' formal address to Atossa (155–8) and her responses to it (159–72). The latter speech is solemnly didactic in tone and ominously resonant in the fears she expresses about the danger inherent in great wealth and so for Xerxes.

This contrasts effectively with the more factual and fluid, though no less ominous, content of the queen's long iambic *rhesis*. In this she first of all narrates her dream of a conflict between two beautiful women, one Persian, one Greek, with Xerxes trying to restrain them by yoking both beneath his chariot. The Greek succeeds in wrecking the chariot and throwing Xerxes out of it; while his father Darius looks on, Xerxes tears his clothes. At several points Atossa's words recall the language of the Parodos: the doom-fraught 'has gone' (178), the chariot and yoke imagery (compare 190–6 with 50, 84), and the rending of clothes (compare 190–6 with 125). Atossa continues with the omen of the hawk, which symbolizes Greece, tearing the eagle, which symbolizes Persia. The dream and the omen explain the queen's tears, but they can also be understood as *events* in a mounting sequence of bad omens which builds up to the entrance of the Messenger. The closing lines of the speech (211–14) follow a deliberately euphemistic pattern which avoids spelling out the implications of Xerxes' possible failure and tries to look on the bright side.

At 215 the regular pulse of the trochaic tetrameters is restored as the Coryphaeus recommends 'apotropaic' action by prayers and libations to the gods, a suggestion to which Atossa responds positively. Her speech is followed by a passage of stichomythia (still in trochees) which leads up to the great moment of the Messenger's entrance to report the disaster at Salamis. Here Atossa questions the Coryphaeus about the Athenians who, despite not being ruled by a single person, have succeeded in defeating Darius. The reference to the Marathon campaign seems gratuitous, and there is a lack of realism in Atossa's ignorance of the information she is eliciting; but the artificiality is irrelevant. Darius' defeat by the Athenians is greeted by the queen as another bad omen (245). Her temporary hopes (228) have once again been turned to fear and the drama has thus been advanced. Enter the Messenger, running (247).

Messenger, Chorus and Atossa (249–531)

The Messenger's grandiloquent opening confirms the Elders' worst fears. "Has gone" (252) is now unambiguously negative. The blow at once (256) drives the Chorus into three strophic pairs of sung lamentation, punctuated by spoken affirmations of disaster from the Messenger, as he hammers his bad news home in spoken iambic couplets. This kind of formalization (known as an *epirrhema*) is strikingly powerful and appropriate to the dramaturgical idiom. The wailing sounds of the Chorus, combined with a good deal of alliteration and assonance, suggest the music of ritual lamentation.[3] <TRACK A4, lines 268–79> ◉

The queen now (290) re-enters the picture to question the Messenger and there follows the long sequence of four narrative speeches describing the Battle of Salamis and the Persian retreat through Greece. The poetic vividness and excitement of these make the role a magnificent one for an actor.[4] In terms of the dramatic continuity, the sinister apprehensions of the Parodos and Atossa's dream are now fulfilled. The roll-call of the dead chiefs (302–30) knocks down a number of the names put up for confidence in the opening anapaests. The long central speech (353–432) is in more epic than lyrico-ritual vein, but the language of religion remains important. The Greeks` cry of good omen (388–9) is as significant an action as their naval performance; and the wreck of the Persian fleet is accompanied by contrasting cries of ritual lamentation (426–7). <TRACK A5, lines 384–411 > ◉ The ensuing account of the Greeks' capture of Psyttaleia and the slaughter of all the Persians on the island reaches its climax in the image of Xerxes rending his garments as presaged in Atossa's dream (199) and in anticipation of the king's eventual appearance onstage (908) in rags.

In all these Messenger speeches the double perspective of Persian disaster/Athenian victory will have involved Aeschylus' audience to a marked degree. The Messenger's all-pervasive, very Greek, theology[5] underscores both the idea that the gods are punishing the Persians but also the *non nobis* theme which applies to the Greeks if they are to preserve their own sense of proportion in victory. The trick which lured the Persian fleet into unfavorable waters is not attributed to Themistocles by name but to the appearance of "an avenging spirit or evil demon" (354). At the final climax of the Messenger's narrative Aeschylus almost certainly invents history when most of the remnant of the Persian army is about to cross the River Strymon in Thrace and "the god" freezes it up "unseasonably" (495–7). The troops attempt to cross the ice, but most of them are drowned, like Pharaoh's chariots and horses in the Red Sea, when the sun-god (502) scatters his rays and melts the frozen water. The attribution of the Persian disaster to divine intervention is all of a piece with Aeschylus' sacral dramaturgy.

In the closing speech of the episode, Atossa sees the Messenger's report as the fulfillment of her dream. In the sequence, once again, of sacral dramaturgy, a causal link may be felt between dream and report. The next step must be for the queen to offer prayers to the gods as the Chorus advised earlier on (215 ff.), no longer to avert the effect of her dream but in the hope of better things to come (526). She instructs the Elders to turn to their role as counsellors and to console Xerxes if he returns before she does. Logical plot construction would place these lines (529–31) much later on, at 851, just before Atossa's second exit; but Aeschylus puts them here to refocus the issue on Xerxes' *nostos* and what this may imply for the future. All is not yet entirely lost.

First Stasimon (532–97)

This fine movement is the play's centrepiece and significant in the dramatic sequence. Ostensibly, it is the Persian Elders' lament for the destruction of Xerxes' host and for the women who have been left desolate; but the Greek standpoint is implicit from the outset. Structurally, the contrast drawn between Xerxes' failure and Darius' (unhistoric) success link the preceding and succeeding parts of the play.

The anapaestic introduction, probably delivered by the Coryphaeus, starts by invoking the Greek god Zeus who, no less than Xerxes, has destroyed the Persian army and assigned grief and mourning to the women of the land. This by itself suggests a prelude to a victory song for the Greeks no less than a dirge for the Persians.

The formal lament follows in three strophic pairs. It is typically characterized by repetitions and inarticulate cries, uttered outside the main rhythmical structure, and probably accompanied by breast-beatings in the second pair of strophes. There is no further mention of Zeus in this lyric section; the responsibility lies heavily with Xerxes (550–3), though the woes of aged parents are "god-sent" (581). The closing pair of strophes (584–97) laments the liberation which the Greek cities have won under Persian rule; they are no longer forced to pay taxes and make obeisance to the Greek king, as his power has vanished; released from the yoke of military force, they enjoy freedom of speech. In all this the Athenian perspective is unmistakable.

The ode needs also to be *heard* to be fully appreciated. Especially powerful are the protracted syllables in the thrice-uttered *Xér-xés* and *nă-és*, ships (550–2, 560–2) – perhaps these words also were accompanied by repeated blows to the breast. The iambo-trochaic rhythm of the first strophic pair recalls the sombre phase of foreboding in the Parodos (114–39) and so reflects the Persian perspective; while the Athenian sense of victory is communicated in the second and third pairs by the rolling dactylic trimeter, which in feeling and association is more like a Pindaric victory song than a lament. <TRACK A6, lines 548–82 > ⊙ Atossa's reference in 605 to the cry she has heard that is "not a song of triumph" suggests that it might indeed be thought of as just that, particularly when the word for "cry," *kelados*, has previously been used for the Greeks' song of good omen just before the naval engagement (388–9).

Second Episode (598–622)

This 'insertion' between two choral movements simply consists of one, not very long, speech for Atossa. Her entrance this time is much less grand, without a chariot or attendants. She is wearing a much simpler costume (608–9), probably black. Moreover, Aeschylus makes her speak in iambics rather than in the more spacious and strongly rhythmical trochaic tetrameters of the First Episode. The visual points and the strongly renewed emphasis on Atossa's fears provide the ominous springboard for the elaborate description of all the *choai*, the libations she will be pouring to propitiate Darius. Interestingly, the actual ingredients of her offerings are typically Greek but the imagery of the qualifying words fits the stereotypical view of Asia. This account of the offerings anticipates the act which is then performed onstage during the ensuing hymn of invocation. This she calls on the Elders, as her friends, to utter in *euphemia*, auspiciously, while she pours her libations to the gods below.

Second Stasimon (623–80)

The invocation of Darius is a ritual performance which has the actual effect, through the power of words, of summoning the dead king's ghost from the grave for necromantic purposes, that is to consult a departed spirit and so find a way out of a troubled situation. The song's liturgical structure and content may well be based on real prayers and rituals.

The introductory anapaests are in straightforward Greek terms: Zeus, Hermes and Hades are all invoked and Darius is referred to as a mortal, though a unique one (632). In the following strophes Darius is referred to in progressively divine terms (634, 641, 643) and finally addressed directly as the language becomes more outlandish and the meter more complex and agitated. In the second antistrophe he is praised for never losing men in war (653–4), words which ignore Darius' own attack on Greece ten years previously and on Scythia to the north in the 490s. Here again Aeschylus has altered history to suit his theme: Darius' proper guidance of his people is designed to throw Xerxes' excessive behaviour into high relief. In the third strophic pair the details of the dead king's Persian costume (660–3) anticipate his actual appearance. <TRACK A7, lines 634–64> ◉ There is also the fine image of the "Stygian mist" hovering over the Persians (669) as they bemoan the death of all their younger generation. The epode mounts to a frenetic climax, with a run of short syllables almost immediately followed by a run of longs (675–9).

The actual appearance of Darius' ghost, with the Chorus prostrating themselves before it,[6] will have been a highly spectacular and impressive moment. The most promising solution to the problem of its management in Aeschylus' pre-*skênê* theater is to posit a lowish retaining wall on the terrace at the very back of the acting space, behind the *orchêstra*. The ghost could then mount a ladder set against it, rising "slowly and majestically" from behind the tomb (if it was represented), then stepping onto it before he speaks (so Ewans 1996).

Third Episode (681–851)

The Darius scene offers a dramatic lull, a pause for calm reflection after the excitement of the preceding ritual and before the two concluding lyric movements. The sacral performance which is enacting the *nostos* of Xerxes is held in suspended animation while the crucial issue is linked with the past and with the future.[7] If the play as a whole is viewed as a choral lyric performance, this section comprises the 'gnomic' element that derives the moral lesson, just as the narrative element is most obviously displayed in the Messenger scene. A parallel might be seen in the part played by the sermon in the Christian eucharistic liturgy.

In his opening iambic speech (681–93) the Ghost makes it clear that his appearance has been conjured up by Atossa's libations and the Chorus's lamentations. After that, it is significant that Aeschylus deliberately chooses to make Atossa tell the Ghost what has occurred rather than the Chorus which has invoked him. In a short exchange with an actor (*epirrhema*) (694–702), the Chorus is shown as too frightened to speak or face Darius. This allows the two solo actors to engage in dialogue with each other and in the measured trochaic tetrameters which have been specially associated with Atossa – a ploy which in itself marks the temporary suspension of the quasi-liturgical sequence and leaves the Chorus detached for the time being. Darius' Ghost can now offer an interpretation of events that sets the defeat and tragic *pathos* of Xerxes and the Persians in their moral and theological context.

After an initial address to her father-in-law's spirit (709–14), Aeschylus has Atossa explaining to the Ghost what has befallen the Persians and why. The stichomythic dialogue (715–38) focuses on Xerxes' folly, under the suspected influence of "some divine spirit," or *daimon* (724), in bridging the Hellespont as the cause of the disaster. <TRACK A8, lines 709–25 > ◉ Then (739–41) the Ghost sees his son's humiliation as the fulfilment of (unspecified) oracles concerning him. Here we meet the typical pattern of causation in Greek tragedy. The *daimon* and the oracles do not exculpate Xerxes; his action in yoking the Hellespont is the consequence of "youthful rashness" (744) and "lack of counsel" (749) as a mortal in believing that he could master the gods who include the sea-god Poseidon. Though we have to wait until later (808) for the first actual mention of *hubris*, the multiple determination is already implicit in 742, "When a man is himself in a hurry, the god also lends a hand." Atossa adds a further reason in the trochaic speech which concludes this section: Xerxes was corrupted by associating with wicked men (753–4).[8]

Iambic trimeters return at 759 in a new section which includes two long speeches for Darius. The first gives an account of the Persian kings who hold their sovereignty through the gift of Zeus (762). Even Cyrus, who subdued Ionia (771) (where Greek colonies had been settled), was not hated by the god. None of the kings caused the suffering for which Xerxes has been responsible. At 787 the Coryphaeus re-enters the argument and asks how the issue will end, as they have sought to know in their invocation (632), and how the Persians can fare best in the future. The Ghost's immediate answer focuses on the second question: "Don't invade Greece again, even with a bigger army than before" (790–1), a reminder to the Athenian audience that this is still a real possibility. Darius' final rhesis answers the first question. The culminating disaster at Plataea turns out to be the final catastrophe, which explicitly points the moral about *hubris*, the arrogant thinking which blossoms and yields a crop of *atê*, ruin. Zeus is there to chastise "over-boastful pride" and call it to account (827–8). This passage (820–31) expounding the *hubris*-syndrome, a *locus classicus* in its own right, has been saved up by Aeschylus until this significant point in the drama's argument and development.

At 829 the focus returns from the Persian army to Xerxes himself. He is now on his way back. The final phase of the episode looks forward to the Great King's entrance in rags after the next choral song and motivates Atossa's exit. The *kosmos* (robe), which she goes off to fetch for her son (849–50) suggests a possible restoration of order and dignity; but the omen in this declared intention – which represents Atossa's final attempt to do and say something positive in a desperate situation – is left unfulfilled. The queen never returns. The omen is invalidated by the ritual of the following stasimon.

Third Stasimon (852–907)

The ritual is resumed in a song which follows naturally on from the preceding episode. In the first of three strophic pairs the Elders nostalgically recall Darius' "all-sufficing" (855) rule and the safe return of his expeditions abroad, so highlighting the humiliation and misery of Xerxes. <TRACK A9, lines 853–62 > ◉ In the second and third pairs they rehearse the place-names of the cities Darius captured and ruled over, with special reference to the lake cities on the river Strymon in Thrace, where the Athenian Cimon had conducted a successful campaign in 476–5. They then continue with a long list of Aegean islands which had formerly belonged to the Persian empire but in 472 were member states of the recently formed Delian League, whose representatives may well have been present for the City Dionysia and been delighted by their mention in Aeschylus' play. The epode similarly refers to the Greek cities in Asia Minor. The double perspective of the First Stasimon is thus once again reinforced. Indeed, the mood of the whole song, as expressed throughout in racing dactyls, once again suggests a celebratory, epinician atmosphere rather than one of lamentation. The long catalogue of place-names is a strongly positive omen for the Athenians themselves and the final lines (905–7) affirm the unequivocal, divinely inflicted, overthrow of the Persian empire, "mightily subdued by blows at sea." Here is poetic justice: the naval defeat at Salamis is the punishment for Xerxes' yoking of the sea. The words amount to a devastatingly bad omen for Persia and lead at once into Xerxes' entrance with a cry *io*. <TRACK A10, lines 880–907> ◉

Exodus (908–1077)

This great finale is the culmination of all the preceding ritual and quasi-ritual in the drama. It consists entirely of a formal lament (*kommos*) in lyric meters for Xerxes in alternation with the Chorus. It follows the conventional pattern of dirge in combining mournful reflections on what has happened with shorter expressions of woe and in making considerable use of antiphony, repetition and formal exclamations, as in the First Stasimon. Dramatically, this movement as a whole expresses the total humiliation of Xerxes and the Persian people.

The climactic visual statement is the entrance of Xerxes, unattended and on foot (1000–1), his clothes torn to rags, with nothing to show for the much acclaimed Persian bowmanship but his empty quiver (1020–2). The rags symbolize the disintegration of the Persian empire, and in such circumstances there can be no oriental prostration of the Chorus before Xerxes as there was for Atossa on her first entrance.

Xerxes first deplores his wretched fate in the rhythmical speech of anapaests. In poignant ring-composition his mention of the "men who are gone" (916) replicates the wording of the opening lines of the play. For four verses the Chorus responds in kind, but their utterance soon changes into song mode in so-called 'lyric' anapaests, with a preponderance of long syllables. Thereafter the singing continues to the end in a pattern of strophic pairs, each stanza divided between Xerxes and the Chorus. This formalization of uninhibited grief in a clearly defined musical structure gives it a shape which avoids banality and allows a tension to be maintained. During the first pair of strophes, while Xerxes loudly laments, the Chorus responds in terms suggestive of professional mourners. <TRACK A11, lines 932–47> ◉ In the second and third pairs they go on the attack and question the king about the fallen Persian leaders in a dismal roll-call of proper names which reprises the catalogue of the Parodos and the Messenger's narration. The rhythms of the exchange are predominantly lyric anapaests in a hideous parody of the Elders' confident utterances at the drama's beginning, but these are broken by eruption into other metrical cola, including a few (934 = 943, 936 = 945) in the irregular 'dochmiac' form associated with great agitation or pathos.[9] At 950 (=962) Xerxes braves a brief return to oriental ionics, but these are broken in form and yield to anapaests which run away with the Great King as though he were racing out of control like the unruly horse in Atossa's dream (194–6). <TRACK A12, lines 950–73> ⊚

Confrontation ceases in the concluding strophes. From 1002 the pace increases and by 1008–9 Xerxes and the Chorus are united in the use of the first-person plural. This may well have been marked by Xerxes no longer facing the Chorus but standing in their midst in the centre of the *orchêstra*. The tension builds up as the antiphonal responses, with the Elders picking up Xerxes' words in single verses, become briefer and more frequent. At 1038 Xerxes starts a long processional exit involving at least one full circuit of the *orchêstra*, and from 1046 the cries of lament must be accompanied by the ritual mourning gestures of beating the head and the breast. Rhythmically, these final stanzas are dominated, with expressive variations, by the relentless throb of the iambic meters, often 'syncopated' (see Appendix B), which pulses through the long threnodic exchange. The rhythm persists through the epode (1066–77) during which one can imagine the Chorus following Xerxes out of the *orchêstra*, as the cries of *oioi*, *io* and *e e* gradually fade into the distance and the dirge brings the ritualistic dramatic sequence to its ultimate, inexorable ending. <TRACK A13, lines 1038–77> ⊚

Conclusion

We are fortunate, for a variety of reasons, to have inherited *Persae* as the first surviving example of Greek (and European) drama. First of all, once the ominous use of words and conventions of ritual performance in which it is composed are properly understood, it emerges as a dynamic, arresting and strangely beautiful play in its own right. Second, it provides an excellent illustration of the kind of performing arts out of which Greek tragedy sprang and was subsequently to develop. Third, it offers a certain kind of evidence to supplement Herodotus' account of the battle of Salamis and throws interesting light on the ancient Greeks' perception of themselves by reference to barbarian stereotypes. Finally, it shows us Aeschylus already as a mature artist but before the crucial developments in the stagecraft of the tragic genre which led to the composition of the *Oresteia* and beyond that to the dramas of Sophocles and Euripides.

Notes

1 Pace Sommerstein 2010, who sees here a deliberate recall of an earlier play about the Persians by Phrynichus.

2 So Garvie 2009, who compares 201–4, 517–31 and 845–51, adding "in this play nothing goes according to plan for the Persians."

3 The 'a' and 'ai' sounds may be the result of an attempt to make the Elders distinctively Persian (so Hall 1989, note on line 256).

4 See the discussion in Rutherford (2012), 203–5, on lines 391–411.

5 The key passages are 345–7, 353–4 and 495–7.

6 The prostration is more likely here than after Darius' first speech (693), as envisaged in the Loeb edition.

7 Aeschylus adopts the same technique in the Cassandra scene of *Agamemnon*.

8 This complexity of motivation will recur again and again in this study. It gives the lie to the standard theory of "the tragic flaw" as the mainstay of tragedy in general.

9 See Appendix B. The dochmius may have occurred once earlier in the invocation to Darius (658–65). Otherwise this seems to be the earliest use in surviving tragedy of a particular exciting rhythm which features importantly in later Aeschylus and the other two tragedians.

References

Text: *Aeschylus Persae* (Loeb edition). 2008. Cambridge, MA: Harvard University Press, edited and translated by Alan H. Sommerstein.

Ewans, Michael. 1996. *Suppliants and Other Plays*. London: J.M. Dent.

Garvie, A.F. 2009. *Aeschylus: Persians*. Oxford: Oxford University Press.

Hall, Edith. 1989. *Inventing the Barbarian: Greek Self-Definition Through Tragedy*. Oxford: Clarendon Press.

Pickard-Cambridge, Sir Arthur. 1968. *The Dramatic Festivals at Athens*, 2nd edn. Oxford: Clarendon Press.

Rutherford, Richard. 2012. *Greek Tragic Style*. Cambridge: Cambridge University Press.

Sommerstein, Alan. 2010. *Aeschylean Tragedy*. London: Duckworth.

Commentaries

Garvie, A.F. 2009. *Aeschylus: Persians*. Oxford: Oxford University Press.

Hall, Edith, 1996. *Aeschylus: The Persians*. Warminster: Aris & Phillips.

4

The *Oresteia*

General Introduction

Aeschylus' final entry into the tragic contests was at the City Dionysia in 458 BC, and we know that it won first prize. The four plays were *Agamemnon, Choephori* (Libation Bearers), *Eumenides* and a concluding satyr-play, *Proteus*, which is almost entirely lost. The first three of these dramas are unique among surviving Greek tragedies in forming a connected whole, known collectively as the Orestes Trilogy or the *Oresteia*. The individual plays, though often read or performed separately, should properly be regarded as three acts of a single drama.

The Trilogy takes its title from the character Orestes who in the second play commits the crime of matricide as a sacred duty. This central act needs to be viewed in the context of Aeschylus' main theme which is essentially concerned with the concept of *dikê*, justice, and the advance of mankind from a code of retribution for wrongdoing, which is purely retaliatory and vindictive, to a more enlightened code based on a legal system such as was enshrined in the Athenian polis or city-state. Orestes' murder of his mother is the climax of a long series of crime and punishment within the house of his grandfather, Atreus; it has its antecedents in the first play and its sequel in the third. The tragedy does not lie so much in the predicament or character of particular individuals as in a situation where justice is pursued in a futile, self-perpetuating chain or cycle of retaliatory violence.

Synopsis of the Trilogy

The first play, *Agamemnon*, deals with the return of Troy's great conqueror to his palace in Argos, only to be murdered by his wife Clytemnestra, with the support of her lover, Aegisthus. Clytemnestra's prime motive is revenge for the sacrifice of Agamemnon's and her own daughter, Iphigenia, which was needed to further the great expedition to Troy to punish Paris and the Trojans for the abduction of Helen. Aegisthus is driven by a desire to avenge his father, Thyestes, for wrongs done in the previous generation by Thyestes' brother, Atreus, Agamemnon's own father: in a dispute over the sovereignty of Argos, Thyestes had seduced Atreus' wife and in return was served with the flesh of his two young children for meat. In the play, Agamemnon is killed by Clytemnestra along with Cassandra (the daughter of Priam, king of Troy), whom he has brought home as his concubine. By the end of the act, it is clear that Clytemnestra and Aegisthus will be the next victims in the retributory process, which is personified in a *daimon*, an evil spirit haunting the house.

Greek Tragedies as Plays for Performance, First Edition. David Raeburn.
© 2017 John Wiley & Sons, Inc. Published 2017 by John Wiley & Sons, Inc.
Companion website: www.wiley.com/go/raeburn

The inevitable follows in Act II, *Choephori*, when Agamemnon's son Orestes returns from exile to kill the two usurpers of his patrimony and exact revenge for his father's murder, at the command of Apollo, the god of the Delphic oracle. He triumphs, but his reward is to be pursued offstage in madness by the agents of his mother's vengeful wrath, the terrifying Furies.

In Act III Orestes, driven by the Furies, has sought refuge in Delphi, from where Apollo sends him on to Athens to appeal to the city's patron, Athena. Resolution is found after the goddess sets up a court of Athenian citizens on the Areopagus hill to try Orestes and adjudicate between the conflicting claims of the Furies and Apollo who represents Zeus, the supreme god. Zeus has been invoked in *Agamemnon* as the deity who guided mortals along a path of "learning by suffering." Orestes is acquitted and the anger of the Furies is assuaged by Athena, who persuades them to accept a benign cult-role in the polis.

Historical Background

The *Oresteia* was first performed at a period for Athens which was characterized by a clash between an older aristocratic class and the development of greater democracy in politics. The former was represented in public life by Cimon who admired the oligarchic Spartans and supported an alliance with them; the latter by Ephialtes, who in 461 successfully proposed an alliance with Sparta's enemy, Argos. The court of the Areopagus had formerly been an ancient aristocratic council, and Ephialtes had also engineered a reform which transferred some of its power to other bodies. Both these innovations were divisive and Ephialtes was murdered. These events doubtless underlie the passages in *Eumenides* which refer to everlasting friendship between Athens and Argos, the dignity of the Areopagus as a homicide court (which it had remained) and the avoidance of civil bloodshed.

Aeschylus, though, was a profound thinker and we may be equally sure that his vision transcended the events of his own time in a universal philosophy that human beings can learn from painful experience; they can develop institutions for the resolution of disputes which avoid the need for ongoing retaliatory violence and rely instead on the power of persuasion. His Trilogy can be seen as a mythological presentation of justice based on the family vendetta yielding to another system which depends on the collective jurisdiction of the city-state.

We might find a modern analogy to this in the evolution, after two extremely destructive world wars, of international law and the United Nations organization in resolving civil or inter-state conflict as far as possible by non-violent diplomatic means.

Other Themes in the Trilogy

Though the theme of *dikê*, justice, is central to this colossal work, it is strongly complemented by some original thinking on the relationship between the two main strands in Athenian cult: the worship of the Olympian gods in the sky (mostly male) and the "chthonian" deities associated with the earth and the underworld (mostly female). The former are typified in the Trilogy by Zeus, Apollo and Athena; the latter by the Erinyes or Furies, avenging spirits who owe their authority to Moira or Destiny. The Furies are, by definition, the natural agents of retributory, tit-for-tat justice; the Olympians are, eventually, associated with a more enlightened world order. Aeschylus also engages with philosophical issues of causation and human responsibility, including the notion of inherited guilt and the danger of excessive wealth and prosperity. Another theme, much emphasized today, is the relative status of men and women in society. Full exploration of these ideas lies outside the scope of this book (students are referred to Raeburn and Thomas 2011, Introduction xxx–xliv). They will be touched on as they affect Aeschylus' dramaturgy.

Dramaturgy

By 458 the third solo actor has been introduced and the dramatic possibilities of this are starting to be developed, as will be seen in the analysis of the individual plays. Stagecraft has advanced a long way between *Persae* and the *Oresteia*. A wooden stage-building is now in use, conceivably for the first time, from which the solo actors can make a central upstage entrance and retire into, in order to change costumes and masks for a different role, if required. It has now become an important feature of the "set," which the dramatist can exploit in a variety of ways.

Fundamental though, to Aeschylus' dramatic technique is the use of "word power," as derived from tragedy's sacral origin in choral lyric (see pp. 2, 17–18). The understanding that words operate like *actions* and can influence what follows for good or evil is the key to the play's dynamic. The drama of the *Oresteia* is controlled not so much by events in the normal plot sense as by *words* conceived as having a kind of magical power to determine what happens.

Another important feature that is illustrated in the dramatic analysis, is Aeschylus' use of lyric meter in his choral movements not only to create a mood or an effect but even to give a unity to his work by associating particular patterns of rhythm with key ideas underlying his Trilogy. A useful analogy to this is the use in Wagner's music dramas of leitmotif, an often repeated melodic phrase which is associated with a specific character or idea.

Finally, we may sense that the characters in the *Oresteia* are rather more fully delineated than in *Persae*. Although they are designed primarily to accord with Aeschylus' dramatic thrust and his main themes, each one is invested, selectively and economically, with enough features and, in some cases, development to come across as a dramatically convincing and vital individual (see Chapter 2, pp. 18–19).

AGAMEMNON

Synopsis

A watchman sights the beacon-signal which will notify the waiting Clytemnestra that Troy has been captured and that Agamemnon's homecoming is imminent. The Chorus of Argive Elders arrives to ask why sacrificial fires are being lit on the city altars. Clytemnestra announces the capture of Troy and describes the chain of beacons which has brought her the news; she also warns that the Greeks need to show respect for the gods in their victory to ensure their safe return. A herald arrives to report that Agamemnon has landed in Greece after razing Troy and its shrines to the ground – though he has lost the whole of his fleet, apart from his own ship, on the homeward journey.

Agamemnon finally enters, with Priam's daughter Cassandra as part of the spoil. Greeted by Clytemnestra, he is lured by her to enter his palace over a line of rich purple garments. Cassandra remains outside to prophesy what is to come before she follows the king indoors. Agamemnon's death cries are heard and throw the Chorus into confusion. Clytemnestra rejoices in triumph over the corpses of her husband and Cassandra but comes, under pressure from the Chorus, to realize that revenge must come to herself in due course. Aegisthus arrives in similar triumph also to be challenged by the Chorus; but he repels them forcibly with his guards. For the time being he and Clytemnestra can reign supreme.

Interpretation

This play, like *Persae*, follows the pattern of a *nostos*-plot, the main facts of which will have been familiar to Aeschylus' audience from Homer's *Odyssey* (Books 1, 3, 4, 13 and 14). In that, however, Aegisthus is the main villain and the prime motive is the adultery between him and Clytemnestra. Aeschylus followed the lyric poet Stesichorus in according the leading role in Agamemnon's murder to Clytemnestra and in the emphasis that he lays on the sacrifice of Iphigenia; this event plays a crucial part in the serial sequence of crime and punishment which constitutes the tragic situation of the Trilogy.

Agamemnon, therefore, cannot be seen as a personal tragedy. His murder is one of a series of crimes. It has its antecedents in the "Thyestean banquet," Paris's abduction of Helen in breach of the laws of hospitality, the sacrifice of Iphigenia and the destruction of innocents on both sides in the Trojan War. It has its crowning sequel in Orestes' murder of his mother. Human psychology, however, is not altogether absent. Agamemnon *chose* to sacrifice his daughter, to enable the Greek fleet to sail to Troy, and Aeschylus is at pains to suggest how that might have brought him to do such a frightful deed (218–27). He may have been paying for the sins of his father or subject to the curse of Thyestes, but he is also accorded the *hybris* or arrogance generated by excess of wealth or prosperity, which allows him to be tempted by Clytemnestra over the purple garments. These examples illustrate the complex amalgam that we find in Aeschylus between human and divine causation or between determination and responsibility (see Raeburn and Thomas 2011, Introduction xxvi–xl).

Agamemnon is not only the longest of the Trilogy's three acts but it is also much the weightiest as it introduces the full range of themes which have been outlined (pp. 34–35). The motif, however, that provides the driving impulse to the drama, as it does to the second play, is above all that "the doer must suffer," the notion of tit-for-tat justice which is self-perpetuating and ultimately futile. The so-called *lex talionis*, the law of retribution, is repeatedly affirmed and in this play is said to have the sanction of Zeus and the Olympian gods on the one hand and of the nether powers typified by the Furies on the other. The more comforting law that Aeschylus attributes to Zeus and is stated by the Elders near the start of *Agamemnon* (176–83) that "from suffering comes understanding" only makes sense in the context of the Trilogy as a whole.

Dramaturgy

The *skênê* representing the *oikos*, the *daimon*-haunted palace of Atreus is a looming presence throughout the play, a place which embodies the curse on the family and where sinister deeds are performed. The central door establishes a threshold which Clytemnestra, as the watchdog of the house, can guard and control and through which the *ekkyklêma* (p. 4) can be wheeled out to display the bodies of Agamemnon and Cassandra at the play's climax. The roof of the building can accommodate the Watchman in the Prologue.

Most of the play is performed by a single actor with the Chorus, as for most of *Persae*. Only in the central confrontation between Agamemnon and Clytemnestra are two actors onstage in mutual responsion. The third actor who plays Cassandra is initially mute and it is something of a surprise when the character breaks into utterance. Though Clytemnestra would have been played by the protagonist and is one of the most challenging parts in Greek tragedy, the largest is played by the Chorus who function ostensibly as the old men of Argos reacting to the play's events. They are also used by Aeschylus to narrate past events and articulate the ideas which underpin his interpretation of the inherited myth. The choral songs are crucial to the play's whole texture and contribute vitally to its dramatic continuity.

The importance to Aeschylus of word power in giving his plays momentum has already been strongly emphasized. In *Agamemnon* it is remarkable that virtually nothing seems to happen during the first half of the play, which leads up to Agamemnon's entrance and lasts over an hour in acting time. All we learn in action terms is that Troy has been captured and that Agamemnon is on his way home. Clytemnestra has been established as a very sinister presence, but we never see her, as we might in a modern play, plotting murder with Aegisthus, who is never even mentioned by name until after Agamemnon has been killed. And yet the tension and suspense have been built up during that hour on great waves of foreboding, so that when Agamemnon is wheeled onstage in his wagon we know with overwhelming certainty that he is doomed. Aeschylus achieves this by an accumulation of words of ill omen prevailing over words of good omen. The Watchman, Herald and Chorus are all anxious for the issue which is Agamemnon's safe homecoming. They try to speak the auspicious word, but again and again their train of thought and utterance leads them inexorably to the expression of the unpropitious. Clytemnestra, on the other hand, uses words to undermine Agamemnon's *nostos* and to promote the downfall of which she is to be the main human agent. Aeschylus makes her use language that is ostensibly well-omened but in fact malevolently ambiguous. Her words in this way can be understood like the spells or the curses of witchcraft. Blessings and curses – therein lies the key to Aeschylus' extraordinary dynamic and powerful dramatic technique.

Dramatic Analysis

Line references refer to the Greek text in the Loeb edition (see Notes at the end of this chapter), which has a parallel English translation. For the terminology of the discrete movements, see Appendix A; for the lyric structure and meters, see Appendix B or hear TRACK 0 ⊚.

Prologue (1–39)

This opening movement to the Trilogy offers a perfect illustration of Aeschylus' characteristic dramaturgy. It takes the form of a monologue delivered by the Watchman who has been posted by Clytemnestra on the roof of the palace of Atreus to sight the beacon-signal that will bring her news of Troy's capture and so of Agamemnon's imminent return. As the speech develops it becomes clear that the Watchman is loyal to his master Agamemnon and unhappy about dark goings-on in the house.

The newly (or recently) introduced stage-building at once comes into its own, with the Watchman intriguingly mounted aloft. His first sentences identifies what the *skênê* is supposed to represent, but later references to "the *oikos* here" give flesh to the location; it is unsatisfactorily managed (19) and has a story it could tell (37–8). A few words operate to give the building a sinister presence.

The opening line of the speech is, "I ask the gods for a release from these toils." Significantly, the Trilogy has opened with a prayer, which immediately establishes the word-power convention. In "release from toils" the Watchman is, of course, referring to his toilsome vigil, but the phrase could also serve as an image for the wearisome cycle of retribution from which humanity is to find release in *Eumenides*. These words were also associated with the Mysteries of Eleusis, the city where Aeschylus was born, and betokened the promise of an afterlife in rites which featured torches of fire blazing out of the darkness at the climax.

The Watchman tells us that his task has brought him to know the stars, both the "commonality" of them and also the "bright dynasts," the constellations that conspicuously mark the seasons. The imagery is not merely decorative. Aeschylus' drama is being accorded a cosmic, as well as a local, setting that includes a scheme or order in society. He is now watching out for a fire-signal at the behest of "a woman's *male-counselling*, expectant heart" (11) – an important first clue to Clytemnestra's characterization. She is a woman with a man's power of initiative, as she has to be in ancient Greek society if she is going to kill her husband.

Lines 12–21 introduce a recurring pattern of thought and utterance. When the Watchman tries to remedy his anxious sleeplessness by singing or humming, he *weeps* for the misfortune of the house, which is "not managed ideally as in the past." The pattern is one of *trying* to say or do something positive in a gloomy situation but ending up feeling more gloomy and miserable than ever. That is exactly what happens in the choral songs and episodes leading up to Agamemnon's entrance.

The paradigm is illustrated immediately. After a long pause, and in a thrillingly dramatic moment, the Watchman sights the beacon and hails it with rapturous joy. He calls on Clytemnestra to raise the *ololugmos euphēmōn*, "the woman's cry of triumph in *well-omened* utterance" (28). He himself will dance the prelude, now that his master's luck has thrown him a triple six. But then the cloud starts to move across the sun. "Well, at any rate" (an interesting combination of Greek particles which suggests an ellipse of something better left unsaid), "I hope to grasp my beloved master's hand in mine when he returns. For the rest, I am silent. A great ox is standing on my tongue (another phrase very possibly derived from the Eleusinian Mysteries). The house itself, if it could find a voice, would say it most clearly. For my part, I *deliberately* speak to those who have learnt; to those who have not learnt – I forget" (34–9). The Watchman has concluded on a deeply sinister note. His joy over the beacon and the capture of Troy has been eclipsed by the thought of adultery in the house. To mention that specifically would be ill-omened and damaging. He can only speak in mysterious terms to the initiated; that must be the audience who are in the know because they are familiar with the myth. There is no more that can be said or should be said.

Parodos (40–257)

This, the longest choral movement in extant Greek tragedy, can be considered as an event of quasi-ritual which, in the dramatic context, is designed to promote a favourable issue for Agamemnon's homecoming. Like the Watchman, the Chorus of Argive Elders keeps trying to say positive things but finds itself saying the opposite, which at the end can only be wrapped up in euphemistic terms. During the course of this sequence, themes are stated which will run through the Trilogy as a whole, much as in the opening movement of a classical symphony.

Detailed analysis should be preceded by a general point. The Chorus in Agamemnon plays only a small part in the physical action (those in *Choephori* and *Eumenides* do more), but its songs are in no sense interruptions but form a vital part of the whole play's structure and momentum; they get steadily shorter as the tension of the drama mounts towards the climax of Agamemnon's death-cries. Where their own separate form is concerned, Aeschylus makes use of two important features in the genre of choral lyric: the narrative element which allows him to elaborate (in magnificent poetry) on the background to the drama's events, particularly the parts played in the story by Iphigenia and Helen; and the "gnomic" element, the proclamation of moral truth which provides the universal perspective. In an important sense, the Chorus in this play has the leading role.

The movement begins with a long section of introductory anapaests (40–103) in rhythmical spoken mode, perhaps divided up between the Leader and the Chorus as a whole (as in the opening of *Persae*, p. 24). The choral song proper falls into three further sections, characterized by different meters: dactylo-iambic (104–59), trochaic (160–91) and "syncopated" iambic (192–257), with excursions into other meters (see Appendix B). The music to be heard in the different rhythms (see p. 35) is an important dimension in appreciation. We are far closer here to a musical composition than to a play as we understand the word.

Lines 40–103 (Introductory Anapaests)

Led on by the aulete to this strong marching rhythm, the Chorus makes a confident start as it tells of the warlike mission of a thousand ships and how Zeus, god of hospitality, sent the Ares-screaming Atridae (Agamemnon and Menelaus) as a Fury – an interesting conjunction of Olympian and chthonian deities – to punish Paris. <TRACK B1, lines 40–59> ◉ But before long, we learn of "many heavy-limbed wrestlings" (63) for Greeks and Trojans alike and the "stubborn anger" (of the gods) which is not to be propitiated by offerings of any kind. At 72 the Elders go on to characterize themselves as weak old men, left behind at home by the expedition, supporting their strength on their staves – a crucial point to make in anticipation of their later impotence at the moment of Agamemnon's murder and against Aegisthus' bodyguards at the end of the play.

At 83 the mood brightens and the tempo quickens as the Elders address Clytemnestra (in her absence, apparently)[1] and ask the reason for the sacrificial fires that are springing up all over the city. Their lively description, however, soon leads to a plea to "heal this anxiety" (98–9), as they describe their shifting feelings of hope and malignant foreboding.

Lines 104–59 (Dactylo-Iambic Triad)

The first sung lyric section takes the formal triadic structure of strophe, antistrophe and epode. Most of it is composed in rolling dactyls, in the grand manner of Homeric epic or of oracles, as befits the story that the Chorus goes on to tell of the omen which attended the departure of the Greek host for Troy. "I have the authority to *utter*," it begins (104). The Elders may be physically weak and infirm, but their narration as a chorus has strength and significance – through word power. The omen is of two eagles observed tearing a pregnant hare. <TRACK B2, lines 104–21> ◉ This is interpreted by the prophet Calchas (126 ff.) as having both a good and a bad side (145). The eagles stand for the two Atridae and the hare is Troy, which is going to be destroyed; but her unborn young signify the innocent victims of the war, of whom Agamemnon's own daughter, Iphigenia, is going to be the prototype. Artemis, as a goddess of childbirth and also the patroness of hunting who controls how animals should be killed, "hates the eagles' feast" (137).

Calchas goes on cryptically to anticipate the heaven-sent storms that will delay the Greek fleet at Aulis and necessitate the sacrifice of Iphigenia. He continues: "For there awaits a frightening, resurgent, crafty housekeeper, a remembering Wrath that avenges a child" (154–5). The thrust of the choral utterance is now that the sacrifice of Iphigenia and Clytemnestra's consequent murder of Agamemnon are implicit in the very launching of the Trojan expedition – a profoundly depressing conclusion to have already reached. Hence the refrain which is sung at the end of all three stanzas: "*ailinon*, say *ailinon*, but let the good win out." The cry of woe, *ailinon*, is particularly associated with dirges. Its rider is a hope-against-hope prayer that is somehow intended to modify the evil omen. <TRACK B3, lines 140–59>

Lines 160–91 (Two Pairs of Trochaic Strophes)

At this point the Chorus breaks off their narrative in a passage commonly referred to as the Hymn to Zeus. There is a switch to a new contrasting meter, trochaics, which Aeschylus seems to associate with a search for an ultimate meaning to the story he is unfolding. To avert the evil effect of their words so far, the Elders invoke the name of Zeus as the supreme god to call on if one is to offload the burden of anxiety. Their reason? "Zeus led mortals along the road of wisdom after validating the law, 'by suffering learning.'" (176–8) What does this mean? The context implies that that it must be a positive doctrine of hope, "From suffering comes under-standing."[2] This cannot be seen to apply to Agamemnon himself, as he evidently learns noth-ing during the course of the drama; it can only be interpreted within the framework of the Trilogy as a whole. It is *mortals* (176) who learn, drop by drop, through the toil of remem-bered pain (179–80), as they do when in *Eumenides* retaliatory justice is replaced by the col-lective justice of the Athenian polis. "Even to men against their will comes wisdom" (180–1). At *Eumenides* 1000 the Athenians who represent enlightened mortals are hailed by the mol-lified Furies as "showing wisdom in time." The burden of the Trilogy is that humanity can "move on," and Aeschylus firmly plants this idea in the "gnomic" part of the *Agamemnon* Parodos; it is far too crucial to be left until the end. <TRACK B4, lines 160–83> The poet skillfully integrates the theme, though, with the narrative of what happened at Aulis, intro-ducing it at an appropriate moment in the choral sequence and at the end dovetailing the resumed story of Agamemnon with the trochees of the Hymn to Zeus. Though Agamemnon himself does not learn from his suffering, his story typifies the sequence of futile retaliation which ultimately *forces* mankind to the "grace of wisdom" (182–3).

Lines 192–257 (Three Pairs of Strophes in "Syncopated Iambics")

In the third lyric section, the contrary winds begin to blow and create havoc in the camp at Aulis. The passage introduces another key meter, the syncopated iambic trimeter (see Appendix C). The rhythm, which involves an artificial prolongation of some long syllables has a taut, exciting effect. It recurs again and again in the *Agamemnon* lyrics and later on in the Trilogy as a rhythmic leitmotif associated with the idea of crime and retribution and the relentless operation of the *lex talionis*. This theme now resumes the sway it was holding in the content at the end of Calchas' prophecy, after the more hopeful theme of enlightenment expressed in the preceding trochees of the Hymn to Zeus. Other rhythms are added for special effect, as when the prophet screams out a "remedy for the bitter storm," implying the sacrifice of Iphigenia, and the frightened Atridae beat the ground with their staffs of office in verses of striking mimetic potential (198–204). <TRACK B5, lines 192–78> ◉

At 205 the story focuses on Agamemnon himself in his dilemma. One choral stanza (205–17) puts his thoughts into direct speech. Eventually, he "put on the halter of necessity" (218) and conjured up the will and the state of mind required to kill his daughter. The narrative tensely builds up to the moment when the gagged Iphigenia is lifted up over the altar and can only appeal to her killers with her eyes – a passage of great poignancy and beauty (239–47). But the Chorus characteristically stops short of the fatal stroke and replaces it with a remarkable euphemism: "The rest I neither saw nor tell of, but the crafts of Calchas were *not unfulfilled*" (248–9). In a final coda they return to the theme of "learning through suffering": in the course of justice the doctrine may be true in the long run, "but for the (immediate), future – you will hear when it happens," yet another euphemism to cover the bleakest possible outlook for Agamemnon (250–2). "*Well, at any rate*," they conclude, "may the issue turn out well" – once again, the desperate expression of hope against hope (255).

How might this rich dramatic movement be summed up? The mood and atmosphere have changed from initial confidence to deep foreboding, but there is much more to it than that. Aeschylus has not faced his audience with twelve old gaffers tediously reminiscing or piously moralizing. Here is a chorus of strength and dignity which, within the convention of lyric utterance, can present the launch of the brilliant Greek expedition to Troy, the ambivalent omens that attended it, the storm that prevented it from sailing and the sacrifice of Iphigenia as *events* no less powerfully – indeed more so, I suggest, with the selective economy of the poetic stylization – than they could be depicted visually in a modern film. Moreover, in the quasi-religious mode, Aeschylus has given his story a religious perspective: retaliatory justice upon Paris has the sanction of Zeus who has sent the Atridae as an avenging Fury. This justice has painful implications, but there is the consoling thought that pain may ultimately prove valuable to human beings generally. The concept is magnificent and the poetic execution consummate, particularly when enhanced by the power of music in a variety of significant rhythms.

First Episode (258–354)

Clytemnestra makes her grand first entrance at the *skênê* doors during the final lines of the Parodos (255–7). This is a solemn moment. The "child-avenging Wrath" (155) is there before us. In her reply to the Coryphaeus who has asked to know the reason for the sacrifices in Argos (261–3) she immediately strikes a note of authority. "Bearing good news … may dawn spring from her *mother* night … The Greeks have captured Priam's city" (264–7). The speech *sounds* like one of good omen; the past night (the Greek word for this means "kindly time") has given birth to dawn with good tidings of Troy's capture. But if the night is kindly, Clytemnestra's words may also suggest a "kindly mother" who wants to avenge her sacrificed daughter, a resonance that could deliberately undercut the good omen for Agamemnon. This may put us on the alert for further resonances and ambivalences.

The Coryphaeus is skeptical about Clytemnestra's announcement. How could she possibly know so soon about Troy's capture which has taken place only the preceding night (279–80)? The rest of the episode is almost entirely devoted to two long *rheseis*: one is an exciting and vivid description of the chain of beacons which has brought the news in one night from Troy to Argos; the other gives Clytemnestra's imaginary picture of the scene in Troy after the sack, followed by a stern warning that the Greeks should not destroy Troy's shrines, as they still have to return home safely. At the end of this the Coryphaeus declares himself convinced.

What are we to make of this as drama? Nothing is happening, apparently, to take the action forward. There are no hints of murder-plots or adulterous goings-on. Is it enough to say that the episode merely demonstrates Clytemnestra as formidable and dominating? Or, in the case of the beacon catalogue, that the Greeks had a taste for romantic geography?

The key lies, once again, in word power. In the beacon speech (281–316) all the various proper names can be shown to have some kind of sinister association with feminine treachery, ambushes, the death of kings and the like.[3] Viewed in that light, it is a more than lively description or a grand metaphor for the vengeance of Zeus, which struck down guilty Troy, now blazing across the sea to strike the palace of Atreus. It can rather be seen as an aggressive *action*: Clytemnestra is hammering verbal nails into Agamemnon's coffin, sticking pins like a witch into his wax image. This would explain the Coryphaeus' extremely odd comment in response to the speech (317–19): he would like to hear it all over again "from start to finish," a strong hint to the audience that there are layers of ulterior significance which might not be grasped at the first hearing. <TRACK B6, lines 281–9> ◉

Clytemnestra's second rhesis (320–50) is even more sinister. After describing the sad plight of the Trojans she goes on to enlarge on the disarray in the Greek army. In 345–7 she rehearses all the dangers in the Greek situation and in mentioning them makes them all the more likely to happen: offence to the gods (for sacking their shrines), reawakening the suffering of the dead (Iphigenia and all the innocent victims of war); then, for good measure, accidental evils. Clytemnestra is again using words as weapons to damage Agamemnon's cause and to further her own.

The result of these verbal acts of aggression is that, by the end of the episode, our sense of foreboding is strongly intensified. We have now met Clytemnestra with her "woman's male-counselling heart" (11) and also the self-assertion as a woman (348) with which she counters the Coryphaeus' scepticism.

First Stasimon (355–487)

At 352 the Coryphaeus has accepted the reliability of Clytemnestra's evidence for Troy's capture: it is now an established fact. Leading on from this there follows another long choral song, though shorter by some 75 lines than the Parodos. The technique which gives the ode its dynamic is very similar. It starts with a hymn of praise and thanksgiving to Zeus for the victory over Paris and Troy; it ends on a theme of public resentment against the Atreidae and a grim comment on the dangers of conquest. This leads the Elders (or some of them), in an after-song, to question whether the beacon messages were to be trusted after all.

The movement as a whole follows a subtle train of associated ideas, whereby the laws which govern Paris's crime and Paris's punishment can be seen to apply no less to Agamemnon. The subject matter keeps shifting, but the metrical structure is largely constant, as though to underpin the principle which gives the song its unity and logic.

In form we have a few introductory anapaests (probably delivered by the Coryphaeus), followed by three strophic pairs and, finally, by an epode in altogether different vein. The strophic stanzas (367–474) are largely iambic – though the final pair is more complex in a peculiarly exciting way – and chiefly based on the syncopated leitmotif of crime and retribution. Each of the six stanzas, unusually, has a metrically identical coda of four lines in a contrasting aeolic meter. <TRACK B7, lines 367–84>

The train of thought and imagery which the chorus "tracks out" (368) starts with gnomic utterances about the punishment of the sinner, as typified by Paris, who is forced on by *Peitho*, Persuasion or temptation, the intolerable child (slave) of calculating *Atê*, Ruin, and eventually, like bad coinage, revealed for what he is and brought to inescapable justice. The song moves on, in magnificent poetry, to the flight of Helen and so to the picture of the abandoned Menelaus, then to the lonely Greek women who sent their husbands to Troy and received them back in unrecognizable form, as ashes in urns. In a famous image, war is presented as a gold-changer who converts human bodies into the new gold-dust of ashes.

The sequence grows even darker: resentment is mounting among the people of Argos in secret mutterings against their kings. The musical impact in the final stanza is particularly striking, as the Chorus voices its anxiety in the light of the people's anger. "The gods do not fail to spy the killers of many and the black Furies in time reduce to dimness a man who prospers without justice ... Over-great glory is a sore burden; the lightning bolt is cast from the eyes of Zeus. I prefer a prosperity that is unenvied. May I never be a city-sacker!" A devastating conclusion has been reached. The song as a whole has driven a huge nail into Agamemnon's coffin. <TRACK B8, lines 457–74>

The epode (475–87) is a kind of appendage, though still in syncopated iambics, in which the Chorus or very probably three individual Elders, cast doubts on the truth of the beacon's message and express sexist sentiments about feminine gullibility. This runs completely contrary to the Coryphaeus' assent at 352 to "trustworthy signs" but is perfectly intelligible if we remember that the beacon's news motivated the start of the ritual song which, in its unity of structure and meter, has led the Chorus inexorably to a conclusion they would now like to unsay.

Second Episode (489–680)

"Soon we shall know", says the Coryphaeus, "whether the beacon-signal told the truth. I see a herald coming" (489–502).[4] Quite a long time, perhaps several weeks, can be taken to have elapsed during the preceding stasimon. Tragedy after Aeschylus treated the presence of the Chorus throughout the play more realistically and only assumed short intervals of time between the episodes, but Aeschylus was not bothered by that.[5] He was composing within the convention of the choral hymn which allows one significant event in a story to follow another without regard for time-gaps.

The function of the Herald scene is to deepen the audience's sense of foreboding still further, in anticipation of Agamemnon's entrance in the following episode. Operating essentially through word power, it follows the, by now, well-established paradigm of confidence clouded over by gloom. It resembles the Messenger scene in *Persae* and later uses of the Messenger convention in containing much rapportage of offstage events; but it differs from the latter by including three long speeches, not just one, and from the former in that the news deliverer is quite strongly characterized in his own right. The Herald is a soldier back from the wars, deeply conscious of his news-bearing role and very involved in the story he is telling. The scene also contains some of the finest poetry in all Greek tragedy.

The episode consists essentially of two speeches by the Herald, one by Clytemnestra and then one more by the Herald. The Coryphaeus is skillfully used to cover transitions and elicit information in stichomythia.

Lines 503–37

The Herald begins his opening rhesis with a deeply affecting greeting to the homeland he has not seen for ten years. Perhaps he kneels and kisses the earth like Agamemnon or Odysseus in Homer (*Odyssey* 4.521–2, 13.354). He then hails the gods of Greece and the royal palace of Argos. The victorious Agamemnon has returned, bringing "light in the darkness" after "digging down Troy with the mattock of justice-bearing Zeus." All seems thoroughly well-omened – until we hear that the Greeks have sacked the seats of the gods (527)[6] and recall Clytemnestra's stern warning in the previous episode (339). As an audience we shudder; quite inadvertently, the Herald has used words of ill omen. At 530 he boldly speaks of Agamemnon as a "happy man" – tempting providence if we remember the old Greek saying, "Call no man happy until he is dead."

Lines 538–50

The speech is followed by a stichomythic exchange with the Coryphaeus. The Herald responds to the Leader's greeting by affirming that death will no more be unwelcome to him. As the dialogue continues, it emerges that, just as the Greeks longed for home while they were at Troy, the Leader missed the army with an uneasiness for which "silence has been the medicine" (548). He, like the Herald (though for another reason) would be happy to die.

Lines 551–82

"Yes, all is now well," the Herald cheerfully continues as he starts his second rhesis. But at once he goes on to describe the horrors which the besieging army endured at Troy in a wonderful passage which, in 458 BC, would have resonated powerfully with men who had served in the campaigns of the previous year. <TRACK B9, lines 555–67> ⏺ But goodbye to all that. In more upbeat vein the Herald envisages the Greeks nailing the trophies of victory to their temple walls as an everlasting memorial and builds up in a blaze of triumph to end, "You have the whole story." But do they?

Lines 583–6

At this point the Herald starts to move toward the palace doors, only to be frustrated by Clytemnestra making a "talk of the devil" entrance as the Coryphaeus names her (585). Critics rightly make much of Clytemnestra as the watchdog (607) who controls the interior of the house and the threshold across which Agamemnon will be lured to his destruction (see Taplin 1977, 299–302). The Herald's second speech has ended on a sunny note, but now the atmosphere suddenly becomes overcast and the clouds grow darker and more thundery as the episode moves to its conclusion.

Lines 587–614

Clytemnestra begins not by welcoming the Herald but by snubbing him. She implies that she already knows his news, and speaks contemptuously of the sexist criticisms made of her reliance on the beacons – as though she knew what had been said behind her back in the coda of the First Stasimon (483–8). She then gives the Herald a message of greeting to her husband and, with outrageous hypocrisy, protests her loyalty to him during his absence. Her final profession (611–12) is deeply sinister: she knows no pleasure or scandalous rumor at another man's hands any more than she knows how to "dip" (temper) "bronze" (the art of the blacksmith), a very damaging utterance when we think of the bronze sword which is soon to be "dipped" in Agamemnon's blood. Ending her speech with a powerful assertion of her womanhood (614), Clytemnestra makes her exit and retires into her kennel.

Lines 615–35

In a further passage of transitional stichomythia the Coryphaeus questions the Herald about the homecoming of Menelaus, and the confident façade cracks. Menelaus and his ship have disappeared in a storm, which the Coryphaeus assumes was due to divine anger (635).

Lines 636–80

The first sentence of the Herald's final rhesis is highly significant dramaturgically: "It is not right to *pollute* a day of good omen with tongue of ill tidings." The speaker is deeply conscious of virtually destroying the beneficial effect of his good news by following it with bad. He describes this paradoxically as a "paean of the Furies" (645); the triumph song has turned to a dirge. For him the storm also bodes the anger of the gods (649). Then he proceeds to his graphic description of the conspiracy between fire and sea which destroyed the Greek fleet, as the winds caused the ships to butt against each other like goats whirled round by a wicked shepherd and left the Aegean sea "flowering with corpses and ships' wreckage." <TRACK B10, lines 650–60> ◉ By good luck Agamemnon's ship was saved, but the fate of the rest of the fleet is unknown. And now the poignant ending: "May it be as well as possible" (674) – the usual cry in despair. "Yes, as for Menelaus, the best thing is to *expect* that he has returned. *Well, at any rate*, if any ray of sun detects him alive, by the plan of Zeus not wishing to *annihilate* the race, there is some *hope* that he will return home. So much you have heard. Know that it is the truth."

   The whole truth has now been told. The Herald can be imagined making a very slow, despondent exit. The sky is now really black and depressing.

Second Stasimon (681–781)

The Herald scene ends on a note of bleak foreboding. The ensuing choral song is the final stage in the ritual performance which culminates in Agamemnon's appearance onstage in person. As in the First Stasimon, the thought shifts ground as it proceeds; the unifying idea is that a name, a word, a song, a situation, an evil deed always contains the seed of something else. The language of "giving birth" dominates the later stanzas, and one might indeed see the whole of the play so far as the process of gestation which brings to birth the dramatic outcome that the audience is going to witness after Agamemnon's return.

   The ode contains four pairs of strophes and their meter this time is much more complex, reflecting the changes implied in the argument. One can imagine that the choreography too becomes correspondingly elaborate as the winding of the spell is completed.

Lines 681–716

The Chorus turns first to the thought of Helen: in the destruction she wrought she was rightly named. The point depends on a play of words and the belief that a person's destiny may be enshrined in their name (p. 18). The syllable *hel-* is the root of a Greek verb meaning "capture" or "destroy." Hence Browning's translation, "Ships' hell, man's hell, city's hell." Helen proved all these things when she was followed to Troy by a host of "shielded huntsmen" who brought a bloody war with them. Similarly, Troy had to endure a "marring marriage," the phrase which Louis MacNeice found to render a pun on the noun *kêdos*, which can mean both a "marriage alliance" and also "grief, sorrow." Word power, as ever, is at work and advancing the movement of the whole drama: names are being translated into realities, words into events. What has only been spoken of so far is shortly to become alive in onstage action.

Metrically, the first five verses of the first strophe are trochaic, as in the Hymn to Zeus with its search for underlying significance in the Parodos. This gives way to two more complicated aeolo-choriambic phrases, quickly followed by a run of ionics in contrasting 3/4 time to describe Helen's flight across the sea, rounded off by three steadier aeolic cola as the Greeks establish their footing in Troy. <TRACK B11, lines 681–98>

Lines 717–49

In the Chorus's narrative of the Trojan War, Paris's and Helen's wedding song has now turned to a dirge of lamentation (709–11). In their second strophic pair and the strophe of the third the Elders continue with a fable about a lion-cub, told to reflect the contrasting situations created by the presence of Helen at Troy. When young this creature is a gentle, delightful pet; but later its inherited wild nature is revealed. It begins to kill the sheep and turns out to have been sent by the gods as a "priest of Ruin." As the situation with the lion-cub changed, so did the situation at Troy. At first, there came a "spirit of windless calm, a gentle adornment of wealth, a soft dart from (her) eyes, a heart-biting flower of desire." Then (with a change of meter) all this delicious sensuality turns out to be a sinister Fury, sent by Zeus, god of hospitality (cf. 59–62), so that the end is bitterness (745) and lamentation (749). Helen has been converted into an avenging spirit, an Erinys in the person of the Atridae, who have now landed, conveyed by Zeus, on Troy's doorstep. <TRACK B12, lines 738–49>

Lines 750–81

As in the First Stasimon the focus shifted away from Paris and the Trojans to the Greeks, and Agamemnon, so now in the last stanzas the Elders turn away from Helen's impact on Troy to gnomic reflections which are more obviously relevant to Agamemnon and culminate in the king's entrance. They consider a traditional view that prosperity always generates sorrow but differ from it in believing that it is "the impious deed" (of the over-prosperous) which generates further sin, while the righteous house has a fair issue. At this point (763) the syncopated iambic rhythm reasserts itself with strong insistence as the Chorus introduces the word *hubris* into the sequence of its utterance: "One act of insolent pride breeds another at the appointed time, together with that invincible *daimon*, unholy boldness of black Ruin for (or in) the palace." This seems best understood as referring to Agamemnon's *hubris* in sacking the shrines of Troy, which is to lead on to a visible act of *hubris* in the following episode. We can also identify the "unholy boldness" (770) with Clytemnestra, who is later (1468–74) to be equated with the *daimon* which haunts the house of Atreus. <TRACK B13, lines 763–71> The train of words runs on relentlessly: "But Justice shines bright in smoky dwellings and honors the righteous man. She abandons gold-spangled abodes which are conjoined with filthy hands and visits what is pure, not revering the power of wealth falsely stamped with praise, and guides all to its appointed end."

Transitional Anapaests (782–801)

Enter Agamemnon, the prosperous sinner, in his wagon, to be hailed by the Chorus: "Come, king, city-sacker of Troy, offspring of Atreus!" The two appellations are hideously ill-omened. A "city-sacker" was what the Chorus in 472 did *not* wish to be; and a Greek certainly remembers what Atreus did to Thyestes' children in a crime so far unavenged. Agamemnon is paying for his own guilty deeds, which he can help, and also for his father's, which he cannot help. As in the words which immediately precede Macbeth's first entrance, "The charm's wound up." No character in drama was more surely doomed before he had spoken a word.

The entrance of Agamemnon is the first of two great climaxes; the second comes at the murder itself. It is also, to some degree, a moment of spectacle. The conqueror arrives not, we can be sure, in a magnificent war-chariot, which would be incompatible with what the Herald has told us, but in a simple cart, more probably drawn on by slave extras than by live horses or mules. He should not be imagined with a bodyguard either. Behind him, almost certainly in a second cart, is his captive Cassandra, not dressed in slavish rags but an august figure in the robes of a prophetess (1264–72).[7]

The passage of introductory anapaests is probably delivered by the Coryphaeus on his own. He confesses that it is hard to find an appropriate greeting for Agamemnon. He is torn between feelings of loyalty and disapproval of what the Trojan expedition entailed; he doubtless has the sacrifice of Iphigenia in mind. In such circumstances many would resort to insincere congratulations, but a "good judge of his flock" will not be taken in by eyes which "seem to fawn with watery friendship." The Coryphaeus concludes with a dark hint at "untimely" activities at home during Agamemnon's absence. The speech is important as a prelude to the engagement ahead. The issue now is: will Agamemnon be taken in by Clytemnestra's insincerity?

Third Episode (810–974)

Agamemnon's rhesis (810–54) opens with an impressive greeting to Argos and the gods who played their part in the justice he executed on Troy. His words are full of rich sound and grandiose imagery, as he describes the smoke rising in the ruined city and the wooden horse containing the shield-bearing host that surmounted the wall like a ravening lion and "lapped its fill of the kingly blood." The tone suggests a man with blood on his hands and proud of it. Then, significantly, Agamemnon turns to the Chorus and picks on the Leader's theme of insincerity. Yes, he agrees that most loyalty is spurious: only Odysseus proved a "ready tracehorse'" (841–2) – an interesting touch. The crafty Odysseus is an odd choice to single out for honesty, and it may cast doubts on Agamemnon's quality as a "judge of his flock." Anyway, he says he will now apply himself to the needs of the polis and, with a final greeting and prayer to the gods, prepares to enter the house.

But his entrance, like the Herald's before him, is frustrated by Clytemnestra. There she is again, occupying the way, so that Agamemnon has to enter his palace on her terms. The queen now embarks on a very long speech of 59 lines (855–913), the longest in the play; but this is no static demonstration of Clytemnestra's hypocrisy. The drama moves all the time. She starts, quite unrealistically, by addressing not Agamemnon but the Chorus. Describing her supposed anxieties during her husband's absence, she dwells on the rumors of his death with a kind of macabre fascination – all, of course, calculated ill-omened utterance. Only at 877 does she turn to Agamemnon himself to explain why his son Orestes is not there with her to welcome his father home: she sent him for his safety to Phocis, on the advice of King Strophius, and adds that there is "no deception" in this excuse – which makes it obvious to the audience that there is. *Cho.* 913 ff. makes it fairly clear that she really wanted her son out of the way, so that she could pursue her affair with Aegisthus (see Sommerstein, Loeb translation 329, n. 180). Whatever her real motive, though, the passage is important here for plot reasons: Orestes is brought into the story for the first time, and his absence abroad is established.

Clytemnestra's next ploy is to greet Agamemnon's return in a long series of gushing metaphors (896–901), probably accompanying this with an elaborate gesture of oriental obeisance, like the Chorus's prostration before Atossa in *Persae*. "Let *phthonos* [jealous resentment] be absent," she adds – but she has been *inviting* the *phthonos* of the gods by larding Agamemnon with all these images. At last she asks Agamemnon to leave his cart and calls on her hand-maidens to strew his path into the house over embroidered garments of rich purple, "so that Justice may lead him into his unexpected home," the home which, like the Herald, he may never have hoped to see again and also the one where he is to meet a very "unexpected" welcome.

The long carpet-like line of purple extending from Agamemnon's cart in the *orchêstra* up to the palace doorway creates a memorable spectacle, but the symbolism here is profoundly important. Clytemnestra is proposing an action of barbaric extravagance and wastefulness which no Greek in his right mind would assent to. She is exemplifying the Chorus's words in the First Stasimon (385–6) as the embodiment of "Temptation, child (slave) of Ruin who schemes ahead" and forces the sinner on until his wickedness is made manifest. Other words in the same ode are similarly echoed: it is the impious man who asserts that the gods are not concerned about men who "tread on the grace of things not to be touched" (369–72). For Agamemnon to do as Clytemnestra urges will also be the act of new *hubris* mentioned at the climax of the Second Stasimon and coupled with "the invincible *daimon* of black Ruin" (763–72) almost immediately before his entrance. Words are indeed being translated into realities, like Helen's name and the "marring marriage," the alliance that turned into sorrow.

Agamemnon's initial response to Clytemnestra's tempting invitation (914–30) is one of out-right disapproval and refusal. He is not a barbarian and, among the Greeks, such honors are due only to the gods. "Do not make my path subject to divine envy!" But Clytemnestra is too strong for him. The crucial pass of stichomythic dialogue which follows (931–43) is the only exchange between two solo actors in the play (as opposed to soloist and Coryphaeus). In a brief, hugely suspenseful build-up of specious argument, Clytemnestra wins every point and asserts her mastery. It occupies only thirteen lines, but Aeschylus has demonstrated Agamemnon's limited perspicacity well enough earlier in the scene to make the great conqueror's surrender perfectly plausible.

In his final speech (944–57), then, Agamemnon assents, though with some unease. As a gesture of humility, he asks for his sandals to be removed and prays that no *phthonos* from the gods will smite him as he walks over the precious materials. Briefly he introduces Cassandra as his prize gift out of the Trojan spoils and insensitively (by ancient standards, probably, as well as our own) asks for her to be kindly treated. Then he steps down from the cart: "I will go into my palace halls, *treading on purples*." The words, marked powerfully in the original by heavy alliteration, no less than the action, seal his fate. As he slowly advances from the centre of the *orchêstra* along the path resembling a great river of blood, Clytemnestra lures him on

Figure 4.1 *Agamemnon*, Greek Theatre, Bradfield College, England 1958. Source: Reproduced by permission of the Archive of Performances of Greek & Roman Drama.

in a magnificent speech (958–74) with a further profusion of imagery vested with sinister overtones. At 972 he is swallowed up in the darkness of the central entrance. She follows him up, but turns back in front of the doorway to deliver two lines in gloating triumph, a prayer to Zeus which is devastating in its malevolent ambiguity.

We now have to imagine Agamemnon's cart being led off, while the purple garments are lifted up and carried back into the house. Cassandra remains, a lonely figure in her separate wagon on the upstage edge of the *orchêstra*. The Chorus can now advance to occupy the circular space for their next song at this crucial juncture.

Third Stasimon (975–1033)

The keynote now is one of overwhelming fear and apprehension. The meter is predominantly trochaic, which takes us back to the Hymn to Zeus in the Parodos, so suggesting that the Elders are still struggling, though in vain, to find a meaning behind the terror-inspiring events that are being enacted. The opening lines of the original Greek are peculiarly expressive in the alliteration of "d" and "t" sounds. <TRACK B14, lines 975–87> 🔊

The text and language of this ode are very difficult, but the essential argument seems to run: Agamemnon's homecoming inspires no victory-song, only a "dirge of the Fury;" excessive wealth may be corrected by jettison, but there is no remedy for blood once shed. That is to say that the wealthy and also guilt-stained Agamemnon must pay for his daughter's sacrifice and the suffering of innocents in the Trojan War. Such is the ordained pattern of Justice, that it would be futile for the Elders to blurt out their fears (in a warning to Agamemnon). <TRACK B15, lines 1019–33> ⊚

All is now set. Agamemnon's murder-cries must surely be about to ring out. But this event does not happen for another 300 lines, about twenty minutes of acting time. An extraordinary scene follows in which the whole drama is in suspended animation.

Fourth Episode including *Kommos* (1035–330)

Cassandra has been in the acting area since Agamemnon's entrance but not, I have suggested, in the main picture until, to our surprise, Clytemnestra suddenly reappears: "Get yourself indoors you too, I mean Cassandra!" This is the first time that we have heard her name; Agamemnon has simply referred to her as "the foreign woman." We are thus reminded that the stranger in the second cart is a prophetess who could be dangerous to Clytemnestra's plans and plainly needs to be "got indoors." But this time the queen's mastery fails. Cassandra offers no response either to Clytemnestra's peremptory commands or to the Coryphaeus's gentler urging. She remains obstinately silent.

This is a very mysterious moment. The third actor was still a comparative novelty in 458, introduced (according to Aristotle) by Aeschylus' younger rival Sophocles during the previous few years. The impression given so far was rather that this character was a mute. At 1050–1 Clytemnestra raises the possibility that she only speaks a twittering barbarian language and cannot understand Greek. Yes, we suppose, she *must* be a mute. However this may be, Clytemnestra is defeated for the first time in the play and returns angrily into the palace. Left alone with Cassandra, the Coryphaeus appeals again in compassionate terms. And now the strange figure leaves her cart (which can then be discreetly moved by attendants down the nearby *eisodos*) and moves slowly into the middle of the *orchêstra*, while the Chorus regroups around her. Suddenly, she bursts out into three Greek cries expressive in turn of lamentation, pained surprise and horror, followed by an invocation to Apollo, her guardian deity. A third actor after all! Aeschylus was renowned for his use of silence for dramatic purposes, and this one must have been among his most effective.

Why does Aeschylus delay the catastrophic crisis of Agamemnon's murder over the long scene which follows? He needs to show that Agamemnon's death is not just a single event but part of a series, in relation to his main theme, the universal problem posed by justice that is purely retaliatory. Cassandra, with her gift of clairvoyance, can look back to the past of which she has no direct experience and also forward to the future. She can thus be used to link the murder of Agamemnon with its antecedents and its sequel in the story of the house of Atreus (p. 33). For this dramatic purpose Aeschylus skillfully exploits the story of how Apollo had pursued Cassandra in love and bestowed on her the gift of prophecy in anticipation that she would yield her virginity to him; she had then refused him and been punished with a curse that her prophecies would never be believed. This makes it plausible for the Chorus to be entirely bewildered by Cassandra's utterances and so creates a vital tension which can be maintained through the scene's full length.

Formally, the sequence falls into two sections. The first (1072–177) is a lyric *kommos* or lament,[8] during which Cassandra is shown in a trance and having strange visions that are expressed in agitated meters, notably the jerky *dochmiac* rhythm (see Appendix C). The Coryphaeus first responds in iambic couplets, then in couplets immediately followed by lyric passages for the full Chorus, until finally the Elders catch Cassandra's wild mood and lyrics take over altogether, while Cassandra herself follows dochmiacs with lyric couplets. This complex alternation between iambic speech and agitated song must have been extremely effective. A similar contrast can be seen, on a larger scale, between the first division of the scene and the second (1178–370), which is purely iambic, as Cassandra emerges from her trance and her prophecies grow calmer and more explicit, although her long speeches are still enlivened by two bursts of frenzy (1214–16, 1256–7).

Lines 1072–177 (*kommos*)

In the opening lines of this first, weirder and more agitated, division of the scene, Cassandra calls Apollo her Apollyon, her "destroyer." <TRACK B16, lines 1072–89> ◉ The god has brought her to a house which is "a god-hated place of kindred murder, a slaughter-house of *men* whose blood is sprinkled on the floor." At 1095 she has a further vision of "children lamenting slaughter, roasted flesh eaten by a father." The reference to the "Thyestean banquet" is clear even to the Chorus, for whom it is a known fact. But then at 1100 Cassandra sees a wife washing her husband at the bath and a "net of Hades," which is itself the wife. <TRACK B17, lines 1114–24> ◉ The audience, of course, can recognize this vision as Agamemnon's imminent murder by Clytemnestra who is to trap her husband in his bath by enfolding him in a large robe; but the Chorus is prevented by Apollo's curse on Cassandra from understanding the meaning of this cryptic utterance. Later (1136) the prophetess begins to foresee her own death and goes on to lament the wedding of Paris which led to the destruction of Troy, so working in two further elements in the chain of crime. <TRACK B18, lines 1136–45> ◉ The exchange ends in a heartfelt cry of perplexity from the Chorus: when will all these sufferings *end*?

Lines 1178–330

The second, iambic, section of this great scene, mostly in more rational vein, recapitulates much of the preceding material but also amplifies it. In 1186–93 Cassandra tells of the "revel-band of kindred Furies" who haunt the house of Atreus, "chanting the hymn of the primal act of ruinous folly," the original offence which was the adultery between Thyestes and Atreus' wife. After her first long speech, in stichomythia with the Coryphaeus, Cassandra confesses the story of her own relationship with Apollo, which leads on at 1214 to a fresh attack of frenzy and a second long speech. Here she has a further gruesome vision of the Thyestean banquet, "children filling their hands with flesh that fed their own kin," and then foretells the vengeance of Aegisthus and Clytemnestra more explicitly than before. But her meaning still eludes the curse-ridden Chorus (1245). Now comes the crucial moment when she comes out with the straight truth: "It is *Agamemnon's death* I say you will witness," to receive the Coryphaeus' appalled response: "Lull your lips, rash woman, to *speech of good omen*!" After all the careful reticence with which the Chorus, like the Watchman and the Herald, have expressed their foreboding, the dreadful words *"Agamemnon's death"* have now been unequivocally spoken. Cassandra, in the Coryphaeus' book, has virtually *condemned* Agamemnon to death by her ill-omened language. He still prays (1249) that it will not happen and asks

(1051) "What *man* is procuring this grievous thing?" He has missed the point; Apollo's curse on Cassandra is still in operation.

Once more (1256) the fire comes over Cassandra and in a third rhesis, she foretells her own murder by Clytemnestra. In another intensely dramatic moment she divests herself of her prophetic garments and insignia; then, in a sudden pathetic return to reason, she realizes poignantly that Apollo is punishing her and leading her to her death. But now a new point: she will not be dishonored by the gods. A "mother-killing offspring" (1281) will return to avenge his father. Here at last is the reference to Orestes whose enforced crime in the second act of the Trilogy will crown the retaliatory series of which Agamemnon's death is a part. The future has finally been embraced along with the past and the present.

The remainder of the episode (from 1285) is perhaps the most moving passage in the whole play. Cassandra advances upstage towards the palace entrance with calm dignity, in the role of a willing sacrificial victim, much to the Coryphaeus' admiration. Suddenly (1307), she recoils in disgust at the horrible smell from the palace within, "like the stench from a grave." But soon she pulls herself together and formally calls on the Elders to be her witness when vengeance arrives for her and Agamemnon. Her final lines (1327–30) are a lament, no longer for herself but for the shadowiness of prosperity and the fragility of all human life. Thus, at the conclusion of this long scene, so integral to his total design, Aeschylus represents his tragedy as a universal situation and not one that simply relates to a particular individual from the legendary past.

Choral Anapaests (1331–42)

In this highly charged emotional atmosphere, the moment we have waited for so long, poised in air, has at last arrived. Instead of another lyric stasimon, the Chorus is given a brief but very impressive passage of pounding anapaests, perhaps (like the opening of the Parodos) divided between the Coryphaeus and the Chorus as a whole. Starting from Cassandra's final theme of human prosperity, they exemplify this in Agamemnon's predicament. He has returned home honored by the gods; but if he is to be caught up in a never-ending chain of crime and retribution, "Who could boast that he was born with a harmless destiny, hearing these things?" The verse lends itself to a grand crescendo of vocal sound which reaches a fortissimo climax in this powerful exclamation of protest and despair. <TRACK B19, lines 1331–42> ◉

Fifth Episode (1343–576) including *Epirrhema* (1407–576)

Lines 1343–71

"Hearing these things." On this cue we *hear* Agamemnon's anguished and repeated death-cry as he is murdered offstage. The Coryphaeus responds in three rapid-running trochaic tetrameters (see Appendix B), the last urging that the Elders consult together to produce a plan. Here at this climactic moment, in what *happens* on stage, Aeschylus comes up with a masterpiece of dramaturgy. The corporate personality of the Chorus, with its orderly controlling ritual, is shattered for a brief but extremely compelling moment and split up into its component parts. The choreographic symmetry is broken as we watch twelve frightened old men arguing in shapeless confusion about what they ought to do. Should they confront the murderers immediately or adopt a more cautious approach? A bomb has dropped on a papal High Mass – a magnificent *coup de théâtre* to express the tragic catastrophe, the disharmony and havoc in nature and society that are instanced in King Agamemnon's death at the hands of his own wife. Each of eleven choreuts is allotted his individual iambic couplet to offer his own view, and the jabbering only ceases when the Leader, in a twelfth, restores order and marshals them all once again into a united body to break into the palace. But as they perhaps advance in a horizontal line towards the *skênê*, the central doors swing open and, in contrary motion, the *ekkyklêma*, the low trolley on wheels (possibly deployed now for the first time) rolls out towards them, in a tableau displaying the bodies of Agamemnon and Cassandra with Clytemnestra standing over the corpses, sword in hand.

Lines 1372–406

In a grand rhesis addressed to the Chorus Clytemnestra proudly discards all her earlier pretences and triumphantly announces that she has done the deed. The wealth of gory detail that is later to be found in the Messenger speeches of Sophocles and Euripides is entrusted to her, as she relives every detail of her hideous murder of Agamemnon: her casting of a rich robe, like a fishnet, to trap him, followed by three ritual strokes of her sword, and her crazy joy in being bespattered by the blood spurting from her husband's body, as the budding crops rejoice in Zeus's gift of the rain. Clytemnestra's frenzied relish in the slaughter of the helpless king suggests nothing short of demonic possession. When the Coryphaeus expresses his shock at her exultant tone, she unflinchingly proclaims her indifference to the Elders' censure: there lies Agamemnon's corpse, the work of a "just craftsman" (1406). This "demonic" self-assertion can be seen as the base-line in the "epirrhematic" exchange with the Chorus that follows.

Lines 1407–576

In the first section of the *epirrhema* the Chorus expresses their horrified reaction in two powerful dochmiac stanzas, each followed by a fairly long iambic speech (14 and 17 lines respectively) in which Clytemnestra attempts to justify herself. The Elders suggest that the queen must have been driven mad by eating a poisonous herb or drinking seawater (apparently) to have been capable of such a hateful abomination which must bring down the people's wrath on her head. She on her side refers to the sacrifice of Iphigenia and affirms that she has nothing to fear so long as Aegisthus, now named for the first time in the play, remains loyal to her. This takes her on to Agamemnon's sexual infidelities and to gloat with vigorous explicitness over her murder of his concubine Cassandra.

The second section introduced at 1448 is a long exchange of lyric or anapaestic stanzas, arranged in quite a complicated musical structure, during which the Chorus and Clytemnestra explore and dispute the question of responsibility for Agamemnon's murder. The Elders are given lyric meters for their sung accusations, lamentations and warnings in words not usually directed straight at Clytemnestra. Each of their three strophic pairs contains a largely anapaestic *ephymnion* (here meaning a song to a person or deity), starting with the cry *io* by way of lamentation, delivered after the strophe. The second of them, which is a lament for Agamemnon, is given centrality by being chanted a second time after the antistrophe. Clytemnestra responds consistently as if she were on the defensive, and her medium is *spoken* anapaests, so offering, as in the Cassandra scene, an interesting contrast between the two utterance-modes of song and speech. The prevalence of judicial language throughout the

Figure 4.2 *Agamemnon*, Greek Theatre, Bradfield College, England 1958. Source: Reproduced by permission of the Archive of Performances of Greek & Roman Drama.

exchange gives this movement the atmosphere of a trial. To explain the dramatic development, the conflicting viewpoints are better summarized separately rather than in piecemeal alternation.

The Chorus, as one should expect, takes Agamemnon's part and bewails all the deaths caused by the two sisters, Helen and Clytemnestra (1455–61). At 1468 the Elders' viewpoint on the murder shifts a little. They see it not as a one-off crime or an act of personal revenge but as part of the calamitous history of the accursed family whose *daimon* or evil genius shares with Clytemnestra the guilt of bloodshed. Vividly, they imagine the evil spirit standing, as Clytemnestra is, over Agamemnon's corpse, like a raven tunelessly singing a song of joy. Zeus is in any case the cause of all (1485–6). But even if an avenging spirit may have been Clytemnestra's accomplice, she is not herself free from guilt (1505–8). The god of destruction is forcing his way on with *new* streams of kindred blood (1509–12). Justice is being sharpened for another deed of harm on whetstones of *Moira*, destiny (1535–6). It is the law that *the doer must suffer* (1564).

Through this important sequence of thought, so fundamental to Aeschylus' conception, the syncopated iambic rhythm, the leitmotif of retribution, becomes more and more insistent, and rings out powerfully in the Elders' final cry of despair: "Who could expel the seed of the curse from the house? The race is *clamped* to Ruin [*Atê*]" (1566).

The shift in Clytemnestra's thinking under this relentless pressure is remarkable, though it is less highly coloured by metaphor, as might be expected in the spoken anapaests which are her assigned medium. At first she eagerly clutches at the suggestion that the *daimon* is responsible, "masquerading as the wife of the dead man here" (1500–1), as she starts to distance herself from what she has done. But little by little the implications of this dawn on her. *She* will be next on the list of the *daimon's* victims in the retributive process. She still clings to her grievance as a mother deprived of her child and, in bitter irony, imagines Iphigenia meeting her father by the entry to the underworld and throwing her arms round him to kiss him. But by now Clytemnestra is frightened. When at 1564 the Chorus reaffirms the law of retaliation, she accords an oracular authority to their words (1567–8). She would like to make a pact with the *daimon* by putting down blood money if it will only go away and haunt some other house. Blood money is a response to homicide mentioned in Homer (*Iliad* 9.632–6, 18.497–500), but this is a forlorn hope. In the world of the *Oresteia* there is no remedy for blood once shed (1019–21, *Cho.* 48). <TRACK B20, lines 1530–76> ◉

In this intriguing dramatization of Clytemnestra we can see the beginnings of what we call "character development" in drama. At the moment of the murder Aeschylus has presented her as demonically possessed; she personifies the "child-avenging Wrath" of Calchas' prophecy (155) and, as such, has embodied the evil genius of the house. But gradually the spirit has left her and she starts to appear more as a normal woman who can voice maternal feelings and now appreciate what is coming for her. She is almost pathetic; her old forcefulness and self-assertion, her masculine power of initiative is deflated and she only longs to be rid of the whole crazy, ugly business.

The drama of *Agamemnon* has not ended with the king's murder. In this last quasi-operatic sequence nothing at all has happened in terms of actual events; but the dynamic has been sustained by an exciting and moving confrontation between the Chorus and Clytemnestra, as both sides in their different ways perceive the significance of past and present, as Cassandra has done, and anticipate an alarming future in the forward march of justice. Our attention to this has been enhanced, as in the Cassandra scene, by the variety of a complex rhythmical structure and some magnificent imagery, of which this account has included only a small sample.

Exodos (1577–673)

What can happen next? Aeschylus surprises us once again with the sudden arrival of a new character, Aegisthus – not, of course, from the house but along an *eisodos* – accompanied by a band of guards. In a splendid rhesis (1577–611) he gloats over the death of Agamemnon. His own ground for satisfaction is the attainment of revenge for the crime of Atreus against his own father Thyestes. He gives a lurid account of the gruesome banquet which leads up to Thyestes putting a curse on the whole house. At 1604 he claims the credit for "stitching" Agamemnon's murder as the instrument of Justice. At this point the theme of inherited guilt comes more to the fore among the complex of motivating factors in the play's action.

We can also note how skillfully Aeschylus uses Aegisthus in the dramatic sequence. Earlier on he would have been in the way and detracted from Clytemnestra's crucial role. But his presence in the palace as a usurper will be important in the second play of the Trilogy when Orestes returns not only to avenge his father but to recover his patrimony. The lateness of his entrance, with the implication that he has been staying out of the way, reinforces his characterization as a coward behind his vindictive and bullying bluster. Where after the preceding *epirrhema* we may have come to feel some sympathy for Clytemnestra, retribution in Aegisthus' case will be humanly warranted as well as inevitable.

At 1612 ff. a verbal confrontation follows between Aegisthus and the Coryphaeus, who warns him of the justice to come. Aegisthus responds with the threats of a tyrant, but the Leader expresses open contempt for the "woman" who waited at home while Agamemnon was at war and who plotted his death without having the courage to strike the blow himself. Does Orestes, he asks, still live to avenge Aegisthus' crime? (1646–8).

This provides the cue for the tempo to speed up. For the final 28 lines of the play, the iambics change to long trochaic tetrameters, the rhythm of which runs more swiftly and sharply than its stately use in *Persae* (p. 25). The mention of Orestes is too much for the blustering Aegisthus who calls on his guards. The tension mounts and it looks as if a fight is going to develop; but the final surprise is a moving intervention by Clytemnestra, who has stood apart upstage, weary and silent. Advancing forward, she implores her "dearest of men" not to add to the sum of bloodshed and begs the "reverend elders" to return to their homes. She would welcome a cure for this troubled situation, unhappily struck as they are by the heavy talon of the *daimon*. "So runs the word of a *woman* – if anyone thinks fit to *learn*" (1654–61). Clytemnestra's modest and deferential tone is in the strongest possible contrast to the contemptuous attitude of her earlier scenes when she is vigorously asserting the force of her intelligence as a woman.

Aegisthus continues to threaten the Coryphaeus, who taunts him once more with the possibility of Orestes' return under the guidance of the *daimon* (1667). But taunts are in vain. Aegisthus' men with their swords are clearly superior to the Elders with only their staves for weapons. Though the Leader gives no quarter verbally, the final word goes to Clytemnestra in a last attempt to put a bold face on a desperate situation. "Pay no heed to these futile barkings. You and I, masters of this house, will order all things well" (Louis MacNeice's translation reconstructing a slightly incomplete text).

The final stage business can only be conjectured. Perhaps the Chorus retreats before the guards' swords and exits down an *eisodos* in sullen silence. Significantly, Aeschylus did not provide the usual passage of anapaests to see his chorus off after the solo actors have made their exit. This might suggest that the Chorus files out of the *orchêstra*, while Clytemnestra and Aegisthus remain in a dominant position before the open *skênê* doors (the *ekkyklêma* will have been withdrawn earlier on, perhaps at 1662). When they are gone, Clytemnestra could lead Aegisthus into the house and the doors then close behind them.

For the moment the usurpers are in control, but this is not the end of the story. The tragic situation is unresolved and, in musical terms, *Agamemnon* ends on a violent discord.

CHOEPHORI (Libation Bearers)

Choephori occupies the central position in Aeschylus' Trilogy. Act I has presented the main theme, the tragic situation posed by the law of retribution, "the doer must suffer," based on the family vendetta. The tragedy is now taken to the ultimate horror and paradox of matricide, a crime committed as a duty, an act of justice.

Plot-wise, Act II follows closely on Act I, though after a time interval of some years. *Agamemnon* had ended with Clytemnestra and Aegisthus asserting their supremacy in Argos, but the Exodos had included two references by name (1646, 1667) to the exiled Orestes whom the *daimon* is to guide back to his house. Thus the second play opens with Orestes praying by his father's tomb and dedicating a lock of hair there.

Synopsis

The action falls into three phases. First a long preparation (1–652), at the start of which Orestes returns from exile, accompanied by his friend Pylades, the son of Strophius, king of Phocis, by whom he has been reared. He goes on to meet his sister Electra in a scene of recognition and together, with a sympathetic Chorus of elderly captive women, they pray to Agamemnon's ghost to aid the course of justice. There follows the central section (653–971) which shows Orestes taking his revenge. He obtains entrance to the palace at Argos, disguised as a stranger from Phocis, bearing false news of his own death to Clytemnestra. Aegisthus is summoned through Orestes' aged Nurse and meets an expeditious death, which is shortly followed by the climactic mother-murder of Clytemnestra. Finally, in an aftermath phase (9773–1076), Orestes publicly denounces his father's murderers. Madness comes on him and he is driven offstage, fleeing from a terrifying vision of the Furies, "the dogs of his mother's wrath."

Interpretation

Orestes' predicament is given added poignancy because, unlike the blood-guilty Agamemnon or the adulterous Clytemnestra, he is not tainted himself by any previous wrongdoing. He comes at the command of Apollo, the interpreter and mouthpiece of Zeus, to kill his mother in revenge for his father. The gods are prompting a hitherto stainless man to pollute himself with his own mother's blood in the pursuit of justice.

The main theme is once again the law of retaliation, this time taken to its very limit and largely uncomplicated, as in *Agamemnon*, by questions of determination, distant hopes for mankind and gender polarity. This thematic simplicity is reflected musically in the predominance of lyric iambics and the near absence of trochaic measures in the choral songs. As in *Agamemnon*, though, Zeus, Apollo, Moira and *dikê* are still moving in the one direction, towards retribution through self-perpetuating revenge. The appearance of the Furies to Orestes at the very end of the play is the first sign of a split in the divine underpinning of the human drama, as is to be seen in the conflict between Olympian and chthonian deities in Act I.

Dramaturgy

In *Agamemnon* Aeschylus used his chorus to exercise the original sacral function of the earlier lyric chorus to influence future events within the context of the drama; the assumed power of words as "performative utterances" allows them to be perceived as events. This is even more obviously the case in *Choephori*. Almost two-thirds of the act is given to the preparatory phase, in which the crucial elements are prayer and ritual performance understood to be efficacious. We can see this all as a "preliminary ritual" to the enactment of the blood-sacrifice which must be offered in atonement for blood already shed. In this the Libation Bearers, who give the play its title, are vital as the quasi-ritual body that in an important sense *controls* the action. The Chorus can also be seen as a link between the priests (Orestes and Electra) and the congregation that makes up the play's audience, which thus becomes involved as participants in what might be called "the liturgy of dutiful crime" which is being enacted for them to hear and see.

Aeschylus' use of theatrical space is important too. The *skênê* representing the palace of Atreus remains a looming presence, as in *Agamemnon*, but the main focus of the action during the preparatory phase must be on the *orchêstra* with its *thymelê* or altar in the middle of it. This, whether permanent or portable, could serve various purposes in ritual scenes, and it is fair to assume that it stood here for Agamemnon's tomb which plays a vital part in this first section. For the latter part of the play, however, the focus shifts upstage to the *skênê* and the area close to it. (For the possible use of two additional doors see p. 64) This has the effect of detaching the audience further from the actual murders than they have been in the preliminary rituals.

Finally, we can note Aeschylus' masterly contrast of pace in the different phases of the drama. The build-up during the long preparation is deliberately slow. Then, after Orestes' second entrance at 653, everything speeds up rapidly as ritual succeeds to lively practical action.

Dramatic Analysis

Line numbers refer to the Greek text in the Loeb edition (see note at the end of this chapter), which has a parallel English translation. For the terminology of the discrete movements, see Appendix A; for the lyric structure and meters, see Appendix B or listen to TRACK 0 ◉.

Prologue (1–21)

The opening lines of the play are regrettably missing from the sole manuscript of this play that has survived. Providentially, a few of them can be recovered from an obvious quotation in Aristophanes' *Frogs*. It is thus clear that this drama (like *Agamemnon*) opens with a prayer. Orestes invokes the god Hermes as the escort of the souls in the underworld and calls on his father's spirit to hear him as he dedicates a lock of hair on his tomb. After sighting the Libation Bearers approaching, with a woman among them whom he identifies at once as his sister Electra (16), he ends his speech with a further prayer to Zeus for aid in avenging his father, before retreating with Pylades to a hiding place, probably just at the mouth of the *eisodos* from which they entered.

Parodos (22–83)

It is very possible that Electra and the Chorus of black-robed household slaves do not enter from the other *eisodos* but, quite unusually, from the *skênê*. This is suggested by their opening words, "Sent out of the house," and also by their entry in iambic rather than the marching anapaestic meter. If this is right, it is a good ploy for reidentifying the *skênê* as the house where Clytemnestra is living, when the visual focus for much of the play is to be on Agamemnon's tomb in the *orchêstra* and not on the upstage area for some considerable time.

All are carrying *choai*, pitchers, containing drink-offerings to appease the dead. The women tell how they have been sent by Clytemnestra who has been frightened by an ugly dream, the details of which are not at this point revealed but are supposed to indicate that Agamemnon's spirit is stirring angrily against his murderers (38–41).

The opening strophe is a kind of dirge, presumably of sorrow for the house, in which the Chorus describes and probably mimes the tearing of cheeks and garments in ritual gestures of mourning (25–31). <TRACK C1, lines 22–31> They indicate their support for Agamemnon by expressing their *fear* of uttering prayers to appease him as there can be no washing away of blood once shed (46–9). Justice, though, must bring retribution in the end (61–5). In the epode (75–83) they bemoan their own status, forced to do as they are told and secretly weeping "for the senseless suffering of their (former) masters."<TRACK C2, lines 75–83>

This entrance-song has established the identity and sympathies of the Trilogy's second Chorus; it contains an element of spectacular ritual; and has reaffirmed the underlying theme of retribution for blood once shed. Given the rhythmical leitmotif so familiar from the *Agamemnon*, it is entirely appropriate that the meter of this movement should be largely iambic, with a lot of syncopation in the epode. This helps to link Act II with Act I and also lends a feeling of excited expectancy to the episode which is to follow.

First Episode (84–584), Including *Kommos* (306–478)

The presence of the Chorus and Electra in the *orchêstra* has been motivated by a ritual office. The ritual issue is now: what *words* should be used to accompany the libations, for on these will depend the effect of the drink-offerings to the earth. In her opening speech (84–105) Electra asks the Chorus for its advice.

In the stichomythia (106–23) that follows, the Coryphaeus suggests that Electra should pray for good to come to right-minded people who hate Aegisthus and that someone, be it a god or mortal, will appear to counter murder with murder. "Do you mean a judge or an avenger?" asks Electra in an alternative question (120), which draws a distinction that means little at this stage but a lot in Act III when judges, in the sense of a civic jury, do enter the picture. "Is this a *righteous* thing to ask?" Electra also enquires. "Yes," comes the reply, but it is significant that Electra has for one moment questioned the law of retribution.

Electra now offers her own prayer to Hermes, mother Earth and to Agamemnon's shade: let Orestes return from exile and (separately) an avenger appear to punish the murderers (123–51). Electra and the Chorus then pour their libations from their pitchers – a spectacular action – with the original stated object of their ritual reversed, as the offerings are used as a kind of curse or anti-spell on Clytemnestra. During this the Chorus chants a short song (152–63) in lyric iambics with some (more agitated) dochmiacs, described in 150–1 both as a lament and as a paean, a prayer for healing to Agamemnon. This concludes with a prayer for the arrival of a great warrior who will heal the house. <TRACK C3, lines 152–63>

As though in answer to the song accompanying the libations, there follows Electra's discovery that Orestes has in fact returned resulting in the eventual reuniting of brother and sister. This big moment affords an opportunity for a tremendous build-up; so here we have the prototype of the *anagnorisis* or recognition scene, often involving the use of one or more recognition "tokens," which is a common feature not only of later Greek tragedy but also of fourth-century comedy and subsequent drama, at least up to Oscar Wilde.

At 166, immediately after the libation song, Electra asks the Chorus to share in a "new *word*." She has sighted the lock of hair which Orestes has dedicated on her father's tomb and it closely resembles her own hair. During an exciting stichomythic exchange the Coryphaeus raises the possibility, though with some doubt, that it could be a secret offering from Orestes. "He *sent* it," says Electra, "to honor his father," then quickly goes on (183) to a long speech which expresses her emotion in poignantly anthropomorphic language. "If only the lock could *speak*, to spare me the torment of uncertainty!" Once again she invokes the gods; and once again, as though in response to her prayer, she sights a second token, two footprints, one with an outline which, like the lock, matches her own. "I'm filled with anguish," she cries; "my wits are destroyed!" (211).

"Proclaim to the gods that your prayers are fulfilled, and continue praying for future success!" (212). So speaks Orestes, emerging from his hiding place and maintaining the language of prayer. The tension is drawn out in further stichomythia. Electra remains hesitant to accept that Orestes is standing before her, until her brother produces the third token. He clinches the matter by asking her to look at a piece of weaving in Electra's own hand, with an animal design on it, which now forms part of the clothes he is wearing. Electra, at last convinced, rushes to embrace her brother and winds off the section with a speech (235–45) of joyful greeting and warm affection.

Some scholars (e.g. Fraenkel 1950), have felt uncomfortable with this scene and even questioned its authenticity, largely on the grounds of the illogicalities involved in treating the different tokens as evidence. (Much later Euripides made play with these same three tokens, for his own artistic purposes, in his *Electra*.) But the naive logic involved sits perfectly easily with this highly ritualized form of drama. Ancient Greek audiences will not at this stage have been looking for tidy realism. What matters is the prolonged suspense, as we identify with Electra's agony and thus rejoice with the brother and sister as they finally meet.

The happiness of reunion, however, is quickly put aside as the language of prayer is resumed and Orestes passionately invokes Zeus (246–63) to have regard for "the orphaned brood of an eagle father who died in a viper's twisting coils" and for the sacrifices he will be missing if he fails to take care of the surviving members of the house. Soon after, in response to a nervous warning from the Coryphaeus, he affirms in a second colourful speech (269–305) that he is under Apollo's protection and catalogues the horrible plagues and social isolation which the oracle has prophesied for him if he fails to punish his father's killers. All pressures, divine and human, conspire to make his revenge inevitable. To all that can be added the compulsive power and musical sonority of Aeschylus' image-rich poetry. Electra's trembling and uncertainty during the recognition have yielded to the unflinching resolution and confidence of Orestes in this latter part of the episode. All is now set, in terms of atmosphere as well as plot, for the culminating ritual performance which lies at the centre of the play and of the whole *Oresteia*.

The long *kommos* or lament is designed first (315–422) to pay Agamemnon the debt of tears which has long been owed to him from his own kindred; second, to awaken his spirit to aid his children in their sacred duty of vengeance. This extraordinary lyric movement probably reproduces a real incantation ceremony, deployed here in the dramatic context to conjure up Agamemnon's ghost. Its anapaestic introduction (306–14) strongly proclaims the law that "the doer must suffer," while the end (466–75) movingly voices the tragic suffering in its operation for the house, which alone has the power to treat the suppurating wound of Agamemnon's murder. Interest and tension throughout are sustained by an interaction between Chorus and soloists. As Orestes and Electra address the spirit of their dead father, the Chorus' contributions serve to encourage and support them. <TRACK C4, lines 315–31> ◉ Towards the end, at 439–43 the women address Orestes directly to confirm his resolve to take vengeance on his mother by describing how she mutilated Agamemnon's corpse; at 451–2 they tell him to *record* the story and let it *pierce* through his ears to the depth of his mind.

The movement's musical form is highly elaborate and extremely striking. The Chorus and the two soloists, Orestes and Electra, deliver their lines antiphonally, in lyric meters for the most part, though the Chorus comes in with anapaests (not sung) at regular intervals. The use of strophic correspondence is unique: antistrophes do not follow strophes in immediate succession, as normal, but are set at intervals in a complicated kind of interlacing (see Garvie 1986, 122–5 on lines 306–478). This unusually elaborate structure brilliantly reflects the intricacy of the spell that is being woven. As in the two *amoibaia* in the *Agamemnon*, an internal dynamic is also present in the metrical patterning: aeolic and ionic cola yield to the tauter, less fluid syncopated iambic rhythm. The total impact is of a highly crafted musical composition, lasting some ten minutes, which can only be fully experienced in a well-informed performance in the original Greek, or just possibly in an "isometric" translation.

Visually, we can imagine the choreography in the *orchêstra* as very formal and static, with Chorus and soloists grouped round the central altar. Ritual gesturing is called for at certain points, especially at 423–8, where the Chorus all beat their heads and tear their hair in the manner of professional eastern mourners. This occurs at the start of a fresh set of interlacing stanzas in the lyric structure and lifts the movement to a higher level of emotional intensity. <TRACK C5, lines 423–28> ◉ From 451 the invocation rises to a climax and is rounded off in a poignant expression of compassion for the afflicted house. <TRACK C6, lines 451–75> ◉

The audience in the ancient Athenian theater may have wondered whether Agamemnon's ghost would actually appear, as Darius' did in *Persae*. It is hard, in fact, to imagine how this might have been staged, but in any case no spirit appears. From 479 the Chorus is silent, while Orestes and Electra continue their prayers in iambic trimeter form. In speeches of symmetrical length, including single lines, they appeal to Agamemnon, using taunts reminding him of how Clytemnestra killed him, to make him rise from the grave. But still no ghost appears, and at 510 the Coryphaeus assures the pair that they have done all that was needed by way of tribute to their previously unlamented father. The temperature has been skillfully lowered before the passage that follows.

At 514 Orestes asks the Coryphaeus the reason for Clytemnestra's sending the women to the tomb with their libations. Only now do we learn the substance of the queen's dream. It was that she gave birth to a snake which drew blood from her breast. At 540 Orestes greets this as a favourable omen: it points to himself and to his vengeance. Aeschylus has purposely reserved the details of the dream until now. The timing of this in the dramatic sequence suggests that the *kommos* has *worked*, that the spirit world is alive and active. In one final long speech (554–84) Orestes outlines his plan of action for himself and Pylades: equipped with baggage to look like foreign travelers and speaking with Phocian accents, they will gain access to the palace and so kill Aegisthus. There is no mention of his mother at this point. That is to be saved up for the climax and we are kept guessing. Orestes and Electra now leave the *orchêstra* and make an exit, Electra into the *skênê* and Orestes with Pylades departing down the *eisodos* to prepare their disguises.

First Stasimon (585–652)

This fine movement concludes the preparatory phase of the drama, before the action of the murder-plot gets going. The Chorus sings a song about the terrible sources of fearful suffering that are reared by the earth: sea-monsters, comets, hurricanes, audacious men – and wicked, lustful women. Of the last they offer specific instances from mythology: Meleager's mother, Althaea; Scylla, the daughter of Nisus, who betrayed her father to Minos; the ultimate abomination of the Lemnian women who killed their husbands. Beside these is then set the crime of Clytemnestra, as though to win for her a similar condemnation and retribution. The meter, as one might now expect, is almost entirely lyric iambic, heavily syncopated.

The closing pair of strophes (639–52) is peculiarly striking. The Greek text is corrupt, but the gist is clear enough. The imagery of Justice predominates in both stanzas and includes some sinister word-play. In the first *Dikê* is associated with a sharp, penetrating wound inflicted by a sword on those who trample on her underfoot; in the second she is an anvil on which Destiny the smith is forging the weapon. "A child is being brought into the house to pay in time for the stain of older bloodshed by the famous deep-thinking Fury." The child is obviously Orestes, but who is the Fury, the avenging spirit? "Famous, deep-thinking" suggests the etymology of Clytemnestra's own name, which means "famous schemer." As Helen was transformed to a Fury for Troy (*Agam.* 738–49), so Clytemnestra, her sister, has now become the avenging spirit who has ensured her own destruction at the hands of her own child. Throughout these stanzas the iambic rhythm is at its most insistent. One can hear the hammer-blows that are forging the sword on Justice's anvil – an image which might be applied to the Trilogy as a whole, which portrays mankind painfully hammering out a new kind of justice. <TRACK C7, lines 639–52> ◉

Second Episode (653–782)

Through the final words of the Chorus re-enter Orestes and Pylades. The next sound we hear is a powerful knocking on the door of the *skênê* to mark the start of the drama's central action. The spatial focus shifts from the middle of the *orchêstra* to the house and the area immediately before it. While the Chorus, as we shall see, contributes to the mounting tension, Orestes is no longer in relationship to the Libation Bearers until the closing scene, while Electra is no longer in the picture at all (the actor is getting changed for his next role). This emphasizes Orestes' growing isolation as he enacts his awful revenge. Furthermore, the pace of the drama grows faster as the Trilogy advances to its main crisis of the mother-murder. Movements for soloists and chorus alternate with unusual rapidity, and this is a major factor in the drama's exciting impact. The spring has been slowly wound up in the earlier part of the act, and the accumulated energy is now released in this central sequence.

Orestes has to knock (the magic) three times before a voice from within asks who he is. As he demands to relay a message to someone with authority in the house, Aeschylus sets up the question in the audience's mind: will it be Aegisthus or Clytemnestra who comes out to greet the strangers? An atmosphere of suspense is already being generated. It turns out to be Clytemnestra who welcomes them in a speech which mentions "warm baths" and "the presence of righteous eyes" (670–1), disturbing words as she becomes the victim of deceit as Agamemnon was before her. In his disguised accent – word power even here – Orestes delivers the news of his own supposed death. Clytemnestra puts on a sham display of grief (her hypocrisy is later confirmed by the Nurse at 737–9), but her words referring to the curse on the house have sinister overtones that are unintentionally damaging to herself, by contrast with the deliberate malevolence of her ambivalent utterances in *Agamemnon*. The scene continues in this kind of vein until, at the end, a servant is ordered to escort the two visitors to the men's quarters and Orestes finally gains his admission into the house through the central doorway. Clytemnestra has ceased to be in control of the threshold.

A brief passage of anapaests (719–29), probably delivered by the Coryphaeus, bridges a gap before the next entrance. "When, serving women," she asks, "shall we display the power of our own lips in Orestes' favor?' Then Earth and Agamemnon's tomb are invoked. It is now time for guileful persuasion, associated with Clytemnestra in *Agamemnon*, to enter the lists and for Hermes, as the god of trickery, to watch over Orestes and Pylades in the murderous task ahead. Suspense is mounting.

But there are no murder cries yet. Enter from the palace Orestes' old Nurse, Kilissa, in tears. She has been sent by Clytemnestra to fetch Aegisthus to learn the news of Orestes' death. At this critical juncture Aeschylus chooses to introduce a wonderful new character, a homely soul, rather a chatterbox, a little like the Nurse in *Romeo and Juliet*. She mourns the death of Orestes in terms of her wasted labor in looking after him and washing his nappies when he was a baby. Her sorrow, by contrast with Clytemnestra's, is obviously genuine, and the earthy details of her speech introduce a human note to complement the more abstract aspect of tit-for-tat retribution. The emphasis on the Nurse's maternal feelings anticipates the confrontation between Orestes and his actual mother. Kilissa's role in the plot is to engineer the entrance of Aegisthus; and the Coryphaeus persuades her, in a most unusual intervention by the Chorus in the action of a play, to tell Aegisthus to arrive alone without the bodyguard that accompanied him in *Agamemnon*. The scene ends with the Nurse bustling on her way after the hint has been dropped that Orestes may not be dead after all (775–8).

Second Stasimon (783–837)

In this conspiratorial atmosphere, the Chorus sings a shortish prayer for Orestes' success, first to Zeus and then to the gods of the house. The text and rhythmical interpretation of this passage are exceptionally uncertain. The three pairs of strophes seem to suggest a groping after the steady trochaic phrases of the Hymn to Zeus in the *Agamemnon* Parodos; but they also contain other metrical elements which serve to disrupt. Each strophic pair is punctuated in the middle by a "mesode" in cretics (5/8 time) or ionics (3/4 time). This musical instability appears to reflect the tension in the dramatic situation, with an implication such as: yes, the long-term will of Zeus that men should learn from suffering is perhaps being fulfilled and the house *will* be released from its bondage; but what is going on now is deeply unsettling. In the final stanzas the women anticipate the immediate issue and urge Orestes to be bold when he is confronted with his mother's cry of "My child!" and to "wreak bloody ruin," like Perseus when he killed the Gorgon. <TRACK C8, lines 819–37> ◉

Third Episode (838–934)

From now on the drama moves very quickly, with much coming and going. Aegisthus arrives in response to the Nurse's message and enters the house within the space of only seventeen lines. Like Clytemnestra he feigns dismay at the thought of Orestes' death but he wants to be sure that the report is true, not based on women's frightened imaginings or a mere rumor. We remember his bullying tone from *Agamemnon* and watch him fall into the trap which we feel he deserves.

In another brief anapaestic interlude (855–68) the Coryphaeus prays to Zeus for Orestes' victory. There is a sinister touch: whether or not Orestes succeeds in overthrowing the usurper and recovering his patrimony, the work of his sword will involve *miasma*, pollution (859). The tension mounts again and culminates in Aegisthus' death-cries from within (869).

At this point (872–4) Aeschylus deliberately draws the Chorus away from the palace, perhaps to the sides of the *orchêstra* close to the *eisodoi*. The motive given by the Coryphaeus for this move is that they must not be seen to be involved in what has taken place indoors. Dramatically, this has the effect of focusing the audience's gaze even more strongly on the crucial confrontation between Orestes and his mother which now follows in front of the *skênê*. I believe there to be a further practical reason.

The staging of the following sequence (875–930) has been much discussed and disputed. At 875 a servant, who must be played by the third actor, rushes out from the stage building to announce the death of Aegisthus. He calls for the gates to the women's quarters to be opened and for Clytemnestra to appear. He has to beat on the door several times before Clytemnestra finally emerges to ask what is up. The text at this point undoubtedly calls for a *second* entrance in the *skênê*. This is something which no other surviving Greek tragedy requires, but the scholars who insist on only one (central) entrance have to justify a lot of impossibly confusing and clumsy movement in and out of the single doorway over the next few lines. It is important that earlier on, at 712, Clytemnestra when welcoming Orestes and Pylades has given orders that they be conducted to the *andrônes*, the men's quarters. At the end of that scene, which is set before the doors of the courtyard, Clytemnestra with Orestes and Pylades would all, of course, go off through the central entrance.

If there *was* a side-entrance in the *skênê*, I think the strong probability is that there were two, for reasons of symmetry if for no other, to the right and left of the central doorway, perhaps half-way between it and the sides of the building. My own view is that 875–930 was played without using the central entrance at all. The passage is to be imagined as taking place *inside* the courtyard and in front of the different rooms of the house. The Servant comes out of one side-entrance, as from the *men's* quarters, where Aegisthus will have been murdered; Clytemnestra at 885 enters from the other side-entrance, as from the *women's* quarters. Orestes with Pylades naturally comes out of the former door at 892, points toward the body of Aegisthus indoors behind him, close to whom he proposes to kill his mother (904–7). This staging, with *two* side-entrances, results in perfect clarity and also explains why the Chorus is at this point removed from the picture. They can thus be imagined as remaining outside the front gate and so entirely detached from what is taking place in the inner courtyard and beyond, *as if* the action was invisible to them.[9]

At 885 Clytemnestra responds to the Servant's summons and quickly realizes that she is now, in her own turn, the victim of deceit (888). Splendidly, she calls for someone to fetch an axe (this can motivate the exit of the Servant, who needs to be out of the way), only to be confronted from the other side-door by the man who has murdered her lover. In a powerful gesture she opens her dress and appeals to her son to show respect for the breast which fed him as a baby. For a brief moment of suspense Orestes hesitates and turns to Pylades who, as usual, is standing nearby. "Pylades, should respect prevent me from killing my mother?" The answer rings out: "Where, then, in future will be Apollo's oracles and sworn pledges? Regard all men as foes rather than the gods!" (900–2). This crucial moment is all the more dramatic, as Pylades is played (except for these three lines) by a mute actor; the third actor was the Servant and could not conceivably have managed the change of costume and mask in time. The audience have so far associated the figure of Pylades, always there with Orestes but in the background, with the silence of a mute character. His "irregular" speech here as the voice of Apollo comes as a dramatic surprise, comparable to the moment in *Agamemnon* when the third actor playing Cassandra bursts into her wild cries, after previously being mute (see p. 50).

The awful confrontation between mother and son is resumed at 908 in twenty fierce lines of adversarial stichomythia. Clytemnestra threatens Orestes with a mother's curse and the "hounds of her wrath," so prefiguring the aftermath that is shortly to come. Her last words are a couplet: "Alas, this is the snake I bore and nursed! The fear from my dream was prophetic indeed." Orestes then drives his mother offstage with the riposte: "You killed the man you should not, now suffer what you ought not!" These closing lines affirm the law that "the doer must suffer;" at the same time they seal Orestes' own fate. <TRACK C9, lines 922–30>

At this point (931) the Libation Bearers return to their role as witnesses and we can imagine the central entrance reasserting itself as the focal point of the *skênê*. In four iambic lines the Coryphaeus briefly deplores the double murder: the hapless Orestes has brought many deeds of bloodshed to a summit, but he is the "eye" or "light" of the house and they would not want him to "fall in utter destruction." On this slightly ambivalent note, the Chorus reoccupies the *orchêstra*.

Third Stasimon (935–71)

Inevitably, there follows a joyful ode of triumph for the deliverance of the house, the song of victory which the Chorus had prayed several times to be able to sing. The meter is the highly excited dochmiac rhythm, used earlier in the prayer to Agamemnon for a deliverer as the Chorus poured their libations (156–63). <TRACK C10, lines 946–52> The text of the final sentence is badly corrupt and cannot be restored with any confidence. I favour an approach which construes the last words (971) as "The metics (resident aliens) in the home will fall back," referring to the Furies haunting the house of Atreus as described by Cassandra at *Agam.* 1186–90.[10] If that interpretation is right, the Chorus is hailing the imminent departure of the Furies as a result of Orestes' act in clearing the house of pollution. In that case, this movement as a whole would be following the pattern, particularly liked by Sophocles, of triumphant choruses which are instantly or (as here) very soon to be belied by what follows.

Exodos (973–1076)

For the second time in the Trilogy the *ekkyklêma* is wheeled out, now bearing the corpses of Clytemnestra and Aegisthus and Orestes standing over them in triumph with his bloodied sword. The visual parallel with *Agamemnon* is a splendid stroke of theatrical art, as is Aeschylus' use of a prop, the bloodstained robe in which Clytemnestra entangled her husband when she murdered him. This Orestes proudly displays and then calls on the Chorus to stand round in a circle and lay it out. We can now see a bloody trail leading away from the palace, as we saw it lead up to the doorway in the crimson garments scene in *Agamemnon*. To cover this business, Orestes is given a number of fine lines describing the robe in various metaphors and comparing Clytemnestra to a deadly sea-serpent or viper. But Orestes' triumph is tempered

Figure 4.3 *Choephori*, Greek Theatre, Bryanston School, England 1987. Source: Reproduced by permission of the Archive of Performances of Greek & Roman Drama.

quite soon by a sense that his victory has brought him "unenviable pollution" (1017); while the Chorus in two anapaestic interjections (1007–9, 1018–20) are already anticipating that further trouble is on its way.

From 1021, just as Clytemnestra's mood changed in the scene after Agamemnon's murder (see p. 55), so does Orestes'. His wits begin to turn and, in a further rhesis, he realizes that he must flee for sanctuary to Delphi as commanded by Apollo, bearing a suppliant's olive-branch wreathed with strands of wool.[11] He accepts that he must now be a "wandering exile" (1042)[12] and be known for ever in Argos as a matricide. At this point, perhaps, he may leave the platform and come down to join the Chorus in the *orchêstra*, after which the trolley can be withdrawn and the central doors closed. The Coryphaeus tries to reassure him: "No, you have done well … You have freed Argos by cutting off the heads of the two snakes" (1044–7). This last word triggers two horrible cries, as Orestes now sees the Furies with their murky-dark tunics and snaky locks. Aeschylus magnificently makes the Chorus unable to see them (as, of course, neither can the audience) and the Coryphaeus suggests that they are all in Orestes' imagination (1056). The dialogue continues to the end in six stichomythic couplets as Orestes recognizes the Furies as the hounds of his mother's wrath, crowding in on him with grisly gore dripping from their eyes. Finally, in one of the most powerful exits in the whole of drama, he runs from the *orchêstra* in terror. <TRACK C11, lines 1048–64> ⊕

In the Chorus' closing anapaests (1065–76) Aeschylus encapsulates his tragic theme. This "third storm" for the royal house has been brought to an end. First came the Thyestean banquet, second the death of the warlord Agamemnon in his bath and now a third savior has come – "or should I say *doom*?" The third storm has been the matricide of Orestes who has come as a savior, but we must be reminded of Zeus the Savior, to whom the third libation was poured at a feast, as recalled in *Agam.* 245, in the narrative of Iphigenia's sacrifice, and later at *Agam.* 1385–6 in the third blow which Clytemnestra dealt the king in his bath. No wonder that the Chorus adds the word "doom," death. And when will it all end and be laid to rest – the strength of *Atê*, Ruin? Act II ends like Act I with a huge question mark.

These concluding lines are, I think, too important to have been delivered as a kind of tag to cover the Libation Bearers' exit. They demand a formal, static grouping. After the final line I would have them file out down one of the *eisodoi* in silence, like the Argive Elders before them, perhaps accompanied in melancholy strain by the pipe-player who leads them. We are left with the house of Atreus, rid of its defilers, but now standing empty of any master. What will become of it? Will Orestes ever return there?

EUMENIDES

Act III of the *Oresteia* offers the answer posed by the Libation Bearers at the end of Act II: where will it all end? The final play shows that mankind can learn from suffering. Retaliatory justice makes way for a new juridical system which avoids the need for violence. The theme is universal, but Aeschylus made it real for his own audience by setting his resolution in the world of Athens and at a particular moment in contemporary history (see p. 34).

Synopsis

As in *Choephori* the drama falls into three phases. In the first Orestes, pursued by the Erinyes or Furies to the oracle at Delphi, is promised protection by Apollo, who sends him on his way to Athens. Clytemnestra's ghost compels the Furies to follow once again on his trail. The second scene takes place at Athens, where Orestes clasps the image of Athena and the Furies catch up with him. After a preliminary investigation, the goddess Athena herself sets up a court of Athenian citizens to try Orestes for killing his mother, with the Furies prosecuting and Apollo appearing as his witness and advocate. The votes are equally divided and Orestes is acquitted. In the third and final phase the discomfited Furies threaten to spit forth plagues on Athens, but Athena wins them round by offering them a cult in the polis as *Semnai Theai*, august goddesses, the title of earth-goddesses who had an actual cult at Athens in Aeschylus' time.

Interpretation

This is a play which, by contrast with the two that precede it, ends in a harmonious resolution. The opening scene is shockingly discordant, but the drama as a whole represents a movement from darkness into light. Crucial to this is the transformation of the Chorus of Furies to benign deities, though the play's traditional title *Eumenides* (a euphemism meaning "Kindly

Ones") was probably not its original one. The word does not appear in Aeschylus' text and is not otherwise known as an alternative name for the Erinyes before the end of the fifth century.

The drama takes on a new dimension with the introduction of the divine characters, Apollo and Athena, both deities with highly potent associations. Apollo as the god of Delphi represents moral enlightenment, and Athena enshrines the concept of the democratic polis, by now so important to the Athenians. The Furies themselves have tremendous emotive power; they are terrifying monsters but also goddesses of the underworld who stand for primeval order and authority. As chthonic deities they are presented as *older* gods by contrast with the *younger* gods of the Olympian cult, with whom in this third play they are in conflict until Athena persuades them to accept a place in the changed world order.

The other new dimension is the sudden transformation of a story from the heroic past into a contemporary Athenian setting. The details of Orestes' trial are, of course, stylized; they cannot be naturalistically accommodated within the form of a poetic tragedy. But the atmosphere is certainly telling; trial scenes make excellent theater and this is the first in European literature.

Dramaturgy

"Word power" in this act is less important in the play's dynamic than it was in Acts I and II. The Chorus of the Furies themselves are characters participating in the action rather than bystanders controlling or interpreting the drama like the Elders in the *Agamemnon* or the Libation Bearers. They are an atypical chorus in that they do not sympathize with the leading character (Orestes) but are actively opposed to him. Their incantatory "binding-song" does *not* prove efficacious, though their prayers at the end for blessings on Athens must be deemed propitious.

Aeschylus' use of performance space follows the reverse pattern to *Choephori*, which shifted the focus away from the *orchêstra* to the *skênê* in the latter scenes of the drama. In *Eumenides* the first section is concentrated round the *skênê*, which no longer represents the house of Atreus but the temple of Apollo. When Orestes arrives at Athens, the action then moves forward to the *orchêstra*, where his fate is essentially to be decided by the Athenian people who are, as we shall see, the audience.

An important prop is the image of Athena that is standing on the altar (*thymelê*) in the middle of the *orchêstra*. This is the olive-wood statue of the goddess which Orestes is told by Apollo to clasp on his arrival at Athens. It needs to be on at the start of the play if a props man is not to lug it on when the imagined location changes.[13] For a justification of its possibly obtrusive presence in the Delphi scene, see below (p. 69).

Finally, we may note a slowing-down of the pace as the Trilogy moves to its end. Just as the choral songs in *Agamemnon* became progressively shorter as the drama moved towards the climax of the murder, so in the *Eumenides* they grow in length as the drama proceeds to its stately conclusion.

Dramatic Analysis

Line numbers refer to the Greek text in the Loeb edition (see end of this chapter), which has a parallel English translation. For the lyric structure and meters, see Appendix B or hear TRACK 0 ⊙. The abnormal nature of the Chorus makes it less helpful to divide this play up into the usual categories of prologue, parodos, episode, stasimon and so on (see Chapter 1,

p. 12 or Appendix A). The following description of the play is based on its three main sections: the Delphi scene, the trial at Athens and the appeasement of the Furies which constitutes a kind of epilogue to the whole Trilogy.

The Delphi Scene (1–234)

This first section is in itself an extraordinarily tight and rapid-moving sequence, similar dramatically to the action in the second half of *Choephori*. It can be subdivided into five fairly short movements.

Lines 1–63

The opening speaker is the Pythia, the Delphic prophetess, who enters from an *eisodos* on her way to taking her prophetic seat on the marble throne of the oracle. She is an old woman, wearing the white dress of a young maiden, by contrast with the black-robed Libation Bearers and the dark-clad Furies (see Sommerstein 1989, 80 and note on line 55). The play, like the two before it, opens with a prayer. The Priestess first invokes all the gods who have been associated with the Delphic oracle and gives a little history of it. At 10–14 Aeschylus skillfully works in a reference to Pallas (Athena) and the Athenians who are going to be so important later in the play. She continues with a secondary list of deities who have not been possessors of the oracle but are otherwise connected with it. Here (21) she gives pride of place to Pallas Pronaia, Athens before the shrine, whose temple in fact stood about a mile to the east of Apollo's temple. I suggest that the actor might have delivered this line with a nod at the image of Athena already set in the *orchêstra*, to justify its presence during this scene.

So far the atmosphere has been solemn, serene and awe-inspiring. But all is suddenly shattered when the Priestess enters through the *skênê* doors and then apparently *crawls* out in horror at the sight of the suppliant Orestes within the shrine, surrounded by the sleeping Furies who are frighteningly described as being like Gorgons or wingless Harpies, black, shooting out foul breath, with a nasty ooze dripping from their eyes. This graphic description is the first stage in Aeschylus' presentation of the terrifying Furies; he begins with an appeal to the audience's imagination in a powerful anticipation of their actual appearance. At the end of her description the Pythia decides the Furies must be left to Apollo to deal with and exits where she entered.

Lines 64–93[14]

The *skênê* doors then open and the *ekkyklêma* rolls out with a tableau of Orestes kneeling in supplication besides a representation of the conical *omphalos* (40), the oracular navel-stone, besieged at this point by *three* Furies (as implied by 140) who are slumped in sleep on *thronoi*, chairs with tall backs to them. At this second stage of the Furies' presentation, these figures are probably no more than a sinister and formidable presence. The priestess has sighted them in front of Orestes (46), so that they will not yet be facing the audience and their masks will not then be visible.

Orestes calls on Apollo for his protection.[15] The god then appears out of the darkness from the interior of the *skênê* and reassures the matricide that he will guard and stand by him against his enemies. He instructs him to flee to Athens and to clasp Athena's image; there judges will be found and "soothing words" which will result in Orestes' "release from toils" (the words echo the Watchman's prayer at *Agam.* 1, 26). At 90–3 Apollo addresses Hermes[16] and asks him to be Orestes' escort; after which Orestes goes on his way to Athens down an *eisodos* and the god retires inside the *skênê*.

Lines 94–142

A second sensational contrast follows when the ghost of Clytemnestra appears, as in a dream, angrily to protest her wrongs and to rouse the sleeping Furies to resume their pursuit of Orestes. After some twenty lines of complaint, her continued taunts are punctuated in a marvellously sinister effect by whines and whimpers from the three sleepers, who then imitate the sound of dogs as they chase Orestes in their sleep with repeated cries of *labe*, "Get him!" At 140 one Fury wakes the other two, and all hell breaks loose.

Lines 143–77

There now follows a parodos movement in three strophic pairs of agitated dochmiacs, inter-spersed in the first with iambic trimeters, as the three sleeping Furies wake up to find Orestes gone. As they individually expostulate during the first strophe (143–8), the rest of the Chorus burst out from the *skênê* until the complete band of twelve is assembled and all join in the first antistrophe (149–54) together. <TRACK D1, lines 143–54> ◉ An ancient commentator records a tradition that the Furies had an extremely frightening impact when Aeschylus brought the Furies on "in scattered fashion" – so much so that pregnant women in the audi-ence had miscarriages and children passed out. The latter details are questioned by most scholars as theatrical performances, like political assemblies, were essentially for men only.

However, "in scattered fashion" would aptly describe what could have happened if the remaining nine choreuts rushed out, not through the central doorway where the trolley in front of it would still have been occupied by the three "thrones," but out of the two side-entrances which I have suggested for the courtyard scene in *Choephori* (p. 64). This would have been a second and extremely effective use of an established staging resource to make a really terrifying impact at this point in the drama.[17] Aeschylus would thus have built up his presentation of the Furies in three progressive stages: first through the Priestess's description, then in the three sinister enthroned shapes on the *ekkyklêma* and finally in their full horror as the three slowly awake and the rest enter in a terrifying swoop out of the two side-entrances in the *skênê* façade.

The substance of the Furies' song with its jerky rhythms is an expression of their wild frus-tration with Apollo and the younger gods who have set themselves up against their authority. They accuse Apollo of polluting his own shrine and declare that Orestes will never escape vengeance for his crime.

Lines 179–234

The final section of this opening phase shows an actual confrontation between Apollo and the Furies. "Get out!" the god cries and goes on in grand Aeschylean verse to denounce them as repellent abominations. But in the stichomythia which follows, the Coryphaeus raises the fundamental issue: Orestes, in murdering his mother, shed kindred blood and must be pur-sued. Apollo justifies Orestes by appealing to the marriage-bond which Clytemnestra broke in murdering Agamemnon. This impassioned dialogue brings the Delphi scene to its climax. It defines the essential point of conflict and argument which will shape the ensuing Trial scene, the relative claims of father and mother.

The Chorus now, quite unusually, leaves the stage in mid-play to pursue Orestes, and Apollo returns again into the temple, after which we can assume that the *ekkyklêma* is withdrawn and the central doors are shut. The empty performance space will naturally indicate that a change in the drama's supposed location is about to take place.

Orestes' Trial at Athens (235–777)

This grand, highly original sequence can be subdivided into eight sections.

Lines 35–43

Orestes re-enters on his own and kneels before the image of Athena in the center of the *orchêstra*. The location must now be the temple of Athena on the Acropolis (242), now repre-sented by the *skênê* in the background, though the focus of the drama has moved forward, closer to the audience. In a speech of nine lines Orestes pleads the authority of Apollo and asks the goddess to receive him as one worn out by travel but now with clean hands (at 282–3 he refers to his ritual purification at Delphi).

Lines 244–75

Very soon the Chorus reappears in a second informal entrance. At first the Furies do not see Orestes; they are still following the trail of blood and probably grouped roughly in a pack where the *eisodos* meets the *orchestra*, while their Leader addresses them in a speech of normal iambic trimeters (244–54). The lyric lines which follow (255–75) are, like the earlier parodos (143–77), not an entrance song in the strictest sense. The lines should probably be broken up between individual speakers or small groups, as the Furies sniff their way into the *orchêstra*, perhaps one by one to begin with (255–6) and then, after Orestes is suddenly sighted with the cry "That's him!" (257), in more of a swarm, as they crowd round him where he is crouching with his arms round Athena's image and fiercely threaten to suck his blood dry. Once again we have a mixture of lyric dochmiacs with normal iambic trimeters, suggesting that the Chorus's act qua united chorus is not yet fully together. <TRACK D2, lines 254–75>

Lines 276–306

Orestes responds tranquilly in the assurance that Apollo has purified him and, confident in the knowledge that his lips are now pure, he invokes Athena to appear in person and to set him free. The Coryphaeus denies that Apollo or Athena can rescue him and inaugurates the remarkable movement that follows.

Lines 307–96 (The "Binding Song")

This exciting passage is a formal act of incantatory ritual with the fixed purpose of "binding" Orestes' mind and driving him mad. It would doubtless have been accompanied by a vivid and energetic choreography, with the Furies circling round Orestes and making bold leaping movements during 372–6, as they describe themselves trampling upon, or tripping up, the presumptuous sinner. This should not, however, be envisaged as a macabre ballet for female hobgoblins. The poetry expresses the *semnon êthos*, the awesome, august character of the

Furies who combine a fearful menace with the dignity and authority of their primeval power which they regard as slighted.

Formally speaking, the Chorus is now at last functioning as a united body. The song is introduced by an anapaestic section (as in the First Stasimon of *Agamemnon* and the start of the *kommos* in *Cho*. 306–14) and there is now a full strophic/antistrophic structure, combined with a pattern of *ephymnia* (as during *Agam*. 1448–566). There is a thrilling variety of meters: iambo-trochaic, cretics (5/8 time), dactylic and, towards the end (381–96), the familiar syncopated iambics as the Erinyes affirm the ever-mindful, inexorable force of their Destiny-ordained charter of retribution. <TRACK D3, lines 321–46> ◉

Lines 397–489

At the unrelenting climax of the Binding Song, enter Athena in response to Orestes' call. However this was staged, it would have been a spectacular moment. The goddess might even have been carried on the so-called *mêchanê*, the crane device for bringing gods down to earth (Sommerstein 1989, p. 153, note on lines 404–5). Anyway. we can certainly imagine her standing centrally in front of the *skênê*, dressed in gleaming bronze armor with her aegis, the traditional tasselled overgarment, probably worn over the shoulder. She may also be holding a spear. Athena first declares that she has come from the River Scamander near Troy, a statement importantly identified as the first reference in the play to the contemporary world of Athens.[18]

The scene which follows is a sort of preliminary enquiry, with Athena in the role of the presiding magistrate who would rule whether a full trial should take place. The Coryphaeus puts the Furies' case in stichomythic dialogue with the goddess and, by contrast, Orestes is made to reply in a formal speech. Athena declares that it would be unwise for her to try the issue herself; she will choose the best of her citizens as *dikasts*, judges of homicide who will serve in a court under an oath which she will establish for all time. She asks the parties to assemble their evidence and departs.

During the ninety or so lines of this scene we have moved into an entirely new world and atmosphere. The keynote is no longer the theme of retributive violence that has previously prevailed. Furthermore, word power as incantation has yielded to the reasoned argument of judicial proceedings.

Lines 490–565

There follows a fully structured stasimon for the Furies. In four strophic pairs they express their strong concern at the lawlessness which will reign if Orestes is acquitted and their authority is undermined. In that event, they themselves will refuse to respond to appeals for vengeance from the victims of crime in a family. <TRACK D4, lines 490–8> ◉

At this central point in the play, the ode occupies a pivotal position in the sequence of philosophical development as well as of dramatic action. Aeschylus now presents the Furies far more as embodiments of Justice than hell-hounds or blood-sucking fiends. Indeed, the moral themes and imagery of *Dikê* recall some of the Elders' utterances in the *Agamemnon*. In particular, the Furies assert two doctrines that are later accepted by Athena at 696–9. First (517–25), fear is an indispensable ingredient in social order: "There is advantage in the wisdom won from pain" (cf. *Agam*. 180–1). <TRACK D5, lines 517–25> ◉ Second (527–9), a middle course needs to be found between anarchy and despotism, an idea hardly relevant to Orestes' situation but important in Athenian political thought.

The meters are, at first, mainly trochaic in the units familiar from the Hymn to Zeus in *Agamemnon*. Towards the end, however, they revert to the iambic patterns, with syncopation, which have predominated so far. This suggests musically that the concept of retributive *Dikê* is persisting despite an inexorable movement towards insight and enlightenment.

Lines 566–753

Now a very solemn and spectacular moment as Athena re-enters with a jury of eleven[19] citizens whom she has chosen (487) to try Orestes. She calls on a herald to sound the trumpet and declare the proceedings open. The trumpet sounds, but the proclamation is forestalled by the entrance of Apollo as Orestes' witness and advocate.

The location has evidently moved away from Athena's temple on the Acropolis. At 570 the goddess speaks of a "council space" not a law court, and this suggests a place of deliberation with the architecture of an assembly area such as a theater, rather than a temple precinct. Later on (683 ff.) Athena says the council space will in future be associated with the Areopagus; but I believe the essential point at this moment of the drama is that *the audience* is being involved in it. The text repeatedly identifies the jurors with the whole Athenian people (569, 683, 681), conceived not just as spectators but participants in the trial of Orestes. I therefore conjecture that the jurors take their seats on pre-set benches at the front of the acting area, at the bottom end of the *orchêstra* immediately before the lowest tier of the audience sitting in the *theatron*, with the archons, the chief magistrates, in the middle. This arrangement makes the practical staging much easier and clearer if the Dikasts are down front to be addressed during the trial by Apollo, Orestes and the Coryphaeus rather than the alternative of sitting behind them upstage in front of the *skênê*.[20]

With this staging the jury in session at the trial of Orestes belongs not only to the world of the play but also to the citizen body of spectators. This, in turn, has the effect of uniting the heroic world of myth with that of contemporary Athens. It is thus in magnificent accord with Aeschylus' resolution of the tragic problem posed by the *lex talionis* within the context of the Athenian polis and its democratic system. Moreover, the poet has created a setting in which contemporary references are entirely appropriate, notably those that relate to the alliance with Argos which was established in 461/2 (see p. 34).

The content of the scene raises several problems much discussed by scholars but outside the scope of this book. The difficulty for us is the peculiar and unconvincing character of the arguments advanced on either side, focusing in the main on the relative claims of the man and the woman. Each side has its stronger and weaker points and Aeschylus may have wanted to reproduce the atmosphere of a typical Athenian trial with all its special pleading. The balance of the arguments is reflected in the votes at the end coming out equal and so (just) ensuring Orestes' acquittal. Commentators debate whether Athena votes with the jury herself and so produces the equalizer or whether she adds a casting vote as the president of the court.[21] Another difficulty arises over Athena's (not very dramatic) speech at 681 ff. where she founds the court of the Areopagus and warns against innovations connected with it. Here Aeschylus seems to have been adopting some political stance of his own, but it is far from certain what that stance precisely was.[22]

If, however, we look at the trial scene purely as drama, there is much to engage our interest and attention in the argumentation and conflict. The composition is well varied, with skillful use of stichomythia, distichomythia and rhesis, long or short. In the Furies' formal questioning of Orestes (585–608) it looks as if Aeschylus has given each member of the Chorus one or two lines to say.[23] <TRACK D6, lines 582–608> ⊙ The scene builds up to an exciting climax as, from 711, the eleven Dikasts leave their benches and advance upstage (I imagine to the *skênê* platform, close to Athena) to cast their individual votes by dropping a pebble in one or other of the two voting-urns (for conviction or acquittal), while the Coryphaeus and Apollo argue with each other in a run of eleven couplets. Suspense mounts as Athena declares her own vote, with the arbitrary reason for it (734–43);[24] and then, when the votes have been counted out, she announces the result (752–3). Visually, the formality of the proceedings, with the Olympian and chthonian deities in their contrasting costumes mingling with the human characters, will have made for a grand and noble spectacle.

Lines 754–77

Apollo has made his exit, his work done, and the scene ends, as it began, with a speech by Orestes. In his thanks to Athena and his oath of permanent alliance between Argos and Athens, there is a moving sense of triumphant release to bring this phase of the drama to its conclusion.

Closing Scene (778–1047)

The story of Orestes is over, but there are still 270 lines, almost a quarter of the text, to run. The concluding phase falls into three subsections: one in which Athens wins round the defeated Furies and persuades them to accept a place in the polis; in the second the Chorus show their change of heart by calling down on Athens the blessings of fertility and internal peace; the third is a grand processional exit.

The overall pace of the drama is now much more spacious and relaxed, as the Trilogy moves towards its tranquil and joyous ending. Where the choral lyric movements in *Agamemnon* became gradually shorter as the tension mounted, in *Eumenides* as the tension ceases they grow longer – an excellent instance in the tragic genre of Greek balance and proportion in design.

Word power becomes important again in the transformed Furies' prayer for Athens and also in the effect of Athena's Persuasion (885–6, 970–3) in mollifying the Furies. *Peitho* has acquired a different meaning from the "temptation" that forces the wrongdoer on to his ruin (*Agam.* 385), exemplified onstage as Clytemnestra tempted her husband into the palace over the purple tapestries. It now represents "diplomacy," perceived as a better way than violence of settling wrongs.

Lines 778–915

In the first section, the Furies loudly express their sense of dishonor and threaten to spit poisons onto Athens, which will blight the fertility of the crops and the people. Each of the two strophes is powerfully repeated in an antistrophe and these four outbursts, largely in dochmiacs and iambics, alternate with four iambic speeches for Athena. In these she tactfully and graciously offers them a permanent dwelling place in the city, with honors and sacrifices, and begs them not to infect the people with a spirit of internecine strife – another reference, doubtless, to contemporary tensions. <TRACK D7, lines 837–57 and 870–80> ⊙ An equation of the Erinyes to the actual cult of the *Semnai Theai* is becoming increasingly clear (see Sommerstein 1989, 10–11) At the end of a brief passage of stichomythia, the Coryphaeus eventually yields to Athena, who rounds the section off with a rhesis outlining the blessings for Athens that she wishes them to invoke, by way of a benign climate and the birth of citizens who will be god-fearing and bring honor to the city in war.

Lines 916–1020

The next section is formalized slightly differently. The Chorus chant three strophic pairs, during which they accept a home alongside the Olympian gods, pray for blessings as Athena has asked, including avoidance of civil strife, and finally greet the people who rejoice in the protection of Athena and are revered by Zeus. These sung stanzas alternate with anapaestic speeches by Athena who outlines the Furies' function and power in punishing sinners and rewarding the good. She attributes her victory to Persuasion and to Zeus, god of assemblies (970–3), and sees great benefit coming from "the frightening faces" (990) who will, if honored in a kindly spirit, prove kindly to their citizens and serve as a basis for order and glory. The mood pervading the singing of the Chorus and rhythmical speech of the solo actor is now one of sweetness and light, an atmosphere in which music and stately choreography must play an important part.

A final link with the Hymn to Zeus (*Agam.* 160–83) near the start of the Trilogy is evidenced in the choral meters which are now firmly trochaic with occasional dactyls, and the Furies' greeting of the Athenians (996–1002) hails the people as "showing wisdom at the last." Out of all the suffering witnessed in the tragic Trilogy wisdom and understanding have emerged. Zeus, through Apollo and Athena, has set mankind along the right path in the social context of the city state. <TRACK D8, lines 996–1020>

Lines 1021–47

The concluding section is introduced by an iambic speech for Athena, which unfortunately has at least one and possibly several lines missing. It seems clear, however, that the Furies are to be led by Athena and conducted to their home on the Areopagus hill in a procession which recalls the Panathenaea, the festival of civic celebration which was held every year in the summer. Aeschylus thus brings his great Trilogy to an end in a magnificent spectacle, which is rich in symbolic as well as literal significance.

The ritual involves women as well as men. A large number of extras are called for (see Sommerstein 1989, 276–8), and some of these will have played Athena's *prospoloi*, the priestesses who guarded her image. It is suggested at 1028 that the Furies are decked in the purple cloaks worn by resident aliens in the Panathenaea and are thus, with great appropriateness, welcomed into the polis as metics. Possibly the goddess's imperative "Honor (them)" (1029) is addressed to the Dikasts, so that they perform the investiture and then join in the procession as Areopagites, members of the court.

Sacrificial victims have already been brought onstage by *propompoi*, escorts, who may well be the same as the *prospoloi*, bearing torches (1022). The image of light in the darkness which was first presented in the Watchman's greeting of the beacon (*Agam.* 22–3) is now finally and physically manifested. His opening prayer for "release from toils" has now been granted by the gods. For many in the audience this will have communicated the further overtone of initiation into a mystery religion (see p. 38).

The procession is assembled and the music strikes up for a grand exit march in vigorous dactyls to a hymn, sung by the escort, which welcomes the *Semnai Theai* to Athens and asks for their goodwill. The ritual verbs used in the last line of the four short stanzas once again recall the Watchman and the "triumphant cry of good omen" (*Agam.* 28) which he called on Clytemnestra to raise for the beacon and now rings out at the very end of the Trilogy. <TRACK D9, lines 1033–47> ◉

The final words (apart from the concluding refrain) are "Zeus the all-seeing and Moira [p. 34] have thus come down together." The ultimate harmony is the reconciliation between Olympian and chthonian deities in a form of Justice which has broken the never-ending chain of crime and retaliatory punishment. The long ritual drama has reached its triumphant conclusion in words of good omen for the Athenian polis and for all mankind.

Notes

1 For Clytemnestra to enter in person at this point and to occupy herself in stage business upstage would be extremely awkward: no other choral parodos is so interrupted and its effect would be very distracting, particularly if the queen remains onstage after 103. However, there are also difficulties in assuming so long an apostrophe (a speech directed to someone in their absence), with questions and a request which receive no response for another 160 lines. The whole passage would fit a great deal better after Clytemnestra has made her splendid first entrance at 257. The structure, with lyrics framed by two anapaestic passages, would then be very similar to the Parodos in *Persae*; and the connection of thought between 82 and 104, contrasting the Elders' physical weakness with their "strength in song", would be excellent. No scholar, as far as I know, has suggested this transposition. The displacement, if it occurred, must predate the "Lycurgan recension' of *c*.330 (see Raeburn and Thomas 2011, Introduction lxx–lxxi) and could perhaps be explained in terms of a fourth century, or even earlier, revival of the play when a view was taken that the exceptionally long choral parodos should be livened up by some adventitious spectacle.

2 The positive connotation of the proverb is confirmed in Herodotus 1.207.1, where Croesus tells Solon, "My sufferings have become lessons."

3 For the associations in full detail see Raeburn and Thomas (2011, 99–104). One example may suffice here: the reference to "the plain of Asopus" (297), where the Greek hero Tydeus was ambushed by fifty Thebans in *Iliad* 4, 392–6. The plain is also mentioned in *Persae* as the site of the Persian catastrophe at Plataea.

4 In the Oxford Classical Text the iambic lines which announce the Herald's entry along the *eisodos* are given to Clytemnestra, but the whole of 489–502 should certainly be assigned to the Coryphaeus. The shape of the scene is badly spoilt if Clytemnestra is on at the beginning. See Analysis for the effect of her entrance at 585.

5 The intervals implicit in the *Persae* are a great deal longer.

6 Pace Sommerstein who deletes 527 in the Loeb text. I think the line is authentic.

7 An ancient hypothesis (summary) of the play says that Agamemnon enters in a wagon, followed by another wagon containing the spoils and Cassandra. Given the focus on wealth in 779–80, this would be admirably appropriate. Most scholars prefer the idea of placing Cassandra in the same cart as Agamemnon to point up the insult to Clytemnestra. I would maintain on practical grounds, among others, that the prophetess is better positioned *apart*, clearly visible but a silent figure in the background until she is needed. For a full discussion see Raeburn and Thomas (2011, 148–9).

8 The word *kommos*, lament, is often applied to a movement between soloist and chorus. The term *amoibaion* is also applied to such movements consisting entirely of (sung) lyric meters. An exchange in which lyrics alternate with (spoken) iambics or anapaests is known as an *epirrhema*.

9 The fact that no other extant Greek tragedy requires such an arrangement really counts for very little. Two doors are certainly needed in three of Aristophanes' comedies. In 458 the *skênê* was a wooden construction which could have been rebuilt or altered for each festival to accord with the tragic and comic poets' requirements.

10 At the very end of the Trilogy (*Eum.*1011) the Furies are accepted by Athena as metics of the city.

11 I would have Orestes pick the branch up from the floor beside him on the *ekkyklêma* rather than carrying it along with his sword at his entrance. The change of props would make an effective point.

12 The same words were used of Orestes by Cassandra at *Agam.* 1282 where she foretold that an avenger would come.

13 Would Aeschylus' audience have seen this as an untidiness? I think myself that it would have been inconsistent with the dignity and economy of the tragic style.

14 A vast amount of scholarly energy has gone into the staging problems of this scene. I believe that the stage directions supplied by Sommerstein in his Loeb translation are essentially right and these are assumed in my account.

15 Orestes' lines at 85–7 have clearly been misplaced in the MS tradition and belong at the very start of this section before Apollo responds at 64.

16 Hermes could be played by a mute extra, but the lines are perhaps better treated as an apostrophe, since Orestes is not accompanied by him when he arrives in Athens at 235 and the tableau on the *ekkyklêma* is already full enough.

17 The fourth-century vase paintings which are thought to offer stylized depictions of this theatrical scene do not suggest that the Furies' costumes and masks were in themselves particularly gruesome, apart from the snakes entwined in their hair or on an arm. Though the short tunics would certainly have been excellent for agile movement during the Binding Song (321–96), the austerely beautiful faces on the masks are more suggestive of the dignified goddesses that they are portrayed as in the later scenes than of demonic hobgoblins. If the vases reflect a tradition that goes back to the original production, one can only surmise that the frightening effect was achieved through the delivery of the verse and vigorous physical movement.

18 Scholars have linked this passage to the Athenian claim to Sigeum at the entrance to the Black Sea and so of strategic importance to their corn supply.

19 This figure is suggested by the number of short speeches composed to accompany the actual voting procedure (711–33).

20 The introduction of seats or benches by stage hands would be an untidy element in the spectacle at this point, and the principals in the trial should not have to face upstage. See note 13 above.

21 If the jurors total eleven (note 19), the former has to be the case.

22 Readers who wish to pursue these matters further are referred to Sommerstein (1989, 216–8).

23 Under this arrangement, the Coryphaeus would deliver 585–6, and a second Fury 587. The opening couplet would be balanced by another for Fury no. 12 at 607–8.

24 Athena's argument is puzzlingly biased: as a goddess without a mother and sprung from Zeus's head she is for the male in all things and so assigns preference to the father against the mother. I have always been attracted by the explanation given by E.R. Dodds (in his lectures in 1946) that Aeschylus deliberately made Athena use an arbitrary, extraneous justification for her vote because he wanted, for reasons of political tact, to imply that that the contemporary issue (p. 34) was not one between right and wrong but between two rights.

References

Text: *Aeschylus Oresteia* (Loeb edition). 2008. Cambridge, MA: Harvard University Press, edited and translated by Alan H. Sommerstein.

Fraenkel, Eduard. 1950. *Aeschylus: Agamemnon*. Oxford: Clarendon Press.

Garvie, A.F. 1986. *Aeschylus: Choephori*. Oxford: Clarendon Press.

Raeburn, David and Thomas, Oliver. 2011. *The Agamemnon of Aeschylus: A Commentary for Students*. Oxford: Oxford University Press.

Sommerstein, Alan H. 1989. *Aeschylus: Eumenides*. Cambridge: University Press.

Taplin, Oliver. 1977. *The Stagecraft of Aeschylus*. Oxford: Clarendon Press.

Commentaries

Agamemnon

Fraenkel, Eduard. 1950. *Aeschylus: Agamemnon*. Oxford: Clarendon Press.

Raeburn, David and Thomas, Oliver. 2011. *The Agamemnon of Aeschylus: A Commentary for Students*. Oxford: Oxford University Press.

Choephori

Bowen, A. 1986. *Aeschylus: Choephori*. Bristol: Bristol Classical Press.

Garvie, A.F. 1986. *Aeschylus: Choephori*. Oxford: Clarendon Press.

Eumenides

Podlecki, A.J. 1989. *Aeschylus: Eumenides*. Warminster: Aris & Phillips.

Sommerstein, Alan H. 1989. *Aeschylus: Eumenides*. Cambridge: Cambridge University Press.

Further Reading

Goldhill, Simon. 2004. *Aeschylus: the Oresteia*, 2nd edn. Cambridge: Cambridge University Press. A student guide with a useful examination of the themes.

Kitto, H.D.F. 1956. *Form and Meaning in Drama: A Study of Six Greek Plays and of Hamlet*. London, Methuen. Still extremely valuable for its approach to the plays as works of art.

Lloyd, Michael (ed.). 2007. *Oxford Readings in Classical Studies: Aeschylus*. Oxford: Oxford University Press. A collection of influential articles on the plays.

Owen, E.T. 1952. *The Harmony of Aeschylus*. Toronto: Clarke, Irwin and Co. A rather forgotten but extremely important set of lectures which emphasize the power of words in Aeschylean dramaturgy.

Scott, William C. 1984. *Musical Design in Aeschylean Theater*. Hanover, NH: University Press of New England. A useful study of the relationship between meter and themes in Aeschylus.

Sommerstein, Alan H. 2010. *Aeschylean Tragedy*, 2nd edn. London: Duckworth. An excellent comprehensive work on the poet and his plays.

Taplin, Oliver. 1977. *The Stagecraft of Aeschylus: the Dramatic Use of Entrances and Exits in Greek Tragedy*. Oxford: Clarendon Press. A very interesting and thorough exploration of the practical "grammar" of Greek tragedy.

Winnington-Ingram, R.P. 1980. *Studies in Aeschylus*. Cambridge: Cambridge University Press. The outstanding critical study of the ideas in the plays.

Also two helpful guides to the plays, recent scholarship and reception:

Goward, B. 2005. *Aeschylus: Agamemnon*. London: Duckworth.
Mitchell-Boyask, R. 2009. *Aeschylus: Eumenides*. London: Duckworth.

5

Sophocles

The Plays

Only seven tragedies by Sophocles have survived complete out of a known output of 123 – there could have been more. Unlike Aeschylus, this poet preferred to compose in single plays rather than in trilogy form. A fairly large part of a satyr-play, *The Trackers* (*Ichneutae*) has also been uncovered in modern times among the Oxyrhinchus papyri.

We only have reasonably firm dates for two of the seven tragedies and I list them in a conjectural order of composition: *Women of Trachis, Ajax, Antigone* (442), *Oedipus Tyrannus, Electra, Philoctetes* (409) and *Oedipus at Colonus* (first mounted posthumously in 401). The two Oedipus plays and *Antigone* are commonly grouped together as "The Theban Plays," but they are in no sense a connected trilogy; they are separate dramas, composed at different dates and with their own distinctive themes.

All these plays reveal Sophocles as a mature artist. Only three of them can be explored in this volume, but the other four are also of a very high order.

Life and Times

Sophocles' life (446/5–406/5) straddled the most famous century in the history and culture of ancient Athens. In his youth he witnessed the two invasions of Greece by Persia and he is said by an ancient biographer to have sung and danced with his lyre, "naked and anointed with oil," at the celebration that followed the Athenian victory at Salamis in 480. His earlier adult years coincided with the development of Athenian democracy and its empire under the great Pericles; his middle and later years with the hostile rivalry of Athens with Sparta which led to the outbreak of the Peloponnesian War in 431. He died roughly at the time when Athens was finally defeated.

Apart from his career as a dramatist, Sophocles held public office, first serving as one of the Hellenotamiae, the treasurers of the Delian league (see p. 88), and in 441–40 with Pericles as one of the ten "generals," though probably in an administrative rather than a strategic role. After the disastrous Sicilian expedition ended in 413, he served as one of a group set up to deal with the ensuing crisis. He was involved in some of the religious cults in Athens, particularly in that of Asclepius, the god of healing, which Plutarch (*Life of Numa* 8) says that he established in 420. The comic poet Aristophanes (*Frogs* 82) refers to him as an "easy-tempered person," and this is consistent with some rather charming anecdotes which may or may not be true (see Lefkowitz 2012, 78–86).[1]

Greek Tragedies as Plays for Performance, First Edition. David Raeburn.
© 2017 John Wiley & Sons, Inc. Published 2017 by John Wiley & Sons, Inc.
Companion website: www.wiley.com/go/raeburn

Achievement as Dramatist

Sophocles must have become involved in the life of the Athenian theatre quite early, first probably as an actor and in due course as a tragic poet. He had emerged as a rival to Aeschylus by 468, when he beat the older poet to the first prize at the festival with a group of his own plays. After Aeschylus died in 456, according to the ancient sources, he won the first prize eighteen times at the City Dionysia and several more at the lesser festival called the Lenaea. He continued composing plays until shortly before he died and those that can be ascribed to his final decade indicate that his talent remained undiminished up to the end.

Aristotle (*Poetics* 1449a) credited Sophocles with the introduction of the third actor, which enlarged the possibilities of the tragic medium in an important way that Aeschylus was evidently happy to exploit in the *Oresteia*. Three actors dividing the speaking roles between them became the norm which evidently served the poets' needs well enough.[2]

Another fact gleamed from the ancient biographer is that Sophocles increased the chorus from twelve to fifteen members. The reason for this can only be guessed at. He may have felt that the larger number allowed a wider range of choreographic possibilities during the choral odes. During the episodes, he might have preferred to divide the chorus symmetrically, seven and seven to the sides of the *orchestra*, with the Coryphaeus' standing apart, like the aulete, to be involved in a more obvious way with the solo actors when appropriate.

Finally, Aristotle tells us that Sophocles invented *skênographia*, scene-painting, which suggests painted panels attached to the façade of the stage-building to represent a different setting for a play than the conventional palace or temple. In *Philoctetes,* for example, the central entrance is the mouth to a rocky cave on a desert island.

These changes will have allowed a rather greater flexibility and more elbow-room to the medium, which does not seem to have been developed further by Euripides in its essentials.

Thought and Outlook

Sophocles, like Aeschylus, can be seen as a great thinker as well as a consummate dramatist. While his tragedies need to be interpreted in their contemporary context, they all touch on themes of universal interest and concern.

Apart from the evidence of the plays themselves, the poet's involvement in religious cult suggests that, for him, as for Aeschylus, the gods and their associated rituals provided an important framework of reference for interpreting the world and human life. His middle and later years, however, coincided with changes in the intellectual climate at Athens, which took place after the arrival of the Sophists at Athens from the earlier 440s. These were professional teachers of rhetoric who questioned traditional beliefs about the gods and ethical values. The three plays in this volume suggest that Sophocles was very much interested in these issues but was unhappy to abandon conventional religious views and practice or to go along with moral relativism. In *Oedipus Tyrannus,* for example (as in other plays), he presents prophecies and oracles as a crucial expression of order in the universe, mysterious and often cruel as that universe may be. Another important theme is that human beings must acknowledge their status as mortals and not attempt to behave like gods in actions that are excessive and high-handed. To "hit the mark" of correct action means subscribing to the two mottoes inscribed in the temple of Apollo at Delphi: "Know yourself" and "Nothing in excess" – reverse sides of the same coin, since avoidance of excessive behavior entails knowing and coming to terms with one's limitations.

The fact that Sophocles held public office implies that he was also a patriotic Athenian. The dramatic festivals were, after all, civic institutions which offered the stage for his talent to flourish and indeed to take the tragic genre to an extraordinary maturity. His didactic role, however, allowed him to bring a moral slant to bear on political issues. If as Hellenotamias he helped to administer the finances of what had become the Athenian empire, it would not have been unpatriotic in a democratic society to question the inhumane treatment of the subject allies who failed to pay their contributions, and the way in which allied funds were spent for the glorification of Athens. Knowing Pericles could well have made him alive to the dangers of prolonged power that are to be evidenced in Creon and Oedipus. Political morality apart, Sophocles also explores the norm of social ethics, as expressed in the doctrine of "doing good to one's friends and harm to one's enemies." This too he finds problematic when viewed in the light of the universal laws of humanity which he regards as the "established laws" of the gods. In *Antigone* and *Electra* he dramatizes the conflict between utilitarian and non-consequential ethical systems.

Sophocles' philosophy of life, together with the place of the gods and of fate in his plays, are a favorite critical topic. The tragic medium was, of course, not one to encourage a cozy optimism in its audience, however exciting it might be as entertainment. However, I would not myself see Sophocles as a fundamentally "bleak" playwright. While there is no pretense that life is anything other than harsh or ugly, his plays, one way or another, seem to affirm the human spirit no less than the divine order. Multiple causation applies to his characters no less than in Aeschylus.

Dramatic Technique

Sophocles arguably took the basic hybrid form of tragedy as far as it could go. It was during his time that the actor grew in prominence, with a prize established in 449 for the best performer in the tragic contests. The Chorus continued to be essential to the form but it ceased to enjoy the dominance that is evident in Aeschylus' plays. The art reflects less of its origin in religious ritual as it grows more concerned with human interaction. Thus the Chorus's importance in Sophocles varies from play to play in accordance with the part he needs it to discharge in the drama. Whether its role is large or small, though, the songs are always integrated very skillfully with the episodes. An ode will often serve as a pivot first to look back to the preceding episode and then to anticipate what is to follow. With Sophocles one never feels that the Chorus has become irrelevant; it remains an essential resource, crucial to the medium, there to be employed in the dramatic sequence as the poet chooses. Continuity remains as important as in Aeschylus and the chorus is a vital element in the seamless quality of Sophoclean dramaturgy.

The extended form of the trilogy had allowed Aeschylus a looser and more leisurely structure. The single, free-standing play enabled a greater tightness and concentration of focus. Sophocles' plots are brilliantly designed on the basis that there needs to be some plausibility in the presence of the Chorus throughout the action after the Prologue, so that the passage of time traversed during the odes is reasonably short (contrast *Agamemnon*, where the First Stasimon covers the whole period between the night of Troy's capture and Agamemnon's landing home on Argive soil). *Antigone* takes its shape from the sequence of challenges to Creon's authority, which leads the king eventually to change his mind, but all too late. *Oedipus Tyrannus* is the buildup, through the gradual revelation of past events, to the climax of the king's appalling discovery, followed by a slow winding down in pathos. The structural unity in *Electra* depends on the impact of her initial situation and of subsequent events on the heroine personally.

An important development in Sophocles is the use and management of the opening scene. The three parts of the *Oresteia* each begin with a monologue, characteristically starting with a prayer. In six of his seven extant tragedies[3] Sophocles introduces two characters at the very outset in a scene which establishes a critical situation and allows him to articulate some of the themes that are going to be important in the play as a whole. This sense of urgency immediately focuses the audience's attention and is an important aspect of the dramaturgy.

A similar development in sophistication can be seen in Sophocles' use of "word power." When in Aeschylus' *Agamemnon* (1246) Cassandra says to the Chorus, "I tell you it is Agamemnon's death you shall look upon," the Coryphaeus reacts in horror not only to what the statement means but to the fact that it has been *spoken* and so more likely to happen. Sophocles' plays likewise abound in prophecies and oracles. Although foreknowledge does not imply predestination and prophecies are usually fulfilled through human action or humanly driven circumstances, these utterances have an *emotive* potency which transcend philosophical distinctions.

As in Aeschylus, the language of prayer is frequently adopted, particularly in choral addresses to the gods. Sophocles, however, does not exploit double meanings or sinister resonance in proper names; his technique is more to exploit the audience's familiarity with the story he is dramatizing and so to establish a compelling ambivalence or ulterior significance in the words as delivered by the character who lacks the audience's knowledge. The most famous, and perhaps the most chilling example of "tragic" or "dramatic irony" is that of Oedipus putting a dreadful curse on the killer of King Laius and on anyone who harbors the killer, when we as an audience know that he is cursing himself. We shudder because we accept that an oath sworn in the name of the gods is a performative utterance with power to affect the future.

Verbal irony quickly spills over into the irony of situation in which Sophocles excels. An important element in the excitement of *Oedipus Tyrannus* is the audience's knowledge that in hunting for Laius' murderer Oedipus is chasing his own tail. Another powerful example is the situation of Electra believing that her brother is dead when he is alive and "disabusing" her sister Chrysothemis who arrives in high excitement to say, on the evidence of a lock on Agamemnon's grave, that he *is* alive and back in Mycenae. When Orestes does at long last slowly reveal himself to Electra, the tension is thus unbearable.

Characterization

Much criticism has been influenced by the notion of the "Sophoclean hero," as developed by Bernard Knox (1964), which advances the idea of the "heroic temper" as the common quality in Sophocles' leading characters. Six of the tragedies certainly center on a man or a woman who holds uncompromisingly to a particular position, but I would not regard this as cardinal to the interpretation of the plays viewed individually,[4] in which the tragic issue is wider ranging. Common humanity seems to prevail over heroic values, as at the end of Homer's *Iliad* when Achilles consents to restore Hector's body to his father Priam. Of the plays discussed in this volume, *Antigone* illustrates the danger of civic devotion that ignores fundamental human values; *Oedipus Tyrannus'* main preoccupation is perhaps with human limitation and self-knowledge; *Electra* explores the destructive effects of revenge on human personality.

A useful guide to characterization in Sophocles is advanced in Winnington-Ingram 1980 (based on Gellie 1972): "Sophocles builds down and he builds up: he builds down from the traditional situation and the mental attitudes which the action implies and he builds up from observation of life in such a way as to create credibility and encourage emotional response." We might thus say that Sophocles' characters are rather more fully rounded than those of Aeschylus who selects those human qualities that are strictly relevant to his thematic purposes. Their motivation is more complex, as in human life, and we are sometimes left to speculate on why they are made to behave as they do (see Easterling 1977). Conflicts of moral stance are between people no less than they are of principles, which may be debated but not necessarily in a conclusive way.

Style

Sophocles composed in a beautiful Greek. His iambic trimeters are less colorful and grandiloquent in vocabulary and less metaphorical than Aeschylus. His style is still a poetic one which often employs words that would not be found in a prose author and distinctive in a way which makes him difficult to translate.[5] Vocabulary and idiom apart, his structure of sentences and paragraphs in the long speeches has its own characteristic flow, with more enjambment of lines than in Aeschylus and comparable with the seamlessness of his dramaturgy. The choral odes, of course, are most elaborately poetic as words, ideas and images are worked into varied and complex rhythmical patterns which are compelling in their own right, as the recordings included with this book aim to show.

Training students to deliver Sophocles' long speeches in the original has taught me how skillfully they are constructed in shaped paragraphs of, perhaps, 8–10 lines and how the phrasing within these makes the verse expressive, varied and interesting for an actor to project. Sophocles well illustrates how the sounds of ancient Greek vowels and consonants can be used to reflect meaning. The pitch accent is exploited to provide an expressive "tune" in its own right; it is particularly valuable to explore the emotive effect of words which carry a circumflex accent, particularly when these are employed in close conjunction.[6]

These qualities are particularly well exemplified in the graphic narrative speeches by Messengers or other characters. How far Sophocles was influenced by the schools of rhetoric set up by the Sophists from the mid-440s on is hard to judge, as the argumentation in the long speeches is not obviously forensic. However, an important feature of the plays is the *agôn*, or formal debate, in which contrasting speeches between two characters are pitted against each other. This occurs less artificially than can be found in Euripides (see p. 140); the contest always seems relevant to the situation and appropriate in the mouths of the characters who deliver the speeches.

Stichomythia is likewise composed in a lively and arresting way, especially in scenes of conflict or recognitions. Sophocles had the artifice and dramatic instinct to lend naturalness to this very formal kind of dialogue and to sustain interest through a considerable number of lines. The splitting of verses between two characters (*antilabê*) to achieve a quickening of pace and mounting excitement at a dramatic climax, is always very effective when it occurs.

In short, Sophocles' style reveals him as an artist with a keen ear for the musicality of ancient Greek and a gift for poetry, who understood perfectly what would work to engage his audience's attention and stir its emotions in the theatre.

Summary

Sophocles' extant plays embrace a range of serious human topics. They are subtly conceived and not always easy to pin down. As works of dramatic art they are astonishingly skillful in the development of irony as a story-telling device, in the vitality of the personalities portrayed in interaction and in the use of the tragic medium to offer a vibrantly moving and thought-provoking experience.

Notes

1 Much of the evidence is very late and ancient biographical writing did not conform to modern standards.
2 *Oedipus at Colonus* requires four actors, unless Ismene was played by three different performers and Theseus by two.
3 An exception is *Trachiniae*, but even there the Nurse and Hyllus are introduced after Deianira's opening monologue.
4 The idea of the "tragic flaw," based on a misunderstanding of Aristotle's *hamartia* is similarly distortive when applied to Sophocles, Shakespeare or modern drama.
5 The standard works are Earp (1944) and Long (1968).
6 Examples picked at random are: *Ant.* 1010–11, 1288–9; *OT* 1201–2, 1399–400; *El.* 804–5, 1326.

References

Easterling, P.E. 1977. "Character in Sophocles," *Greece and Rome* 24, 121–9.
Knox, B.M.W. 1964. *The Heroic Temper*. Berkeley, LA: University of California Press.
Lefkowitz, Mary, R. 2012. *The Lives of the Greek Poets*, 2nd edn. Bristol: Bristol Classical Press.

Further Reading

Burton, R.W. 1980. *The Chorus in Sophocles' Plays*. Oxford: Clarendon Press. An excellent analysis of the Chorus's contribution to the dramatic sequence in the plays.
Earp. F.R. 1944. *The Style of Sophocles*. Cambridge: Cambridge University Press.
Gellie, G.H. 1972. *Sophocles – A Reading*. Melbourne: Melbourne University Press. A good full survey of the plays.
Goldhill, S. and Hall, E. (eds). 2009. *Sophocles and the Greek Tragic Tradition*. Cambridge: Cambridge University Press. An interesting collection of papers.
Long, A.A. 1968. *Language and Thought in Sophocles*. London: Continuum Press.
Winnington-Ingram, R.P. 1980. *Sophocles – An Interpretation*. Cambridge: Cambridge University Press. A crucial and profound critical study.

6

Antigone

General Introduction

Of all Sophocles' tragedies, *Antigone* is perhaps the most frequently revived today, as it is felt to be particularly relevant to the modern world. The heroine seems to enshrine the protest of the individual conscience against the authority of the state as embodied in Creon, and this concept is certainly dominant in twentieth-century plays based on this one, such as Anouilh's *Antigone* or Fugard's *The Island*. Whether this was Sophocles' governing idea is rather doubtful; Antigone herself disappears from the stage two-thirds of the way through the action. Of all the poet's extant plays this one most needs to be understood in terms of its historical context. Dramatic analysis suggests that the central, truly tragic character is Creon rather than Antigone. If we can read the text in the light of what can be identified as its chief preoccupations, it emerges as an exceptionally powerful piece in which the ideas and their realization within the tragic form are perfectly at one.

Synopsis

Events before the play begins relate to the quarrel between the two sons of Oedipus over the sovereignty of Thebes. Eteocles prevailed and the exiled Polynices raised an invading army from Argos to assert his claim. The Thebans were victorious, but the rival brothers killed each other in single combat. Sophocles' drama begins after Creon, the brothers' uncle, takes over the city and, in the interest of civic order, decrees burial with funeral honors for Eteocles, while the rebel Polynices is to lie unburied for the dogs and vultures to devour. Only their two sisters survive from the whole house: Antigone, who is betrothed to Creon's son Haemon, and Ismene.

Antigone tries to persuade Ismene to help her bury Polynices' body in defiance of Creon's decree, but her sister refuses. A guard later reports to Creon that the body has been mysteriously buried. Antigone is subsequently arrested and brought before Creon who pronounces her death in accordance with his proclamation. Deaf to the earnest appeal of his son Haemon on Antigone's behalf, he is only persuaded by the prophet Tiresias to change his mind – but too late. Antigone has hanged herself in the cave where she has been immured, and Haemon commits suicide, to be followed by his grief-stricken mother Eurydice. At the end Creon is left alone, bereft of his loved ones.

Historical Background

Although the evidence is not conclusive, there are reasonable grounds (Griffith 1999, 2) for dating *Antigone* to 442, when Athens was flourishing under the leadership of the great Pericles. At that time too, the magnificent Parthenon, the new temple of Athena, was being built on the Acropolis, directly above the theatre of Dionysus, where the play was performed. It was Pericles' ambitious vision to make Athens the cultural center of the Greek world, and fundamental to this was his plan to rebuild the temples on the Acropolis previously destroyed in the Persian Wars. The Parthenon was thus something of a symbol and work on it began in 447 BC. It was paid for out of a fund which originally consisted of contributions made by the league of Greek cities formed under Athenian leadership for defense against Persia. When in 454 the accumulated contributions were transferred from the Aegean island of Delos to Athens itself, the league effectively became an empire. Furthermore, though peace was finally concluded with Persia in 449, Athens continued to levy contributions from her subject allies, bringing rebels into line by force if necessary, and to use the money for her own purposes.

In this context the moral basis for an empire involving extortion and repression must have been open to question. Many in the spirit of the new rationalism and relativist morality associated with the Sophists (p. 82) would doubtless have argued that might was right and that the end of Athenian glory and excellence justified the means used to attain it. Others, however, could have been conscious that, besides the written laws and decrees which expressed the interest of the state, there were other unwritten laws of justice and common humanity which man disregarded at his peril.

In 442 Pericles himself held the public office of *stratêgos*, normally translated 'general' (the word applied at Athens to the ten representatives of each tribe who formed the executive government of the polis) and continued to do so until he died in 429. In *Antigone* Creon is referred to by this title when he is first mentioned (8), rather puzzlingly as he is presented as the sole ruler of Thebes and not as a military commander. The view of Ehrenberg (1954) is attractive, that Sophocles used the term to suggest some kind of contemporary relevance to his Athenian audience. It would certainly be misleading to regard Creon as a portrait of Pericles, but the two personalities could be said to share an outlook that is fervently patriotic, self-reliant and rationalistic.

Similarly, there is no reason to suppose that Sophocles was opposed to Athenian imperialism as such or that he actively disapproved of Pericles' building program (see p. 81 for the public offices he held). He was, however, primarily a dramatist, not a politician; and at least two other of his extant tragedies, *Ajax* and *Philoctetes*, suggest that he was well alive to the moral issues of contemporary politics.

Interpretation

Central to *Antigone* is the conflict between written and unwritten laws, as expounded by the heroine herself in her great speech of defiance to Creon (450–9). The plot hinges on one of the latter: the religious duty of burying the corpse of a dead kinsman. In the interests of civic order, Creon issues his edict prohibiting the burial of Polynices who died attacking his native city. Under Athenian law traitors were refused burial in their native soil; but to expose a corpse to be devoured by the dogs and vultures was an act of impiety which could offend the gods both below and above the earth. This Creon chooses to ignore.

The play demonstrates the tragic consequences of a civic devotion which subordinates values such as religious duty, family loyalty and, interestingly, sexual love to the needs of the state. In disobeying Creon's edict, Polynices' sister Antigone is affirming other absolute and overriding claims and so sets in motion the train of events which leads not only to her own death but to the ultimate catastrophe of Creon's moral annihilation through the loss of his son and his wife. Too late Creon learns the need for wisdom, good counsel and reverence for the gods.

Another important theme of particular appeal to the modern mind is that Antigone is presented as a woman setting herself against male authority. Ismene opposes Antigone on the grounds that they are women who are not intended by nature to fight against men (61–2); and Creon regards giving in to a woman as the ultimate disgrace (484–5, 525, 678–80). But the play is not to be seen as a feminist tract. As the heroine prepares to go to her death, she laments the non-fulfilment of her biological role as a woman, to marry and so to bear children (813–16, 876).

Antigone's tragedy is evidently incidental to Creon's and some have wondered why the play takes its name from her. The titles of Greek tragedies do not always correspond with the longest or the leading role. Enough to say in this case that it is Antigone's action which gives the drama its drive and she is the character with whom the audience is chiefly asked to identify with until she leaves the stage.

Crucial, finally, to the play's thought is the famous "Ode to Man," the First *Stasimon* (332–75), which is more fully explored below in its dramatic context. In this remarkable poem man is presented in a quasi-evolutionary context as the lord of creation, whose resourcefulness and ingenuity are equal to any challenge, except death. Yet these formidable qualities can incline to evil as well as to good. The justice sanctioned by the gods needs to be upheld no less than the laws of the land. Sophocles seems to be posing the question: in an age of growing rationalism, can all notions of the divine be dispensed with?

Dramaturgy

Antigone is very much a play of conflict and suspense. The bulk of the plot consists of successive challenges to Creon's authority until he finally cracks, a structure well served by tragedy's episodic form. Suspense is largely concentrated on the fate of Antigone first in her conflict with Creon and then after she has been condemned to die.

Characterization is developed to express the essential conflict of attitudes, but Sophocles' creations are always men and women of flesh and blood. We are conscious of clashes of personality no less than of principle. Antigone is made to display the tiresome intolerance and intransigence of which martyrs are often made; while Creon's aggressive concern for the city is allowed its positive aspects and Sophocles clearly intended his audience to sympathize with him at the end of the play. Nothing in this piece is a matter of black and white, and it is this which makes it so subtly compelling.[1]

The Chorus of Theban Elders is perfectly integrated into the play's action and their songs play a crucial part in a powerful dramatic sequence. Ostensibly, they are there to represent the Theban community, but the voice of the poet is also apparent in several of the odes, which can mostly be imagined as stately and processional. The play's action lends itself to a degree of visual splendor and dignity in the presentation, though never to spectacle for spectacle's sake. The *ekkyklêma* is called for near the end of the play and its deployment there is artistically perfect.

Dramatic Analysis

Line numbers refer to the Greek text in the Loeb edition (see the end of this chapter), which has a parallel English translation. For the terminology of the discrete movements, see Appendix A; for the lyric structure and meters see Appendix B or hear TRACK 0. ◉

Prologue (1–99)

In place of the monologue with which Aeschylus (and later Euripides) opens his plays, Sophocles launches his audience straight into the drama with a dialogue for the two, strongly contrasted, sisters, Antigone and Ismene. This gives the audience the ground facts of the situation created by Creon's decree and also articulates some of the basic themes, while presenting a clash between two different viewpoints and personalities. Antigone has brought her sister out of the house, so that they can talk privately and not be overheard.[2] The purpose is to obtain Ismene's cooperation in burying Polynices' exposed body, but her sister's response in the scene is such that she has to go it alone.

An issue mentioned very early on (2–3) is the murky history of Oedipus' family. Antigone speaks of herself and Ismene as the surviving victims of a family curse, thus sounding an Aeschylean note with which Sophocles' audience could have been familiar. Although the theme is picked up later by the Chorus at 594 ff., it quickly disappears from view at this stage, to be superseded by the oppositions which will be dominating the play's action. The first of these is obedience to the law versus justice in an absolute sense (23–4). For Antigone the latter must be overriding: she cannot ignore "what the gods hold in honor" (77), and the burial of Polynices will be the paradox of a "holy crime" (74). For Ismene, however, there is no point in resisting the powerful (59–60, 63–4) and to do so is to "act excessively" (68). The second conflict is that between the claims of the city and those of the family. The key concept here is *philia*, the instinctive human quality which unites family and friends, as distinct from outsiders who may well be perceived as *echthroi*, enemies. The girls' brother Polynices has shown himself an *echthros* in attacking his native city; hence Creon's decree that his body must have the same treatment as the dead of the Argive invaders. For Antigone, though, a brother is a *philos* and always a *philos*; the edict is entirely unacceptable, and she will win glory among the dead for her devotion (72–3). Here the gender issue also features: Ismene, as already noted, is again the pragmatist, while for Antigone "being a woman" can afford no excuse for failing to do the right thing.

What makes these conflicts dramatically compelling, however, is the contrast in character between the two sisters. Antigone is passionately indignant at Creon's decree, which she evidently takes personally (31–2). She is totally committed to what she is certain is right in terms of loyalty and duty to kindred, but also unsympathetically intolerant of her sister's attitude and apparently set on self-martyrdom. Ismene is far more reasonable and practical. She clearly loves her sister and is deeply concerned for her but sadly content to admire rather than to act. In all this the writing engages the audience's interest and attention from line 1 and the argument is flexibly expressed in shorter or longer speeches which alternate with passages of *stichomythia*.

When the sisters go their separate ways at the end of the scene, Antigone down an *eisodos*, Ismene back into the house, the drama's exposition is virtually complete. We have only to hear from Creon himself before the challenges to him begin.

Parodos (100–54)

Now, in solemn procession, enter the Chorus of Theban Elders, representing their city at large. Their song begins in the form of a hymn; and the public, spectacular quality of their ritual makes a powerful contrast with the private, more intimate, atmosphere of the Prologue. The movement provides a splendid build-up to Creon's proud first entrance.

The ode has an unusual musical structure for a parodos. Sung strophes in expansive aeolo-choriambic phrases are punctuated by 9-line passages of anapaests, martial in their effect and, I would judge, in faster tempo.[3] The four strophic stanzas are, by and large, more oblique as well as more grand-sounding, while the anapaests are more factual and explanatory. Within this musical structure, the content varies: Strophe A opens the ode impressively with a greeting to the sunrise which has seen the retreat of the Argive invaders. Anapaests 1 uses the imagery of an eagle to describe Polynices swooping down on the land with his host. <TRACK E1, lines 100–16> ◉ In Antistrophe A the eagle turns into a monster besetting the city with ravening jaws but repelled before the fire-god could secure a grip on the buildings. Anapaests 2 announces that Zeus hates boasters and struck one of the attacking warriors with his lightning just as he was scaling the battlements.[4] Strophe B portrays the boaster swung down to earth in two runs of three rolling dactyls followed by two bumpy trochees. The demise of

Figure 6.1 *Antigone*, Whitgift School, Croydon, England 1977. Source: Reproduced by permission of the Archive of Performances of Greek & Roman Drama.

other invaders by war-god Ares is described in an exciting complex of 5/8, 3/4 and 2/4 bars. Now, in a peculiarly exciting rhythmical entry (141),[5] Anapaests 3 extols the defeat of the seven Argive champions at the seven gates of Thebes – except (here the tempo might slow down) for the ill-starred brothers (Eteocles and Polynices) who fought and destroyed each other. <TRACK E2, lines 134–47 > ◉ The joyful tone of victory is resumed in Antistrophe B, in ring composition with Strophe A. War can be forgotten and the temples revisited in all-night dances presided over by earth-shaking Bacchus, who balances Ares in the replication of the complex coda of the strophe.

On these lines we can imagine the double doors of the *skênê* opening to reveal Creon making a proud and majestic entrance attended by guards. He is thus presented to the audience on a tide of victorious celebration, modified only by the warning against boastful behavior, which foreshadows the fate that eventually awaits Creon's own loud talk, and by the mutual destruction of Eteocles and Polynices, the treatment of whose bodies has already triggered the drama.

Transitional Anapaests (155–61)

Seven verses introduce Creon as the new ruler and ask why he has summoned this special council of elders. Although they formally balance 141–7, they are in very different vein and probably delivered by the Coryphaeus. They should not be seen as an integral part of the Parodos.

First Episode (162–331)

The function of this episode is to reveal Creon as the man he is, both in the formal declaration of his long first speech (162–210) and then in two confrontations, first fairly briefly with the Coryphaeus, next at much greater length with the Guard who comes to report the mysterious covering over of Polynices' body.

The opening rhesis is a peculiarly skillful use of the form. In essence, Creon is outlining his decree and justifying it to the Elders as good governance.[6] In many ways what Sophocles gives him to say would have struck the Athenian audience as thoroughly admirable, particularly in the opening metaphor of the ship of state which has come safely through a storm and now must be firmly kept on even keel and, after that, in Creon's assertion that he means to rule without fear or favor: rebels, whoever they are, cannot be treated the same way as loyalists.[7] Thebes in the play is, of course, not a democracy like Athens. Creon is presented as a king and an absolute ruler, but in ancient times kings could have an advisory council and this is what Creon's elders might be expected to represent (159–60). However, in his opening words to them he makes it clear that he expects their steadfast loyalty to himself as to his predecessors and is strongly assertive in his insistence on his personal authority (173–4, 207). Moreover, he presents his decree not as a matter of consultation but as a fait accompli. His statement that a man's proper character is not revealed until he has stood the test of responsibility in office is something of a hostage to fortune, since the course of the drama will show how he himself stands that test, only to be found wanting.

Creon receives his first challenge in the stichomythia which immediately follows. The Coryphaeus responds to his categoric declaration not with a profession of congratulatory support but only with grudging acquiescence. Creon, he says, is of course free to act as he thinks fit (211–14). When the king demands that he should not side with the disobedient, he receives the sullen answer, "No man is so foolish as to court his death" (220).

There now occurs a very extraordinary change of tone with the entrance of the Guard who, to Creon's irritation, starts by explaining at some length how he has dithered in fear of punishment over bringing Creon his unwelcome news. The speech is in almost comic vein and can be seen as a deliberate contrast to the self-important quality of Creon's pronouncements. The Guard's earthiness serves as a delightful touchstone of common humanity by which the audience is being invited to judge Creon's general stance.[8]

When, under pressure from Creon, the Guard eventually comes out with the information that Polynices's corpse has received a ritual covering from some unknown person, Creon's dumbfounded reaction is ironically compelling: "Who was the *man* who dared to do this?" (248). The scene develops in the Guard's narrative speech (249–77) in which he describes the mysterious lack of evidence on the earth or any sign that the corpse had been mangled by animals. This prompts the Coryphaeus to suggest that the *gods* might be at work in this burial, a hint to which Creon reacts with fury in a second rhesis (280–314): the burial must be the work of longstanding[9] malcontents (289–92) and money is behind it all. Here Sophocles is giving him the obsessive suspicions of a typical tragedy tyrant (like Oedipus in *Oedipus Tyrannus* 380–6, 541–2). This combined with the bullying threats with which he dispatches the Guard to find the culprit, rapidly establishes Creon as distinctly unsympathetic. The episode is brilliantly rounded off by a passage of stichomythia, in which the Guard cheekily provokes Creon still further by needling him about his reactions to himself (317, 319) and so probes the king's inner insecurity. The final lines of the scene are delightfully human: Creon has stormed off with an angry threat and the Guard himself exits with the words, "Anyway, you won't see *me* back here. Thank God for my lucky escape!" (329–31).

Where the plot is concerned, we may ask why Sophocles, somewhat superfluously, chose to introduce this first abortive burial before the second which results in Antigone's arrest. The answer must be that the poet wished to use the Guard in this sequence of challenges to Creon and so to illuminate Creon's character before his confrontation with Antigone. By the end of this episode it is clear that the two of them are on collision course.

First Stasimon (332–78)

Now follows one of the most celebrated poems in the whole of Greek literature, the "Ode to Man," which begins: "Formidable things are many, and nothing is more formidable than man."[10] The transition is abrupt and it is not easy to trace any immediate connection with what has preceded it. Better, I think, to see the switch from the earthy tone of the Guard's exit lines to grand "gnomic" mode as marking a pause for reflection on the overall issues with which the play is concerned.

In the first three of the four stanzas, the chorus enumerates what human beings have achieved through their own unaided intelligence: navigation, agriculture, the subjection of other living creatures through hunting and harnessing; then speech, "wind-swift" thought, life in communities and building of homes, medicine – though not immortality. Human resourcefulness is all-pervasive. Some of the vocabulary has sinister overtones of cunning or craftiness (347, 365–6). Scholars have related this poem to similar accounts of human development which can be dated to the period of *Antigone*. An obvious parallel is Prometheus' account of his gifts to man in *Prometheus Bound*.[11] There is also a myth of human evolution, attributed by Plato in his dialogue *Protagoras* to the sophist of that name who arrived in Athens about 447 and is famous for his saying, "Man is the measure of all things," implying that moral values are not absolute but relative to different societies.

In Antistrophe B, however, Sophocles makes it clear where his thinking is leading. Human beings, clever as they are, can incline to evil as well as the good (367). The man who observes the laws of the land and the justice of the gods upheld in oaths is high in his city (or makes his city high); cityless is the rash offender with whom the Elders wish never to share their hearth (368–75). Here at the end the Elders are affirming the values of the polis but they have also mentioned the justice of the gods alongside the laws of the land. They may, in their limited understanding, be unconscious of a dichotomy here, but the entrance of Antigone with the Guard makes the distinction explicit to the audience. In burying her brother she has defied the law but obeyed a divine imperative. Man may not, after all, be the measure of all things.

The varied meters of this song (aeolo-choriambic, iambic and dactylic) lend it richness and splendor. Some of the imagery is beautifully reflected in the rhythm: the steady motion of the ship crossing the sea and the plough churning up the soil (336–41). <TRACK E3, lines 332–41 and 365–75> ⓐ

Transitional Anapaests (376–83)

Compassionately the Coryphaeus identifies the Guard's prisoner as Antigone. He hails the entrance as a "supernatural portent," as though the Chorus's words about human law and divine justice have conjured it up. The continuity between stasimon and episode is consummately contrived.

Second Episode (384–581)

Creon's confrontation with Antigone herself is the third challenge to his authority and central to Sophocles' statement of his main theme. The Guard this time is in triumphant mood. He had vowed never to return, but Antigone has now been caught burying Polynices' body and he has claimed the honor of bringing her to Creon. The king is again appalled (403) at seeing his niece before him and cues in another narrative rhesis (407–40) from the Guard with all the details of the second burial. There is mystery again in the Guard's description of the dust-storm which allowed Antigone to reapproach her brothers' newly exposed corpse – the gods at work again? (421). This is immediately followed by the detail of Antigone in her wild frustration "screaming like an angry bird when she finds her nest without her chicks" (423–5). In the bird image we have the quintessential Antigone in her passionate fury and profound sense that her ritual burial *must* be performed again. She is not merely the embodiment of a principle but a woman of natural, animal-like instinct.

Throughout the speech, Antigone has been standing with her eyes averted and bent on the ground (441), a powerful pose suggestive of resignation as well as defiance. When interrogated by Creon, she confesses at once to the prohibited burial before launching into her great speech of self-justification (450–70), in terms of the "unwritten, unfailing laws of the gods which no human decrees can override." She knew she had to die, but that was nothing

Figure 6.2 *Antigone*, Whitgift School, Croydon, England 1977. Source: Reproduced by permission of the Archive of Performances of Greek & Roman Drama.

compared to the pain of leaving her brother unburied. <TRACK E4, lines 441–57 > ⊚ Here we have reached the drama's very core. Creon's rhesis in reply (473–96) demonstrates his own intractability: Antigone is guilty of *hubris* in gloating over her crime, and a woman cannot be allowed to triumph over a man; blood-ties can be as close as Zeus can sanctify (470) – here he is treading on very dangerous ground – but that will not excuse Antigone, or Ismene either whom he assumes, on the strength of her distracted behavior indoors, to be no less guilty. This anticipates Ismene's entrance at 526.

First, though, a further speech from Antigone (499–507), reaffirming the theme of public approval which will be hers for burying her brother, whatever Creon chooses to do. This leads on to a stichomythic confrontation (508–25) in terms of the other conflict of principle relating to "friends" and "enemies". For Creon *philoi* and *echthroi* cannot and must not be treated alike. Antigone's position is that, if a *philos* becomes an *echthros*, her nature is to prefer the claims of *philia* to those of *echthra* (523). At the end Creon gives up and reduces the argument to a personal and sexist issue (525).

The episode moves to a fresh phase with the entrance of Ismene in distress (526–30), at once to be vilified irrationally by Creon. There follows a highly emotional passage of stichomythia for the two sisters (536–60). Ismene now wants to die with her sister and falsely claims a share in the burial. Antigone will have none of this and indignantly repudiates this evident change of heart. Her motivation here is much disputed. Does she want all the glory to herself?

Or is she trying to save the sister? I believe myself that the clue lies in the line, "You chose to live and I to die" (555). They each have made their "existential" commitment and have to accept the consequence: Antigone to die for performing her "holy crime", Ismene to go on living with *her* decision not to help; anything else simply confuses the issue. This is clearsighted, but Creon regards both sisters as mad (561–2).

A new element suddenly enters the plot when Ismene asks Creon, "Will you kill your own son's bride?" to receive the brutal reply, "There are other fields for him to plough!" (568–9). This is the first mention of the close relationship (570) existing between Antigone and Creon's son Haemon. It means nothing to Creon any more than the ties of *philia*.[12] On this note of total insensitivity the scene ends with Creon's servants conducting both sisters indoors, while he himself probably remains onstage as a figure in the background during the following choral song.

Second Stasimon (582–625)

This choral ode falls almost halfway through the drama and occupies a central, pivotal position in Sophocles' scheme. As in the previous stasimon, he is inviting his audience to reflect on the profounder, universal implications of his story at a critical juncture in the action. The Chorus is used to suggest a perspective for viewing first Antigone's and then Creon's predicament. The song is worth examining in detail, so I first offer a translation which aims to communicate the essential meaning, though by no means all the music of the original Greek.

> Happy are they whose life has not tasted evil.   (*Strophe A*)
> When a house is shaken by heaven, disaster never
> Fails from one generation to another.
> As when the stormgusts drive the surge
> Across the murky sea, the black sand
> Is churned up, the wind howls,
> The lashed capes roar.

> This house of Thebes is doomed to perpetual sorrow.   (*Antistrophe A*)
> The ancient curse of the dead continues. A demon
> Smites and no release appears for the living.
> And now the last hope of the line,
> For a handful of bloodstained dust tossed to the dead,
> Is mown down by rash words
> And mad frenzy of spirit.

> Great Zeus, what pride of man   (*Strophe B*)
> Can limit your power? Unconquered
> By sleep or the months or age,
> Supreme master, you reign
> In Olympus' radiant splendor.
> This law holds good for all time:
> Greatness never comes to mankind
> Without disaster.

Hope is a boon to many,   (*Antistrophe B*)
But to many a snare and delusion
Till the ashes burn under their feet.
Wise is that famous saying:
Evil seems good to the man
Whom the god is leading to ruin.
For one brief hour he flourishes,
But then disaster.

Strophe A begins with a beatitude, only to demonstrate that it is never realized; human life can never be free of trouble. A house afflicted by heaven is continually subject to disaster or ruin (the word *Atê* occurs four times in the poem), which is compared to waves relentlessly beating against a headland in a storm. The theme is exemplified in the antistrophe by the royal house of Thebes, viewed rather in Aeschylean fashion as subject to a family curse. This leads on to the fate of Antigone, explored in terms of "multiple determination" (p. 16). The event which has "mowed her down" is the ritual burial of Polynices, but she is also possessed by a mental fury and guilty of "folly in speech." For a Greek it makes sense to regard Antigone as the victim of her heredity (cf. 1–2), but she has also been presented in her own right as daringly outspoken and persistent in her defiance of Creon's edict.

Strophe B changes tack in an invocation to Zeus who reigns immortal on bright Olympus, and whose power no man can rival. Here it is more obviously pertinent to think of Creon, standing before his palace in view of the audience, towards whom the play's center of gravity is shifting. He has already defied Zeus once by implication in his defiance of family ties (486–7, see p. 95) and will do so again at 658–9 and 1040–1. "Greatness" (614) with all its dangers, has certainly come his way. The imagery of the antistrophe accords well with what is yet to befall him. He does turn out to be deluded in his hopes for restoring order in Thebes, and the ashes do eventually burn under his feet. Evil does seem good to him, and from now on we can see *Atê* creeping up on him as the drama advances.

The ode thus typifies Sophocles' technique of combining backward and forward references (p. 83). In sound and rhythm it is magnificent. Strophe A starts with three long majestic cola in dactylo-epitrite rhythm to express the intergenerational succession of *Atê*, followed by iambic units in which we can *hear* the waves of the sea being ruffled by the winds and then, through syncopation, the sand being churned up from the depths and breaking in a roar against the headlands. Similar effects are produced in the antistrophe for Antigone's "mowing down" by the various forces at work in her tragic life. <TRACK E5, lines 383–92>

In Strophe B various aeolic-choriambic units are deployed to build up to the splendor of Zeus on Olympus and to suggest the relentless creeping up of *Atê* (note the repeated "pendant" phrases, punctuated by rests, in the Greek). The antistrophe similarly mounts towards the foot-burning image before resuming the inexorable onset of *Atê* as the god leads on the deluded man. <TRACK E6, lines 604–14>

Transitional Anapaests (626–30)

The Coryphaeus announces the arrival of Creon's youngest son, Haemon. Has he come in distress at the sentence on his promised bride?

Third Episode (631–780)

The next challenge to Creon comes from his own son. We have learned that a strong attachment exists between him and Antigone. The confrontation ends in a blazing quarrel, built up to in a masterly fashion through the characteristic forms of iambic speech.

The start, with four-line speeches for each character, is quiet with Creon tactfully adopting a submissive tone. Two long rheseis of almost equal length follow. Creon (639–680) preaches the importance of family solidarity and patronizingly urges his son to forget about Antigone, whose public insubordination he condemns. Authority, he insists, must be obeyed in all circumstances, right or wrong. No giving in to a woman! In his reply, Haemon (683–720) approaches his father very delicately, but suggests gently that public opinion is sympathetic to Antigone and urges the king not to claim a monopoly of wisdom; he needs to think again. The temperature rises rapidly in the ensuing stichomythia (726–57) with the son urging the claims of the democratic polis (he does not plead his love for Antigone) and the father insisting on his personal authority. Creon grows angrier, while Haemon becomes more and more frustrated by his father's intransigence. He eventually rushes off in an exit of wild despair. <TRACK E7, lines 742–65>

But Creon's resolve is starting to crack. In dialogue with the Coryphaeus (766–72) he now accepts that Ismene is innocent and announces his intention not to kill Antigone outright but to wall her up in a cave with a little food, in the casuistic notion that her blood will not then pollute the polis if death later takes her by starvation.

Third Stasimon (781–800)

Sophocles, however, has not altogether ignored the theme of sexual love, the universal force callously disregarded by Creon, just as he has trampled upon the claims of *philia*. At this highly fraught moment he has his Chorus sing a short but very beautiful hymn to Eros, the invincible and all-pervasive god who "stands sentinel in the soft cheeks of a girl," raids possessions and stirs up quarrels in families. The song is notable for its sensuously lilting rhythms, and its relevance to Creon will be all the more evident if he has once again remained onstage in the background. <TRACK E8, lines 781–800>

Transitional Anapaests (801–5)

As the ode concludes, Antigone is led on by guards through the *skênê* doors. The Coryphaeus expresses his own inordinate feelings and cannot refrain from tears.

Kommos (806–82)

At this point in the drama pathos reigns and a movement for soloist and chorus is exactly what is required. Antigone sings her own death lament – there is no one else to do it for her (881–2) – in two strophic pairs, followed by a poignant epode. The Chorus is used as a foil to her in the exchange, and this is reflected in the meters as well as the argument.

Antigone's sad strains focus largely on the loneliness of her limbo condition, between life and death, in her coming imprisonment and on the absence of the marriage and burial rituals which she might have expected. She will only be the bride of Acheron, the river of sorrow in the underworld; immured in the rock, she will be like Niobe who was turned to stone in grief for her children. At first the Chorus try to comfort her: her independent choice of death will win her glory, as will the sharing of Niobe's fate. Later, though, when she rejects this support, they attack her for her over-boldness and return to the themes of inherited guilt (856) and her own self-willed temper (875) in defying civic authority. Here the tension in the exchange lends a variety to the dominant note of pathos and helps the dynamic of what is quite a long and (presumably) a visually static movement. It ends in a deeply poignant epode in which Antigone expresses her sense of total abandonment. The sequence as a whole, with the Eros ode before it, contrasts strikingly in mood with the heat and excitement of the conflict at the end of the preceding episode.

In the first pair of strophes, Antigone chants her lament in looser, more flexible aeolic cola, which the Chorus responds to in rhythmically spoken and more insistent anapaestic dimeters. In the second, though, aeolics yield to lyric iambics, as do the Chorus's anapaests. Their important lines 856 and 875, referred to above, are composed in the relentless syncopated trimeters associated with sin and retribution in the *Oresteia*. Antigone is given a variety of rhythmical phrases for her epode. <TRACK E9, lines 853–82> ◉

Fourth Episode (883–943)

Creon now orders his guards to take Antigone off to her immurement, but Sophocles has not finished with his heroine. The actor is given one more iambic rhesis, before being finally swept away. In poignant rhetoric, Antigone greets her grave, her bride-chamber, her prison in the rock which will take her on her way to her loved ones in the underworld, who, she trusts, will welcome her arrival – especially Polynices for performing whose burial she is being punished.[13] The pathos mounts as she expresses her sense of betrayal by the gods whose laws she has so boldly defended. At the end Sophocles revives the old passionate Antigone (927–8) in her prayer that, if her persecutors were wrong, they will suffer as she has done. No meek forgiveness there.

The tempo quickens in anapaests (929–43) as Creon scolds his guards for their tardiness. As Antigone sees death in front of her, she is suddenly frightened. Forced away, she is given a powerful exit as she loudly calls the Elders to witness how she is being treated for performing her religious duty. Once again, Creon probably remains onstage during the following song.

Fourth Stasimon (944–87)

The agitated mood and tempo of Antigone's exit is taken up instantly by the Chorus who occupy the *orchêstra* in a very exciting song which advances the drama in a peculiarly menacing way.

The subject matter is rather obscure to us and may have been so to some in Sophocles' original audience. It is an address to Antigone which enumerates three mythological parallels to her imprisonment, all attesting to the inexorable power of fate. In formal terms it appears to be an exhortation to the heroine, after her departure, to submit to her fate as the characters in three other stories had to submit, but the parallelism is far from obvious. There are, however, overtones in the poetry which suggest a relevance to Creon (still on stage) and his coming punishment for ignoring the claims of *philia* and *eros*.[14] In Strophe B the reference to the blinded children of Phineus, whose bleeding eyes cried out for revenge, anticipates the entrance of the blind prophet Teiresias with his awful warning of the retribution awaiting Creon's impiety.

I suspect that the main impact of this movement lay more in its sound and rhythm than its content. The first pair of strophes opens with a run of five long aeolo-choriambic cola in which the basic 2/4 time is interrupted by bars in 3/4. These are followed by *marcato* iambics expressive of the relentless force of destiny, the last unit being the syncopated iambic trimeter used once again as the "retribution" leitmotif, as at 856/875. The two meters are again contrasted in the second pair of strophes. <TRACK E10, lines 944–54 and 979–87> ◉

Fifth Episode (988–1114)

In this scene Creon meets his final challenger, the prophet Tiresias, whose fearful warnings of the gods' anger finally shake him and cause him to feel the menace of the world he has so obstinately despised.

The prophet's threatening presence is felt immediately in a brief stichomythic exchange. "Know that you are standing on a razor's edge!" (996), and Creon shudders. At once Tiresias embarks on a magnificent rhesis (the sound of the Greek here is particularly compelling) describing the hideous omens revealed to him in his burnt sacrifices and observation, through the boy attending him, of the birds. The city is sick and its altars defiled by the carrion from Polynices' body carried there by the dogs and vultures. <TRACK E11, lines 998–1015 > ◉ Creon is warned to yield but his first reaction is to accuse Tiresias of being bribed in a plot to oust him; the gods, he says, cannot be polluted even if the eagles carry Polynices' flesh to the throne of Zeus (1040–4). The emotional temperature rises in the stichomythia that follows (1048–63), with Creon's threats stinging the prophet into a second powerfully damning rhesis (1064–90) in which he foretells that Creon will have to forfeit one of his own flesh and blood for his impious acts. The Furies are lying in wait for him! Tiresias makes his exit on a note of terrible denunciation and Creon is left alone with the Chorus, clearly humbled in the realization that he must at last give way and bury Polynices. On the Coryphaeus' advice, he orders his servants to release Antigone and exits with the thought that "it is best to observe the established laws till one's dying day" (1113–14).

Fifth Stasimon (1115–52)

The mood of the Chorus is now one of ecstatic hope. Their song takes the form of an invocatory prayer to Dionysus, Thebes' special god, to heal the city in its present affliction. This follows the conventions of a "cletic hymn" which addresses the god with his epithets and other ritual formulae. It mounts to a frenzied climax in a final appeal to the god to manifest himself. So Sophocles works up his audience's feelings in optimistic vein, only to dash them down in tragic fashion with the entrance that follows.

Once again the meter is largely aeolo-choriambic with a few iambic cola mixed in. Griffith (1999, 315) describes the general affect as one of "unsettled, pulsing energy." <TRACK E12, lines 1115–25 and 1146–52> ◉

Exodus (1155–353) including *Amoibaion* (1261–346)

There, along one of the *eisodoi*, appears the Messenger. The scene opens in grand style with an address to the Chorus bemoaning the instability and chanciness of human life. The illustration is Creon, the "living corpse" (1167) whose joys have forsaken him. In dignified stichomythia with the Coryphaeus the speaker then reports his news: the death of Haemon by his own hand.

There now (1180) enters from the *skênê* a new character of whom we have heard nothing before – Creon's wife, Eurydice. She has overheard the Messenger's news and asks for further details. This evokes a superbly graphic narrative of all the events since Creon's change of heart. He has performed the burial rites for Polynices before going to free Antigone, as the gods must be instantly placated and she has only to be released. But Antigone has already hanged herself and Haemon is in the cave clinging to her body. A bitter altercation between father and son has resulted in Haemon's suicide – a monument, says the Messenger, to the curse of human folly (1242–3). <TRACK E13, lines 1219–43> At the end of the speech, Eurydice, in an extraordinary moment of theater, turns and re-enters the house in complete silence. The Messenger follows to investigate (1256).

The Coryphaeus turns to see Creon approaching, bearing his son (presumably represented by a dummy) in his arms. The king is doubtless attended on his return to the palace, as Antigone was when she emerged from it at 805 to lament her fate. The two processions and the two laments mirror each other to the most moving effect. In the formal exchange that follows Creon's cries of sorrow are expressed in two strophic pairs of agitated sung dochmiacs, as he mourns his son and reproaches himself. These contrast beautifully with the (spoken) muted comments of the Coryphaeus and later of the Messenger, when he returns to report the suicide of Eurydice who has died with a terrible curse on Creon as his son's murderer. The queen's body is revealed on the *ekkyklêma*, for a visual demonstration of the poetic justice which has struck Creon down. In defying the claims of kinship he has destroyed his wife and son, and so lost all that was personally precious to himself. The closing stanzas express his sense of moral "annihilation" (1325) and he longs to die at once. But Sophocles makes him re-enter the house to live on in remorse and desperate loneliness. At the very end Creon claims our sympathy. <TRACK E14, lines 1317–46>

The closing anapaests (1348–53) of the chorus assert wisdom and reverence for the gods as the heart of happiness. The proud man's boasts are punished and we learn wisdom in old age. All of which is clearly relevant to Creon.

Conclusion

Antigone can be seen as a model Greek tragedy, perfectly constructed, with its themes unfolded logically and economically in a masterly dramatic sequence which grips throughout. The skillful dramaturgy is matched by characterization of human beings who are not presented in black and white terms but endowed with a mixture of qualities. Analysis of the work as a play suggests that it is more concerned with the need for humility in rulers than the conflict between state and individual. If the implications of the Ode to Man have been correctly understood in their historical context, we might consider their bearing on our own sophisticated, technological and humanistic society.

Notes

1 For an admirably balanced explanation of all the play's issues, students can do no better than to read the introduction to Griffith's edition. Particularly helpful is his demonstration of characterization as expressed in patterns of speech (pp. 6–7).

2 This runs counter to the supposed convention that the acting area outside the *skênê* signifies the *public* domain, but the inside–outside distinction is certainly blurred at this point and is not invariably relevant.

3 Are these rhythmically spoken or sung (so-called "lyric" anapaests)? Doric forms which characterize lyric were transmitted in 110–16 but not where they might be expected in 127–33 or 141–7. I suggest that the spoken mode is preferable as it offers the more striking contrast and that the doricisms in 110–16 should be reatticized (as in the Loeb text).

4 The reference here is to Capaneus, one of the seven against Thebes, who had boasted that not even Zeus' lightning could stop him.

5 Dactyl plus spondee substituted for anapaestic metron against the prevailing beat (see Appendix B).

6 For an excellent discussion of this speech, see Griffith (1999, 155–6).

7 Creon's sentiments are echoed in the funeral oration put into the mouth of Pericles by Thucydides (II.38–46) and quoted with approval by the fourth-century orator Demosthenes (19.247).

8 Jebb (commentary on 227) compares the Guard's entrance speech to that of Lancelot Gobbo in the *Merchant of Venice*. The quasi-comic effect is very unusual for Greek tragedy before Euripides; we might possibly compare the Nurse's speech in *Choephori*.

9 This notion of longstanding opponents is a curious touch, as Creon has only just assumed power. I believe Sophocles wanted to invest him with the paranoia of those whom power has for some time corrupted.

10 My attempt to translate the Greek *deina*, an adjective which combines the notions of both wonder and fear.

11 P.V. 436–506. This play, attributed to Aeschylus, is now agreed by most scholars to have been composed by another hand whose thought was informed by the Sophists, in a style which blends Aeschylean with Sophoclean features.

12 In the Loeb edition, Lloyd-Jones is reluctant to interrupt the stichomythic flow, and allocates the whole of 565–76 to Creon and Ismene. I prefer Jebb's much more dramatic arrangement which allows Antigone suddenly to break in at 572 with the cry, "Dearest Haemon, how your father slights you!" and assigns 574 and 576 to the Coryphaeus, the natural character to cue in Creon's confirmed decision that Antigone must die.

13 In 904–20 Antigone argues that she would not have done for a husband or a child what she did for her brother. The passage has been much debated and I side myself with those who regard it as inauthentic, the interpolation of a fourth century actor based on a gross misapplication of a story in Herodotus (3.119). Dramatically, the lines seem to me totally at odds with the stance Antigone has taken on the basis of the divine laws. For a full critique see Brown (1987, 199–200). The passage is defended by Griffith (1999, 277–9) and Cropp (1997).

14 The whole ode is excellently elucidated in Winnington-Ingram (1980, 105–8).

References

Text: *Sophocles Antigone* (Loeb edition, Vol. 2). 1994. Cambridge, MA: Harvard University Press, edited and translated by Hugh Lloyd- Jones.

Cropp, M. 1997. "Antigone's Final Speech," *Greece & Rome* 44, 137–60.

Ehrenberg, V. 1954. *Sophocles and Pericles*. Oxford: Clarendon Press.

Winnington-Ingram, R.P. 1980. *Sophocles, an Interpretation*. Cambridge: Cambridge University Press.

Commentaries

Brown, Andrew. 1987. *Sophocles: Antigone*. Warminster: Aris & Phillips.

Griffith, Mark. 1999. *Sophocles: Antigone*. Cambridge: University Press.

Jebb, R.C. 1900. *Sophocles: The Antigone*, 3rd edn. Republished by Bristol Classical Press 2012.

7

Oedipus Tyrannus

Introduction

Oedipus Tyrannus (*OT*)[1] has enjoyed an archetypal status in the canon of Greek tragedy. Aristotle in his *Poetics* gave it six mentions as an example of a play inducing the emotions of pity and fear, which are the source of "pleasure" in tragedy. In its own time, though, the set of plays including *OT* was only accorded the second prize in the competition. Today it comes across as an intensely gripping drama, a masterpiece of construction within tragedy's characteristic form and outstanding in its use of dramatic irony, both verbal and situational.

The story of Oedipus would have been familiar to Sophocles' audience from the cycle of epic poems relating to the city of Thebes. It had already been treated by Aeschylus in the trilogy which ended in the surviving *Seven Against Thebes* and incorporated a family curse as a prominent theme, besides introducing Oedipus' self-blinding into the tradition.

We have no certain date for the original performance. The opening situation of a plague sent on Thebes and identified with the war-god Ares has been reasonably linked with the great plague at Athens which started in 430, soon after the beginning of the Peloponnesian War with Sparta. A date around 425 would be consistent with the play's style.

Although the character of Oedipus is in some respect reminiscent of Creon in *Antigone*, he can hardly be linked with Pericles who was a victim of the plague and died in 429. *OT* is not a political play in the sense that *Antigone* is.

Synopsis

The plot depends to an unusually large extent on past events, the essentials of which would have been familiar to Sophocles' audience. The starting point is the oracle that came to Laius, king of Thebes, that a son born to him and his wife Jocasta would cause his father's death. To obviate this when a child was born to them, the king arranged his exposure on Mount Cithaeron with a pin driven through his ankles (hence the name Oedipus, "swell-foot"); but the man entrusted with the task handed the boy over to another herdsman from Corinth, who delivered it to the childless king and queen, Polybus and Merope, to rear as their own. Oedipus grew to manhood believing that he was the son of Polybus and Merope until one day his parentage was challenged. Anxiety led him to consult the oracle of Delphi, where he was told that he would lie with his mother and kill his father. Determined to avoid Corinth at all costs, he set out on the road to Thebes and on the way had an angry encounter with an old man in a

Greek Tragedies as Plays for Performance, First Edition. David Raeburn.
© 2017 John Wiley & Sons, Inc. Published 2017 by John Wiley & Sons, Inc.
Companion website: www.wiley.com/go/raeburn

chariot whom he killed, along with all his companions except for one who escaped undetected. Arrived in Thebes, he rescued the people from the destructive presence of the Sphinx by solving the famous riddle, "What is it that walks on four legs in the morning, two legs at noon and three in the evening?" (answer: "a man"). The Thebans duly made Oedipus their king since Laius had died abroad in mysterious circumstances, and he married Laius' widow.

Sophocles' drama enacts Oedipus' appalling discovery that he has unknowingly killed his father and committed incest with his mother. As the play progresses, past events are gradually unfolded until they finally slot together like the pieces of a jigsaw puzzle. In the opening scene Thebes is in the grip of a plague, from which the citizens ask Oedipus to deliver them. An oracle arrives from Apollo at Delphi to demand the expulsion of the man who murdered King Laius and is defiling the city with his presence. The main action consists in Oedipus' hunt for this murderer, only to find that he has been hunting down himself and, far worse, that Laius was his father and that Jocasta who has borne him four children is also his own mother. The revelation leads Jocasta to hang herself and Oedipus to strike his eyes out in his sense of immitigable pollution. At the end he asks to be expelled from Thebes, but this request is for the time being denied him.

Interpretation

OT has been subjected to numerous interpretations, some rather wide of the mark. All students should read the famous essay by Dodds (1966). Not all critics have resisted the influence of Freud who identified an unconscious wish in the human male, which he called the Oedipus complex, to kill his father and sleep with his mother. It is highly improbable, though, that this psychological phenomenon (if it exists) could lie behind Sophocles' treatment of the inherited myth.

Another frequently advanced view of the play attributed to Sophocles a pessimistic fatalism: Oedipus was throughout at the mercy of a cruel and malign providence; the poor man was doomed before his birth and nothing could rescue him from his frightful destiny. This interpretation could be criticized for its confusion of divine foreknowledge with actual predestination (see Dodds 1966). More telling, however, is that the drama portrays Oedipus as energetically exercising his free will in the quest for Laius' murderer and subsequently in the search for his own identity (Knox 1957). Here again the principle of multiple causation (see p. 16) applies.

How much importance should be attached to the theme of *hubris*? In the central Third Stasimon (873–9), the chorus articulates the doctrine of insolent pride, the product of kingly power, which can scale the heights, only to topple over the precipice. Oedipus is certainly made to behave in an arrogant and self-willed way towards the prophet Tiresias and then to Creon, but it would be wrong to say that his pride *causes* his fall rather than *accompanies* his fall. Indeed, it is Oedipus' searching intelligence that leads him to pursue his enquiries to the end and so to his fatal discovery. Aristotle's dictum (*Poetics* 1452b) that the downfall of a person who is *perfectly* good excites repugnance rather than compassion may be pertinent here. Oedipus needs some kind of weakness to be convincing as a human being with whom an audience can identify.

Linked with the *hubris* theme, I have found it helpful to latch on to the parallel established in the opening scene between the remedy for the plague (and so the riddle of Laius' murder) and the riddle of the Sphinx (35–9). In all there are eight references in the text,[2] either direct or by implication, to the Sphinx, including Tiresias' prediction that Oedipus will eventually leave Thebes leaning on a stick, "the third foot." The Priest's appeal to Oedipus to repeat his brilliant performance rises out of his assertion that he and others are supplicating their king "*not* as one equal to the gods but as *first among men* in the trials of life and encounters with beings divine" (31–9). In showing *hubris* to Creon and Tiresias, Oedipus is inflating himself above his human station; but the ultimate solution to the second riddle, the identity of Laius' murderer, gives him the same answer as the first. That riddle has now shifted to the riddle of his *own* identity, the answer to which is "the son of Laius and Jocasta;" it is also "a man" – and not a god. Hence the potency of all the references to the Sphinx.

At the end of his play, however, Sophocles chooses to emphasize Oedipus' state of pollution rather than of humiliation. He may have discovered his true identity, but he does not emerge in the aftermath as a *wiser* man. We might say, though, that Sophocles is reaffirming the two famous mottos inscribed on Apollo's temple at Delphi, "Know yourself" and "Nothing in excess," for the benefit of his audience. In the play's closing lines he also restates the usual proverb on the uncertainty of human prosperity: call no man happy until he is dead.

Does the governing philosophy of this intensely exciting drama boil down merely to these three clichés? Dodds (1966, 75), was surely right to point also to the Third Stasimon which emphasizes the need for piety and respect for oracles regarded as a crucial medium through which the gods communicate with men and so an aspect of the world order which the gods represent. In this, at least, we can see an affirmative message in a period where rationalism is gaining ground and life is felt to be a matter of chance, as Jocasta declares at 977–8. "It's best to live at random," she says (979). Sophocles evidently disagrees.

Dramaturgy

In the final analysis we may find *OT* less compelling for its moral and philosophical thinking than for its power as a theatrical experience. No Greek tragedy employs suspense to such a high degree. We watch Oedipus as the vice in which he is gripped closes in on him ever more tightly with each turn of the screw. The drama builds up inexorably to the agonizing, explosive climax when Oedipus at last realizes the truth. The horror is sustained through the Messenger's narrative of Oedipus' self-blinding and slowly relaxed in the closing scenes to leave the audience fit to endure another tragedy in a series of three or, if it was performed third, to be slightly more in the mood for the satyr play.

The story of Oedipus coming to realize that he had incurred the guilt of parricide and incest – two crimes of exceptional abhorrence to the Greeks' moral sense – was also ideal for the use of dramatic irony. He has tried to escape his destiny but walked straight towards it before, in the play's action, instigating the hunt for himself. Until the truth finally tumbles out, Oedipus and all the other characters, except Tiresias, do not know who he is or what he has done, but the audience is aware of these things from the outset and can see an ulterior significance in all that is said or happening on stage.

The dramatization of the story, however, posed several problems. The details of Oedipus' past, including his childhood history and the circumstances in which he had come to kill his father, had all to be included. But the tragedy could only cover a comparatively short timespan, given the continuous presence of the Chorus after the prologue; the details of past events would have to emerge piecemeal during the course of the action. This necessitated the improbability of Oedipus showing ignorance of the details regarding Laius' murder which he might have been expected to know already. Another awkwardness is that his narration has him visit the Delphic oracle because he is uncertain of his parentage but, as soon as he is told that he will kill his father and marry his mother, he assumes without further question that his Corinthian parents are referred to: Sophocles manages these details in his dialogue in such a way that in performance they are barely noticed.

A more serious problem was that, if the story was to be milked for suspense, Oedipus must not discern the truth too early, not until the last piece of the jigsaw is in place. Hence, I believe, Sophocles' characterization of his king. He had to be intelligent enough to have solved the riddle of the Sphinx and a relentlessly enquiring person, determined to pursue the truth to the end. He had also to be given the hubristic arrogance already noted, with the blinkered vision of those who have held absolute power for some time and are supremely confident of their own rightness. This allowed Sophocles to portray Oedipus as only discovering the truth about himself at the last possible moment, when it could no longer be resisted.

Sophocles also showed remarkable skill in his choice of detail to flesh out his main story. Oedipus survived as a baby because the servant instructed to expose him handed him over, out of pity, to a shepherd from Corinth, on the other side of Mount Cithaeron. These same characters are introduced on stage to feature in the discovery: the former as the sole surviving witness to Laius' murder; the latter to report to Oedipus that his presumed father Polybus, king of Corinth, is dead and to advise him that Polybus and Merope were not his true parents. This economical doubling of roles in two people could be seen as straining probability and extending the long arm of coincidence too far. In dramatic terms, though, it makes perfect sense: the coincidences are ironic and intensify the audience's sense of the net closing in on Oedipus all the more inexorably. We can now see how Sophocles used the tragic medium to work out the drama of Oedipus' self-discovery, movement by movement.

Dramatic Analysis

Line numbers refer to the Greek text in the Loeb edition (see the end of this chapter), which has a parallel English translation. For the terminology of the discrete movements, see Appendix A; for the lyric structure and meters see Appendix B or hear TRACK 0 ⊚.

Prologue (1–150)

The play begins unusually. Apparently a crowd of Theban males enters bearing suppliant branches. Led by an old Priest, they form up in sitting positions in front of the *skênê*. Exactly what this crowd consists of is not entirely clear. The text at 15–19 suggests that young boys and old men are present; and the Priest himself may be attended by a group of unmarried youths, possibly young priests. These are probably a sizeable enough body to open the play with an impressive spectacle; they are there to represent the citizens of Thebes in a humble appeal to release them from the plague that motivates the start of the drama. When all are assembled, the *skênê* doors are opened and Oedipus the king comes out to address the crowd. I suspect that Sophocles may have directed his protagonist to embrace the whole audience in his opening lines (1–8).[3]

The opening tableau is very striking. Oedipus is not a god, but the fillets and suppliant branches suggest that he is being appealed to for help as though he were *like* a god. Though the Priest corrects this at 31–2, as already noted (p. 107), his speech adopts the prayer formula of, "You helped us before, so help us now." Sophocles is evidently presenting Oedipus in all his kingly splendor and as the father of his people (1, 58, 143) to whom all look in the confidence that he has the power to deliver them from the plague, as he delivered Thebes from the Sphinx before he became king.

The pace of 1–77 is appropriately solemn and slow. Oedipus' first speech establishes a grave note: he is aware of the plague and asks the old Priest to explain what the supplication before him betokens. The Priest's long rhesis (14–57) enlarges vividly on the plague's effects and appeals to Oedipus as the "best of mortals" (46) to set the polis upright. In his second speech (58–77) Oedipus asserts his full sympathy with his people in their plight and informs the Priest that he has already acted by sending his brother-in-law Creon to the oracle at Delphi. The pace quickens as anticipation mounts in a passage of distichomythia (78–86) which culminates in the entrance of Creon, crowned with a laurel, as the bearer of good news.

This Creon is very different from the insecure ruler we saw in *Antigone* (Chapter 6); his tone is authoritative, but calm and assured. He is a generation older than Oedipus. In a longer, largely distichomythic run between himself and Oedipus (87–131), he conveys Apollo's response that the plague is due to a pollution on the land caused by the presence of the man who murdered the former king, Laius. Creon's answers to Oedipus' questions are confident but thoroughly respectful. The steady formality of the couplets in the exchange supplies the audience with important information about the details of Laius' death in such a way that they would not have been too conscious of the artificiality entailed in Oedipus' apparent ignorance of the facts.

The exchange is straightforward but for one disturbing detail. Creon mentions the report given by the one witness who escaped from the scene of the crime: Laius was set on by an organized band of robbers. "How could the robber [*sic*] commit such a crime?" continues Oedipus, "unless he had been bribed from here?" (124–5). This apparent slip of the tongue is ingeniously ironic and plants the question which becomes so crucial to the plot later on: was it one or many?

The Prologue draws towards its conclusion with Oedipus' pledge (132–46) to root out the pollution. Another touch of verbal irony follows as he asserts that the cleansing act will not be a service owed to a distant kinsman but one performed for himself. He then dismisses the crowd and retires into the palace. The Priest (147–50) calls on the boys to rise and a prayer to Apollo brings this grand and formal opening scene to an end. The acting area is emptied.

Parodos (151–215)

Enter the Chorus of Theban Elders, an impressive body of dignity and authority. The Messenger's address to them at 1223 as "men most highly honored in this land" is reflected in the tone of all their songs. Gold features five times in the imagery of their opening movement, which could suggest that they are richly dressed and that their entrance would have been solemn and spectacular in continuation of the Prologue's grandeur. The song is the longest in the play with its three strophic pairs (the others have two). The subject matter recapitulates that of the Prologue but in an emotionally heightened way through chanted lyric, choreographed movement and musical accompaniment; and it follows the Priest's address in adopting the form and language of prayer.

Strophe A begins with an invocation to the word of Zeus which has prompted the Delphic oracle and inspires the Elders with fear and apprehension. In the antistrophe they appeal formally to Athena, Artemis and Apollo to banish the plague, described as a "flame of woe" (166), from the land.[4] The second pair of strophes concentrates on the plague and its effects that have motivated their prayer. In the third the gods who have been invoked are asked to unite against Ares, the god who destroys men in war and pestilence. The prayer then extends to Thebes' own patron god, Dionysus, the companion of the maenads, and this gives an ecstatic lift to the poem's conclusion.

The meters of the poem are mainly rolling dactyls (the meter of oracles) and jabbing iambics, a little reminiscent of the long triad in the Parodos of *Agamemnon* (104–59). The dactyls predominate in the first pair of strophes, slightly less so in the second; while the iambics, some with taut syncopation, largely prevail in the third. The overall effect is thus magnificently liturgical to start with, more menacing towards the end. <TRACK F1, lines 151–8, 168–77 and 203–15> ◉

In his Parodos, Sophocles has used his choral medium to enhance the theme of the plague's terrible danger which Oedipus has been called on to confront. He has also articulated a strongly religious perspective and the importance of oracles as a means of communication between gods and men.

First Episode (216–462)

The emphasis on the gods' power in the climactic stanza of the Parodos reinforces the sense of Oedipus' own power and majesty as the king makes his second entrance as though in answer to the Chorus' prayer. His investigation now begins and the drama starts to move forward. This episode falls into two main sections:

a) 216–75: a long address by Oedipus to the people of Thebes in an unsuccessful plea for information regarding Laius' murder; then, after a transitional passage of stichomythia between Oedipus and the Coryphaeus (276–99)
b) 300–462: Oedipus' confrontation with the prophet Tiresias who has been sent for in the hope that he will elucidate Apollo's oracle.

Oedipus' Address to his People

I suggest that the assembled Thebans (summoned in 144) are represented by the spectators, as in the opening lines of the Prologue. Also the actor should direct 216–54, immediately followed by 269–7, towards the whole audience. Lines 255–68, which emphasizes Oedipus' personal position, might be better directed at the smaller group of Elders in the *orchêstra*.[5] I explore the speech on that assumption.

Lines 216–54 plus 269–75 comprise a brilliant piece of dramatic writing. Oedipus appeals for information three times, to be greeted (after 226, 229 and 232) by a wall of silence – Sophocles well understood the effects of a pause. The actor will doubtless communicate Oedipus' growing frustration during this sequence. It leads on to the blood-chilling passage (233–51) in which Oedipus pronounces his dreadful curse of social and religious excommunication on the man who is polluting the city and then, for good measure, includes himself in the imprecation if the murderer is found to be sharing his own hearth. In 252–4 plus 269–75 he demands his people's backing, with a supplementary curse on any who disobey him. Turning to the Chorus at 255, he emphasizes his personal responsibility in the matter as the heir to Laius' throne and to the wife who has borne him his own children, concluding in a solemn genealogy of five proper names in Laius' family tree, unaware that he himself is the next in line of descent. This recital I would see as an ideal climax.

The whole speech is probably the classic example of the dramatic irony for which Sophocles is renowned. The situation is, of course, profoundly ironic; but we can also feel all the dynamic word power that has been noted in Aeschylus, as we hear Oedipus cursing himself, twice over, in language that cannot be unsaid. For sheer theatricality the rhesis is a tour de force.

In the transitional, largely stichomythic, passage that follows, the Coryphaeus recommends the summoning of Tiresias, which Oedipus says he has already done, much as he has announced to the Priest that he has sent Creon to Delphi, and is expecting his arrival shortly. The build-up to these entrances may strike us as a little contrived, but the appearance of the two characters "on cue" helps our sense that the gods with whom they are linked are slowly closing in on Oedipus.

Oedipus' Confrontation with Tiresias

There follows an extraordinarily powerful engagement. The blind prophet's initial reluctance to speak makes Oedipus unpleasantly angry until he quite irrationally accuses Tiresias of engineering Laius' murder, so stinging him into naming the king himself as the killer and going on to tell him that he is living in an incestuous relationship. The ensuing conflict is expressed in three formal speeches and some compelling stichomythia. There is a magnificent rhetoric in Oedipus' rhesis (380–403), in tragedy tyrant mode, accusing Tiresias of being bribed by Creon to denounce him, and then in Tiresias' reply (408–28), warning his slanderer of the troubles ahead; likewise in the prophet's final predictions (447–62), filled with paradoxes that are beyond Oedipus' understanding but not the audience's.

The drama has moved forward in a very significant way. The emphasis has shifted from the danger posed by the plague to the community to the danger threatening Oedipus, which now becomes the central focus of interest. The theme of sight is important: at 370–1 Oedipus cruelly taunts Tiresias with his blindness and the prophet replies that Oedipus himself will be physically blind before long (372–3, 454). We are witnessing the situation of a blind man who can see the truth in conflict with a sighted person who is willfully blind to the truth. In the context of the drama as a whole, it will thus make excellent sense for Oedipus, when he does see the truth, to blind himself physically. Finally, an actor playing Oedipus may well think of this whole episode as the one in which he is dethroned from his divine-like pedestal as the father of his people and revealed as an arrogant, hasty-tempered individual, whose blinkered outlook makes it impossible for him to see the truth at this stage.

First Stasimon (463–511)

The Chorus sweeps forward for their second song, musically much faster-moving than the majestic Parodos. There are two strophic pairs:

a) The underlying emotion is "The hunt is on!" The Elders imagine the fugitive murderer spoken of by the oracle speeding to escape the pursuit of Apollo and the Furies, while the oracles "hover" around him.

b) They now express their anxiety and confusion, torn between their trust in oracles and their loyalty to Oedipus who solved the riddle of the Sphinx. The gods may know the secrets of men, but prophets (like Tiresias) may be no better off than ordinary mortals.

This ode picks up the idea of the hunt for the criminal from the preceding episode. The thought that prophets may be endowed with no special insight anticipates Jocasta's skepticism towards prophets and oracles in the following episode and also what they assert themselves in their next stasimon regarding the reliability of oracles.

Rhythmically, this is a very exciting number, in which the two strophic pairs are strongly contrasted. In the first the relentless pursuit of the criminal is expressed in iambic and aeolo-choriambic phrases in 2/4 time, with a run of anapaests towards the end. The second pair is in 3/4 time, starting with six bars of choriambs (tum-ti-ti-tum) but then, in a striking effect, swinging round to ionics (ti-ti-tum-tum). In this context the former expresses an emotion of fear and apprehension; the latter can be associated with a more rational, if puzzled, speculation. <TRACK F2, lines 463–72 and 483–97> ◉ The ode progresses the momentum of the drama and leads perfectly into Creon's agitated entrance that marks the start of the following episode.

Second Episode (513–862)

This long episode falls into three sub-movements:

a) lines 513–648: the quarrel between Oedipus and Creon, interrupted by the entrance of Jocasta
b) lines 649–96: a lyric dialogue, which allows the Chorus to engage with both Oedipus and Jocasta, with Creon departing in the middle
c) lines 697–862: a scene between Oedipus and Jocasta, during which Oedipus begins to suspect that he could be the murderer of Laius.

Oedipus and Creon

Creon's entry in anger at the suggestion that he has plotted with Tiresias to depose Oedipus follows well on the pace of the preceding stasimon. When Oedipus reappears, his aggressive speech confirms his irrationality and leads well into a run of heated stichomythia. Creon's speech of defense is in calmer vein but extremely interesting in its argument: he enjoys the highest influence in Thebes without the ultimate responsibility of government and so has no motive for a conspiracy to unseat Oedipus. After this the acrimonious tone is resumed and the quarrel reaches boiling point in the use of half-lines for the two speakers (*antilabe*), which provides a fine build-up to the first entrance of Jocasta, Oedipus' wife – and, as the audience knows, his mother – to chastise the two men for airing a private quarrel in a public crisis.

Amoibaion (Chorus, Oedipus and Jocasta)

This section in lyric mode usefully offers a break between the preceding and subsequent sections of iambic dialogue, by involving the Chorus in support of Jocasta's efforts to make peace between the husband and brother. In the strophe the Elders' entreaties lead Oedipus to sulkily climb down and Creon exits. In the antistrophe Jocasta first takes Oedipus' place in the exchange, to be moved out by him in an angry protest at what he perceives as the Chorus's disloyalty.

The formality and balance of the strophic construction lends this sub-movement strength in its own right. The alternation of song with speech offers variety and interest as the Chorus intervenes in irregular cretic or dochmiac rhythms, which here express a powerful urgency, while Oedipus responds in steadier iambic trimeters (contrast, for example, 656–7 with 658–9).

Oedipus and Jocasta

Creon gone, the drama continues on a quieter note. When Oedipus tells his wife of Tiresias' accusation, she tries to reassure him in a speech of skepticism regarding the prophetic art: the oracle that Laius was destined to die at a son's hand had been disproved, since the baby she bore him had died exposed on the mountain and Laius was killed by robbers "at a place where three roads meet" (716). These words are a turning point. The phrase stirs Oedipus' memory of crossing paths with the old man in the cart and his entourage on the road from Delphi. "Zeus, what have you purposed to do to me?" (738) is the anguished cry which betrays his profound insecurity. His anxiety launches his long and vivid narration of his early life and the fatal encounter (see synopsis). Telling details include the irascibility of both parties in the quarrel (like father, like son) and the brutal terseness of Oedipus' "I killed the lot." <TRACK F3, lines 794–813> 🔊

Figure 7.1 *Oedipus Tyrannus*, Cloisters, New College, Oxford 2015. Source: Reproduced by permission of the Archive of Performances of Greek & Roman Drama.

The last part of the rhesis is deeply poignant; it exposes Oedipus' vulnerability as he contemplates the possibility that his victim may have been Laius and so that he may have cursed himself. Sophocles is careful to make it clear that Oedipus still believes his parents to be Polybus and Merope (827), and the speech reaches its climax in a heartfelt prayer for obliteration before he incurs the stain of parricide and incest – tremendous irony here. His only hope at the end of the scene is that the witness to Laius' death will confirm the plural number of his assailants (122–3) and leave him in the clear. After expressing further skepticism about prophecy, Jocasta agrees to summon the witness in from the fields and guides her husband back into the palace. The audience will now be in a mood of sympathetic concern for Oedipus and left wondering how and when the truth of his identity will be established. A new riddle is beginning to replace the original one of "Who killed Laius?"

Second Stasimon (863–910)

The ode which follows occupies a central position in the structure and thought of the drama. The previous two songs have picked up the mood and atmosphere in a fairly obvious way, and the Theban Elders were allowed to voice their own feelings of apprehension, and of loyalty to Oedipus. They remain involved now but in a more detached way. In their *gnomai*, general utterances, we may also detect the voice of the poet and find the clues to his universal stance on the story which his players are acting out. The song merits slightly fuller treatment and is first summarized. There are two strophic pairs:

a) *Strophe A*: I pray for reverent purity in word and deed, in obedience to eternal laws born in heaven, which cannot be forgotten because the god is great in them.[6]
b) *Antistrophe A*: Kingship begets *hubris*.[7] Bred of surfeit, this leads a man to fly too high and casts him down to destruction. May the god who is my champion never quash the emulous struggle that is good for the city.
c) *Strophe B*: May evil overtake the luxuriant pride of a person with no fear of justice, who fails to reverence the gods' shrines. No sinner is proof against the gods' darts. If honor is paid to unholy ways, why should I dance?[8]
d) *Antistrophe B*: No more shall I visit Delphi and other holy shrines if these things are not validated. Zeus, take regard! The oracles regarding Laius are being set at naught and Apollo is nowhere high in honor. All worship is ended!

The relevance of this poem to the drama has been much explored. The prayer for purity derives naturally from Oedipus' dread of pollution as he has just expressed it (813–23). The *hubris* theme is inescapably pertinent to his arrogant treatment of Tiresias and Creon (for *hubris* in the play's scheme, see p. 106). Moreover, the insistence on eternal laws can be linked with Jocasta's skepticism. In Antistrophe B "these things" suggests something specific: the oracles about Laius which Jocasta has challenged. The implication seems to be that if Apollo's oracles are discredited, all ritual dancing and religious worship are pointless.

In this central ode, then, Sophocles appears to be affirming the values of traditional Greek religion, in which oracles feature as the understood way by which the gods communicate with human beings. Despite all the uncertainties of human life, as exemplified in the tragic story of Oedipus, the gods represent a kind of order in the universe and certain absolutes in human behavior that are enshrined in religious practice and the avoidance of *hubris*. Summing up the ode's function, Burton (1980, 157) put it admirably: "The song provides a pause for reflection within the gathering menace of the tragedy." It can fairly be compared with the First Stasimon, the "Hymn to Man," in *Antigone*.

Interestingly, the meter is very similar to that of the *Antigone* ode: aeolo-choriambic combined with iambic or trochaic units. Sophocles apparently liked to combine these two elements to lend a grand and spacious rhythm, with a solemn tone, to songs with a fundamentally religious or philosophical content. <TRACK F4, lines 870–96> ⓞ

Third Episode (911–1085)

The tense atmosphere at the end of the preceding episode may have been mitigated by the "pause for reflection" in the stasimon but it now starts to return, though quietly at first. The last words of the choral song were "All worship is ended!" But at this point Jocasta re-enters with a handmaiden to bring garlands and gifts of incense to the temples. Her fears for Oedipus' anxious state prompt her to address Apollo with a prayer for "some release that is free from pollution" (921). This contrasts forcefully both with the Chorus' closing words and with Jocasta's cozy skepticism. Oedipus' fears have frightened her too.

But then, as though in ironic answer to her prayer, a Messenger (who later turns out to be the Corinthian herdsmen who accepted Oedipus as a baby) arrives. The opening exchange of courtesies between him and Jocasta creates a new atmosphere of anticipation before he delivers his news that the Corinthians want to make Oedipus their king as Polybus has died. Jocasta's skepticism about oracles is joyfully renewed; and when Oedipus re-enters to learn the tidings, his first reaction is one of huge relief: he cannot now kill his father! But another fear soon returns: he might still sleep with his mother, "No need to worry," urges Jocasta. "Chance rules; best to live at random. Many men have slept with their mothers in *dreams*!" – implying that they have never done so in reality (977–83).[9]

From now on more and more of the truth emerges and the tension steadily mounts. On learning that Oedipus fears returning to Corinth on account of Queen Merope, the Messenger, delighted at the prospect of a larger reward, cheerfully declares that Polybus and Merope were not his real parents; they had accepted him from the Messenger himself, who had received the child on Mount Cithaeron from a Theban herdsmen, whom the Coryphaeus identifies as the man who has been sent for to confirm the details of Laius' death. Through all this, the technique of single-line stichomythia is used to the most striking effect as Oedipus ruthlessly hammers the information out of the old Corinthian. The burning question, the riddle, for him has now firmly shifted from "Who killed Laius" to "Who am I?"

There in the background, though, is the third onstage character, Jocasta, who has listened in silence to the long dialogue and already realized the truth long before Oedipus does. She now (1056) advances and implores her husband/son to stop his relentless enquiring. But he still cannot see where it is all leading and is determined to persist. A powerful crescendo culminates in her desperate cry, "You ill-starred man, may you never learn who you are!" "Go, someone," shouts Oedipus, "and bring me that herdsman here and leave this woman to glory in her noble birth!" At this point Oedipus is wildly terrible to his wife; and with two final lines of anguish, Jocasta makes her highly emotional exit – one of the most powerful in the whole of Greek tragedy. <TRACK F5, lines 1054–72> ⓞ

In the closing speech of the episode Oedipus resolutely asserts his determination to establish his origin, however ashamed Jocasta may be of it. In frantic exhilaration he hails himself as the child of Fortune, whose brothers, the months, had marked the changing seasons of his life.

Third Stasimon (1086–109)

At this moment of high exaltation, Sophocles makes his Chorus take on Oedipus' deluded mood. They play the prophet: Cithaeron will be honored with rituals as Oedipus' mother and nurse. He could be the child of a god – Pan, Apollo, Hermes or Dionysus! "The effect," as Burton (1980, 171–2) puts it, is "to invest Oedipus, as he stands on the brink of doom, with an aura of transcendental mystery." The excitement is short-lived, only to be dashed to the ground in the following scene. The dramatic technique replicates that of the Chorus' lively prayer to Dionysus in the fourth Stasimon of *Antigone* (1115–52), after Creon has relented and gone off to bury Polynices and release the immured Antigone, only to be followed by the Messenger's account of their deaths.

This song is short with only one pair of strophes. The chosen meter, as in the *Antigone* ode, is largely the fast-moving dactylo-epitrite, which was particularly associated with Pindar's odes celebrating victories in the athletic festivals. <TRACK F6, lines 1086–97> 🔊

Fourth Episode (1110–85)

This scene, culminating in Oedipus' recognition is one of the most exciting in all dramatic literature. It also perfectly illustrates what Sophocles was able to do with three solo actors.

The Theban herdsman who saved Oedipus' life as a baby, originally sent for to confirm his evidence about the death of Laius, is confronted with the Corinthian messenger and asked about the baby he received from Jocasta. The suspense, already extremely high, becomes unbearable as, in another stichomythic inquisition, Oedipus forces the poor old Theban, very reluctantly and under threat of torture (attendants come forward), to spell out the truth piece by piece – with *antilabe*, of course, at the ultimate climax – until the last piece of the jigsaw is in place. Oedipus' final speech of four agonized lines (1182–5) is preceded by two cries of profound anguish; he prays to see the light for the last time, so tainted is he in his birth, his marriage and his parricide. Oedipus' exit, like Jocasta's before it, is a great theatrical moment; but we should not forget the two old herdsmen as they depart dejectedly along their different *eisodoi*. Both had believed that what they had done in pity for that tiny child would be all for the best, but it has all turned out so disastrously.

Fourth Stasimon (1186–222)

The drama's harrowing climax has now been reached and the aftermath of Oedipus' discovery is devoted to the horror and pity of his *pathos*. The springs of tension are gradually relaxed, but the play remains emotionally compelling to the very end.

Sophocles has his Chorus sing a song of despair, which develops into a dirge. In the first of the two strophic pairs, Oedipus' tragedy is universalized in characteristic Greek fashion: life is an illusion and happiness a mere seeming; witness the tale of Oedipus who rose to kingship (another reference to the Sphinx) and has now fallen so low. In the second pair the horror of the incest motif comes to the fore, and the Elders deplore Jocasta's ambivalent role before returning to Oedipus, whom they wish they had never seen. The substance of the ode thus sums up the conclusion which the drama has reached so far but also focuses on the separate plights of Jocasta and Oedipus in anticipation of the Messenger narrative that follows. The emphasis on sight will also dominate much of what is to come.

The meter in the first strophic pair is aeolo-choriambic, mostly with four pulses to a colon, which gives the song a weighty regularity. The second pair is more varied in its colometry, with some longer phrases of six pulses and a run of four three-pulse cola (1208–10 = 1217–19) which might suggest a formalized movement of bodies from side to side in a physical expression of lamentation. <TRACK F7, lines 1186–96 and 1213–22> ⊙

Exodos (1223–530)

In the formal terminology all the rest of the play is included in the closing scene, as it is unpunctuated by a choral stasimon. For our purposes it is better to explore the text in five separate sections.

Messenger Speech (1223–96)

The narrative of Jocasta's suicide and Oedipus' self-blinding is introduced in a mood of powerful solemnity. The Messenger addresses the Elders in their full dignity, first emphasizing the pollution that has befallen the royal house of Thebes and the deliberateness of the violent actions he is to describe. The rhetorical build-up is deeply impressive.

The vivid narrative speaks for itself and is spoilt by summary. A noteworthy feature is the skillful focalization of the detail as observed through the eyes of the Messenger himself and other witnesses. The masterstroke is the picture that greets them when Oedipus bursts through the barred doors of his marriage chamber to reveal Jocasta's hanged body swinging in a halter. The description of Oedipus' self-blinding is horrifying but not gratuitously so, as Euripides might have done it. The reason for his action is clear: he is determined to cut himself off from all that has meant most to him in life. The self-punishment is more than a terrible physical injury; he is carrying out the sentence of human and social excommunication that he pronounced in the First Episode. <TRACK F8, lines 1258–79> ⊙

The grand tone at the end of the main rhesis balances that of the Messenger's introductory lines. His final speech heralding Oedipus' entrance in his blinded state creates a lively sense of anticipation. As the doors open, the eyes of the audience will be focused on Oedipus and the Messenger fades from view in an unobtrusive exit.

Lament for Oedipus with Chorus (1297–368)

At this moment of supreme pathos, within the Greek tragic medium, Sophocles would naturally have chosen to use the heightened mode of singing in lyric meter and to allow his protagonist scope for displaying this additional skill. For good measure, he precedes a strophic *kommos* with a brief passage in the halfway house meter of anapaests, mostly delivered by the Chorus, probably the Coryphaeus. This guides the audience's involvement in its expressed feelings of shock and compassion as Oedipus comes into actual view, doubtless with a new mask which shows his eyes dripping with blood and probably a bloodstained costume. He can now only feel his way as he totters forward outside the palace, uncertainly extending his arms. His opening cries of despair are also in anapaests.

The formal lament which follows (1308–68) is composed in the same interesting mixture of song (with *aulos* accompaniment) and speech that characterized the earlier *amoibaion*

(649–96). In the first strophic pair Oedipus himself is made to alternate poignant dochmiacs in song with spoken iambic trimeters, while the Chorus responds in the latter. In the second pair the emotional pitch is raised still further as Oedipus combines his dochmiacs with shorter phrases of *sung* iambics, with one such phrase for the Chorus, though they round off the stanza with another spoken trimeter couplet. This variety of delivery and meter would, I think, have been extraordinarily effective (as in the Cassandra scene of *Agamemnon*) and avoided dull turgidity. <TRACK F9, lines 1308–18 and 1327–36> ⊚

I suspect that the dramatic power of this movement lay at least as much in this formalized structure as in the content of the words. The themes are, of course, entirely appropriate to the situation: Oedipus' sense of darkness; his gratitude for the Elders' presence; the part played by Apollo in bringing about his suffering, though his blindness has been self-chosen; a curse on the man who saved him from death as a child. The Chorus on their side bewail the searching intelligence which had led Oedipus to discover the truth and concludes by asserting that Oedipus would be better off dead than alive. All this material is very apt, but its pathos is the more compelling for the stylized framework.

Oedipus' Speech of Self-Justification (1369–415)

Oedipus now changes to the mode of formal rhesis, with carefully structured argumentation boosted by the power of rhetorical verse. Delivered by an actor with a sense of this speech's architecture and with appropriate light and shade in the detail, it is another compelling "number" in its own right which contributes to the graded descent in temperature from the peak of the discovery.

The "aria" has three clearly defined sections. In the first Oedipus justifies his self-blinding by asking impassionedly how, with seeing eyes, he could confront his parents in the underworld or face his own children or anyone else in Thebes. He wishes he could be deaf as well as blind, to cut himself off still further. In a moving middle paragraph he mentally revisits the places that featured in his history – Cithaeron, Corinth, the triple crossroads and, in an emotional climax, the bed where he was born and lived to beget children in incest. Finally, he implores the Chorus to cast him out quickly, whether to banishment or death.

Taken as a whole, the rhesis expresses Oedipus' sense of appalling pollution and his wish, therefore, to be deprived of all communication with his fellow human beings. At the end the question is raised: what now is going to happen to Oedipus? Will the oracle's command and Tiresias' prediction be fulfilled in his expulsion?

Oedipus Confronts Creon (1416–523)

Oedipus does not, in fact, get his way. He is not expelled. This section lends some tension and suspense, as well as further pathos, to the end of the play's wind-down after the catastrophe.

After 1415 Creon returns, attended by his servants, and is introduced by the Coryphaeus as the only person now left as "guardian of the land" (1418). The man who earlier preferred influence to power (583–615) must now take charge. He assures Oedipus in sympathetic tone that he has not come to mock him but firmly orders the servants to take him indoors, to avoid polluting the sun-god. When Oedipus begs to be expelled and allowed to die on Mount Cithaeron, Creon insists that Apollo must be reconsulted as to the proper course of action. But Oedipus still has two long speeches to go. In the first (1446–75) he *charges* Creon with instructions for Jocasta's burial and the welfare of his children, then asks to hold his two

Figure 7.2 *Oedipus Tyrannus*, Cloisters, New College, Oxford 2015. Source: Reproduced by permission of the Archive of Performances of Greek & Roman Drama.

daughters in his arms. To this Creon agrees and Oedipus hears Antigone and Ismene come out of the palace weeping. The pathos is drawn out in the second and final rhesis (1478–514) as, in a visually powerful tableau, he embraces the girls and sadly laments their future fate. He asks Creon to serve as father to them, which we may assume the new regent assents to with a touch of his hand (1510).

But the mood then changes and a new meter with a quicker and more insistent pace is heard, the long trochaic tetrameter, in lines effectively split between Oedipus and Creon for a last adversarial exchange. Creon orders Oedipus indoors. He agrees, but on condition that he is expelled. "That's for the god to decide," replies Creon and tells Oedipus to let go of his daughters. When their father protests, the answer is "Don't wish to rule in everything!" A director will need to decide at this point whether Oedipus should resignedly release his daughters voluntarily or whether the attendants should force them away. However this is played, the ensuing little procession into the palace will offer finality. <TRACK F10, lines 1515–23> ⓐ

This ending is excellent. Sophocles does not want to detract from Oedipus' sense of pollution by showing him too humble and meek. In his resistance to Creon the old Oedipus survives, even if he can no longer control his destiny and must return to the house where he cannot escape from his painful memories.[10]

The Chorus's Closing Lines (1524–30)

The trochaic tetrameters continue, but now, I think, in slower and statelier tempo. Sophocles chooses not to dispatch his Elders in the usual anapaestic tailpiece. The longer, more spacious lines befit a solemn ending to this majestic drama and may have been assigned to the

Coryphaeus. The formal address to the inhabitants of Thebes involves the audience, as earlier on (p. 108 and note 3).

Oedipus' has fallen from high to low. Call no man happy until he is dead. The sentiment is conventional, but the grand tone carries it off. After the final line, the aulete will have struck up to lead the Chorus off in a dignified procession.

Some Concluding Thoughts

OT merits its canonical status as a brilliantly constructed drama of exceptional tension, excitement and pathos. Thematically, gods and oracles as a principle of order seem to be a central preoccupation, but the tragic story of Oedipus suggests a universe that is far from benign and cruelly delusive. The *hubris* motif may give an impression that Oedipus is not altogether undeserving of his downfall, and the repeated emphasis on the Sphinx story may imply the moral warning I have suggested (pp. 106–7); but these are more incidental than fundamental to a tragedy which ultimately consists in the processes and consequences of a terrible discovery. In the end we may feel that the aims of Sophocles the dramatist and Sophocles the teacher are not fulfilled in quite such an integrated way as they are in *Antigone*.

Notes

1 This title is a latinization of the Greek *Oidipous Turannos*. The play is often referred to by the Latin title *Oedipus Rex* or *Oedipus the King* in English. This distinguishes it from Sophocles' other surviving Oedipus play, composed some 20 years later, *Oedipus Coloneus* or *Oedipus at Colonus*.

2 Lines 35–6, 130–1, 439–44, 455–6, 506–10, 694–5, 1198–201, 1525.

3 I suggest this happens again at 216–54, also at 259–75 (see note 5), 629 and 1524.

4 The pervasive fire imagery may well be inspired by the burning of crops in Attica by the Spartans who invaded the country annually during the early years of the Peloponnesian War.

5 Some disturbance in the transmitted order of the lines has been recognized and editors have suggested various transpositions and deletions. My own inclination is to place 269–75 after 254 and to conclude the speech with 255–68.

6 No particular deity seems to be implied, more a general notion of "god" as a divine principle.

7 Here I accept an emendation commended by several scholars. The transmitted text "*Hubris* begets a tyrant" is difficult to understand, particularly as the word *tyrannos* did not carry "tyrannical" overtones in Sophocles' time.

8 The question has been regarded by some scholars (e.g. Henrichs 1994–5) as "metatheatrical," viz. the Athenian chorus are referring to themselves as tragic performers. The words seem to me more naturally interpreted in the context of the drama. To "dance" is to engage in religious ritual.

9 There is no need to suppose that Sophocles anticipated Freud and the subconscious in this speech.

10 We can only speculate whether Sophocles chose to end his play this way to take account of the myth which is the basis of his much later play, *Oedipus Coloneus*: that Oedipus in his old age was expelled from Thebes and came to Athens, where he died and was buried in Colonus,

Sophocles' own birthplace. Some modern scholars have been unhappy with the ending of *OT* as it is and detected interpolation because the drama does not conclude with Oedipus' expected expulsion. Where language is concerned, there are some corrupt lines but these can fairly easily be amended and the style is consistently Sophoclean. Though the whole Exodos is long, it is admirably constructed as drama.

References

Text: *Sophocles: Oedipus Tyrannus* (Loeb edition, Vol. 2). 2004. Cambridge, MA: Harvard University Press, edited and translated by Hugh Lloyd-Jones.

Burton, R.W.B. 1980. *The Chorus in Sophocles' Tragedies*. Oxford: Clarendon Press.

Dodds, E.R. 1966. "On Misunderstanding the *Oedipus Rex*," *Greece & Rome* 13, reprinted in Dodds. 1973. *The Ancient Concept of Progress*, pp. 64–77. Oxford: Clarendon Press.

Henrichs, Albert. 1994–5. "'Why Should I Dance?': Choral Self-Referentiality in Greek Tragedy," *Arion* 3, 54–111.

Knox, B.M.W. 1957. *Oedipus at Thebes*. New Haven, CT: Yale University Press.

Commentaries

Dawe, R.D. 1982. *Sophocles: Oedipus Rex*. Cambridge: Cambridge University Press.

Jebb, R.C. 1887. *Oedipus Tyrannus*, 2nd edn republished by Bristol University Press (2012).

8

Electra (Sophocles)

Introduction

While we know that a number of myths were dramatized by more than one of the three great tragic poets, there is only one story which was treated by all of Aeschylus, Sophocles and Euripides among the plays which survive; that is the myth of Orestes who killed his mother to avenge his father. The three different "takes" on the story well illustrate the differences between the three poets as dramatic artists, which is why all three are explored in this volume.

We have already seen how Aeschylus in his *Oresteia* used the trilogy form to unfold the universal tragedy of justice conceived purely as retaliatory and also to suggest a resolution to a self-perpetuating and self-defeating sequence of crime and punishment. Orestes' crime is paradoxically also a duty and presented as the climax to a long series of retributive acts within a single family.

Sophocles and Euripides chose to concentrate the dramatic action within single plays and with a narrower focus. Both assigned the protagonist's role to Orestes' sister Electra whose role in the *Oresteia* was much more limited. We do not know for sure whether Sophocles' *Electra* preceded or followed Euripides' tragedy of the same name. These two plays share certain formal features and both owe a great deal, though in different ways, to Aeschylus; but they are hugely different both in substance and tone. Recent scholarship, largely based on stylistic considerations, tends to favor an earlier date for Euripides' treatment – about 420 as against about 413 for Sophocles.[1]

Euripides' *Electra* has its own chapter in this volume. Enough for now to say that it focuses less on the ethics of revenge generally and more on matricide as such. The poet was evidently repelled by the idea that Orestes' hideous act as ordained by Apollo could be in any sense a duty and was very much concerned to explore the sort of people who would murder their mothers and how they would feel when the act was done.

If Sophocles' tragedy was composed later, he reverted essentially to the same theme of revenge and concentrated principally on the harrowing effect of the retaliatory process on the personalities of its perpetrators. This *Electra* is arguably the most disturbing and dramatically powerful of the three treatments. As we have no certain date for it, it can hardly be related to any particular events in Athenian history. The message, if I have correctly described it, is pertinent at any time.

Greek Tragedies as Plays for Performance, First Edition. David Raeburn.
© 2017 John Wiley & Sons, Inc. Published 2017 by John Wiley & Sons, Inc.
Companion website: www.wiley.com/go/raeburn

Synopsis

For the background to the story, see on the *Oresteia* (pp. 33–4). For the purpose of Sophocles' play, it is important that the young Orestes, at the time of Agamemnon's murder has been entrusted by Electra herself to his father's tutor (the Pedagogue) to smuggle away to safety at the court of Strophius, king of Phocis.

Sophocles' play begins when Orestes, accompanied by the Pedagogue and (as always) Pylades, returns to Mycenae in secret to take revenge on his father's murderers and to recover his patrimony. His plan is to gain access to the palace through a stratagem: the Pedagogue will deliver a false report of his death in a chariot race to Clytemnestra, and he himself with Pylades will follow bearing an urn with ashes purporting to be his own.

His sister Electra is not informed of this plan, as she is in Aeschylus' *Choephori*. She has persistently angered her mother and Aegisthus by publicly mourning for her dead father and praying for the return of her exiled brother. Treated as a slave by the usurpers, she is contrasted with her sister Chrysothemis who offers no resistance and so enjoys a more comfortable existence.

Convinced, as is Clytemnestra, by the Pedagogue's false report Electra is plunged into despair and rashly contemplates the murder of Aegisthus on her own. When her brother finally arrives at the palace and allows her to handle the urn, he is sufficiently moved by her grief to reveal his identity. She is now driven by the extremity of her joy to virtual madness. When Clytemnestra and Aegisthus are duly murdered, the tragic effects of the revenge process on her personality are fully revealed.

Interpretation

The most significant feature of Sophocles' treatment of the myth is the apparent absence of any aftermath to Orestes' murder of his mother. Where Aeschylus has him pursued by the Furies and eventually put on trial at Athens and Euripides indicates that these consequences are in prospect, Sophocles ends with the murders of Clytemnestra and Aegisthus (in that order) and seems to leave the matter there. This has resulted in two strongly divergent lines of interpretation.

One view[2] has taken Sophocles to have returned to the Homeric account of Orestes' revenge on Aegisthus in the *Odyssey*,[3] where it is treated as laudable and final. The moral basis of the drama is simply that of doing good to one's friends and harm to one's enemies, and the re-establishment of order through retribution. The deeper issues explored by Aeschylus and Euripides are apparently shelved. Hence the famous description of the play by the German critic A. W. Schlegel as "a combination of matricide and good spirits," which might be paraphrased as "matricide without tears."

The other approach, espoused by several modern scholars,[4] has found this melodramatic interpretation too simplistic. It is certainly quite uncharacteristic of the more complex ethical stances evident in Sophocles' other extant tragedies. It ignores the centrality of Electra in the piece; Orestes' drama is clearly secondary to hers. Tears are shed in plenty during the action and there is no escaping the tragic pathos of the whole, the predominant mood of suffering. Indeed, of the three dramatic treatments of the myth this one is certainly not the most cheerful but arguably the most unrelentingly grim.

Scholars who have looked more deeply at this play have drawn attention to several important features. One is that, although Orestes is not made to see the Furies after his mother-murder, they are still mentioned or referred to at several points in the text.[5] The word Erinys is applied metaphorically to the various characters who have been involved in the retributive process, with the implication that they will eventually become the victims after serving as the agents of that process. As in Aeschylus, Furies feature no less than the Olympian god Apollo, whose authority also broods over the action and its tragic effects.

Sophocles' decision to place Aegisthus' murder after Clytemnestra can be regarded in a similar light. For Aeschylus (as for Euripides) the matricide is the climax and so comes second, and the *Oresteia* presents the Furies as visible agents of Clytemnestra's wrath (*Choephori* 912, 924, 1054). Sophocles, by contrast, places far less emphasis on the mother-killing as such.[6] If the Furies in this play stand for the actual characters who are engaged in revenge *generally*, Clytemnestra's murder can just as well precede Aegisthus' and so enable the peculiarly horrible *coup de théâtre* which ends the play (see p. 133).

Indeed, the theme of retaliation is all-pervasive. The picture we are offered by Electra from the start is of a noble nature *compelled* by loyalty to her father to adopt an aggressive attitude towards her mother which is impious and excessive. Her public lamentation for the dead Agamemnon is bound to be extended indefinitely while the murderers remain unpunished and secure in their usurped power. Moreover, the vituperation and harsh treatment meted out to her by Clytemnestra and Aegisthus *enforce* a retaliatory response of non-cooperation and active defiance. Electra herself is aware of her excess but is, at the same time, sure that she has no choice but to behave towards her mother as she does (616–21). The constant iteration of the retaliation motif suggests that Sophocles was less concerned with retribution as a one-moment *event* but more as a continuing *process*. While the play's action appears to show Orestes and Electra triumphing over their foes, the tragedy is that, by a hideous irony, they themselves are destroyed in the process. The dramatic analysis that follows demonstrates this line of thinking.

Dramaturgy

As a theatrical experience *Electra* is possibly the most moving of all surviving Greek tragedies. Paradoxically, for a very large part of the piece, the plot is at a standstill or else nudged forward by false starts which do not come to anything. One critic, Gellie (1972, 106), has observed that it is only when the male characters are around that anything seems to happen; the bulk of the play consists in women arguing or lamenting. Yet in performance, the drama has an organic progression and a quality of suspense that makes it increasingly absorbing.

The characterization is extraordinarily memorable, particularly in the light of the overall interpretation that I favor. Orestes is a cold fish from the outset and Sophocles allows him no word of compunction or hesitation over the killing of his mother. Chrysothemis is a beautifully delineated role in her own right no less than a crucial foil to Electra. Clytemnestra is portrayed as hard and cruel enough to provoke Electra's excessive conduct towards her but still human in her fear of retribution and in the momentary qualm she feels when she learns that her son has been killed (770–1). The central role of Electra, in her extremities of love and hatred, grief and joy, is a truly great part that has attracted several distinguished actors in modern times. For the ancient Greek audience, her tragedy, like Oedipus' (p. 107), would well have illustrated the Delphic motto of "Nothing in excess" and also the counterpart maxim of "Know yourself;" at the end, though, she is so unhinged by all that the retributive process has done to her that she loses her self-knowledge together with her reason.

The Chorus of Mycenaean Women plays a smaller part than those in *Antigone* or *Oedipus Tyrannus*. In their opening *amoibaion* with Electra, they are a defined character in the drama, sympathetic to Electra, though critical of her excess. In subsequent movements, through the music of their rhythms, the poet uses them to provide transitions which reflect the mood of the drama in the action's development (First and Third Stasima) or to help Sophocles' presentation of Electra (*Kommos* and Second Stasimon).

Sophocles' deployment of tragedy's other forms are fully explored in the dramatic analysis, including his use of the three modes (iambic, anapaestic and lyric). The rhetoric of the long speeches of Electra in her confrontations with Clytemnestra and Chrysothemis is full of strikingly vivid detail and suggests the atmosphere of a public debate. The Pedagogue's false description of Orestes' death in a chariot race is one of the very finest in the Messenger convention. Stichomythia is used (as in *Antigone*) to articulate the conflicts of principle and personality and to make these vibrantly theatrical, as well as to build up overwhelming suspense in the Recognition scene.

Dramatic Analysis

Line numbers refer to the Greek text in the Loeb edition (see the end of this chapter), which has a parallel English translation. For the terminology of the discrete movements, see Appendix A; for the lyric structure and meters, see Appendix B or hear TRACK 0. ◉

Prologue (1–85)

The drama has a very strong beginning. Orestes enters with his cousin and friend Pylades[7] and the old Slave, known in Greek as the *Paidagôgos* who rescued him and brought him up in Phocis. The party has walked boldly into the citadel of Mycenae to set about the task of avenging Agamemnon's murder.

The opening lines are delivered by the Pedagogue, who introduces his master to his birthplace with its various landmarks and establishes an upbeat, businesslike atmosphere: the sun is shining, the birds are singing, it is time for action! (17–22). Orestes' rhesis (23–76) occupies most of the scene. He first commends the Slave's loyalty and compares him to a sturdy old warhorse. This sets the tone for the cold, almost military, precision with which Orestes communicates the deception plan enjoined on him by Apollo at the Delphic oracle (see synopsis). He cynically rejects the notion that a false report of his death could be a bad omen but is still pious enough to pray to the gods of his land to welcome him home. But enough of words; the moment has come!

Suddenly (77), a moan of anguish is heard from within the *skênê*. "Could that be Electra?" asks the Pedagogue. "Should we stay and listen?" "No, no! Apollo's orders first!" responds Orestes. "Libations first at the grave. That is the way to victory!"[8] Orestes' decision to ignore the possibility of meeting his sister is crucially significant. Both Aeschylus and Euripides contrived a reunion between brother and sister before the murder plot was formulated. Sophocles moots this possibility here for it to be deliberately rejected. Much of the action which follows depends entirely on Electra's ignorance of Orestes' return. Orestes and Pylades will then exit briskly down one *eisodos*, the Pedagogue by the other.

Electra's Monody (86–120)

We now might expect the Chorus to enter, but Sophocles first brings on his lead actor to establish Electra's character and situation in a monody of lamentation for her father, with a prayer to the gods of the underworld, including the Furies, to punish her father's murder and to send her long absent brother home to help her. Electra's lamentations, we learn, have been often repeated. Her emergence from the palace shabbily dressed (191) into the open air and the sunlight (86) points to their *public* nature. She is performing what the ancient Greeks regarded as a woman's duty: to keep the memory of a murdered man alive by constant lamentation. Her song can also be seen as an aggressive action against the usurping murderers, which we learn later (379–81) is a source of profound annoyance to them.

This is the only instance in Sophocles of a monody following an iambic prologue and preceding the entrance of the Chorus.[9] The meter which Sophocles gave his actor for this first "number" is "melic" anapaests (see Appendix B) which will have been accompanied by the *aulos* and delivered in a mode closer to singing than to speech. The aria reflects both the pathos and the splendor of Electra's isolation. <TRACK G1, lines 86–120> ◉

Parodos (121–250)

Electra's monody leads naturally to the entrance of the Chorus, which engages at once in a formal lyric exchange rather than a separate entrance song. The Chorus consists of noble Argive women (129), probably more mature than Electra, who admonish her and maintain that her prolonged lamentations are immoderate and futile.[10] They use various conventional arguments of consolation and remind Electra that Orestes is still alive, but she is not to be comforted: Orestes has failed to show up and she must go on chanting her laments in resistance to Clytemnestra and Aegisthus. She is aware of her excess (222), but the alternative means the collapse of *aidôs*, the sense of shame before other human beings, and *eusebeia*, religious piety which includes the notion of familial duty (245–50).

The sung *amoibaion*, accompanied by music throughout, consists of three strophic pairs, with lines in each stanza divided more or less equally between the Chorus and Electra, followed by an epode.[11] The first two strophic pairs are mainly in fluid dactyls, with some syncopated iambic elements, which appropriately recall Aeschylus' retribution motif (p. 40). <TRACK G2, lines 121–36> ◉ In the third pair (at 193), there is an effective change to anapaests, given weight by frequent spondees, when the Chorus recalls the night of Agamemnon's murder – the crime that calls for vengeance. <TRACK G3, lines 193–212> ◉ In Antistrophe C (213–32) the women warn Electra against making trouble for herself and the movement builds up as she insists with great passion that she cannot act otherwise. The epode (233–50) is unequally divided: in three lines the Chorus reassert their good, mother-like intentions, but this triggers a longer protestation from Electra in a more elaborate complex of metrical coda to bring this long, revealing movement to an end in one final syncopated iambic trimeter.

First Episode (251–471)

The lyric movement passes on seamlessly to the following scene in a spoken iambic dialogue. After a brief opening restatement of solidarity by the Coryphaeus (251–3), Electra starts a very long rhesis (254–309) by reiterating her sense of shame in her excess but insisting once more that her situation compels it. Vivid detail follows in her description of her life in the palace, confronted by the usurper Aegisthus and her mother's wild reaction to rumors of Orestes' return – though she herself, after so many disappointments, has abandoned all hope of that coming about.

Dialogue between Electra and the Coryphaeus (310–23) establishes the current absence of Aegisthus, which is important to the plot; and Electra's despair of Orestes' return is ironically restressed. The audience knows that Orestes is already back and will be uncomfortably conscious of his insensitivity in failing to seek her out.

At 324 Electra's sister Chrysothemis is announced as she enters from the palace carrying burial offerings. Chrysothemis is the foil to Electra, as Ismene was to Antigone. She has accepted the rule of the usurpers in return for an easy life. Her ethics are utilitarian where Electra obeys a categorical imperative. A speech of criticism from her (328–40) prompts a passionate reply from Electra which points up the difference between their viewpoints. The argument raises the question of how "wisdom" or "being sensible" should be defined: does it mean a practical realism in the face of a difficult situation, or does it consist in uncompromising loyalty to values such as family duty?

Moral issues are brought to earth at 374, when Chrysothemis warns Electra that trouble is on the way for her: the usurpers plan to suppress her embarrassing outcries by walling her up in a cave – we think of *Antigone* again. In terms of the plot this comes to nothing, but the news heightens the tension. The argument continues in stichomythia (385–416). Electra is undeterred by the prospect of immurement and expresses her contempt for her sister's compromising attitude. Chrysothemis is about to give up and go, when Electra asks her about the offerings she is carrying. The plot here receives a genuine nudge forward when Chrysothemis discloses that she is on her way to take offerings from Clytemnestra to Agamemnon's tomb, to avert the danger foreshadowed in a sinister dream (described in 417–27) which the queen has had about her murdered husband's return to life. In great excitement Electra hails the dream as an omen and implores her sister in one more rhesis (431–63) not to lay their mother's libation on the grave but to substitute offerings of their own and pray for their father's return from the underworld to champion their cause. The scene ends with Chrysothemis acknowledging her duty and making a rather timorous exit, while Electra herself remains onstage.

First Stasimon (472–515)

The drama's dynamic is gathering momentum. Clytemnestra's dream that Agamemnon's spirit is now stirring inspires the choral song which follows. Justice, personified as a Fury, is an army on the march; the metaphor optimistically asserts the Aeschylean theme of inevitable retribution for Agamemnon's killers. The excitement is expressed in the meter of the two strophic stanzas, in which long choriambic cola of mixed time signatures are combined with syncopated iambic phrases where some adjacent heavy syllables are protracted to produce a strong pounding effect. <TRACK G4, lines 473–86>

But an epode follows in unexpectedly different vein and rhythm. The long phrases of the strophe and antistrophe yield to quite short ones in a poignantly expressive lilt. Here the Chorus turns to the idea of a curse on the family which goes back to the story of Agamemnon's grandfather, Pelops,[12] since when "cruelty full of travail" has never left the house. The reference to Myrtilus "cast headlong from his chariot" looks forward to the supposed death of Orestes in a chariot race, which will shortly be reported. More importantly, Sophocles has chosen to associate the relentless onset of retribution with ongoing suffering and sorrow, as has already been emphasized and will continue to be demonstrated over the rest of the drama. <TRACK G5, lines 504–15> 🔊

Second Episode (516–822)

This scene divides into two sections: an *agôn* between Electra and Clytemnestra, followed by the Pedagogue's false description of Orestes' supposed death in the Pythian Games, with the two women's reaction to the news.

The *Agôn* (516–659)

"Out and about again, it seems, and off the leash!" The Chorus's final sad words are the cue for this imperious bark of Clytemnestra's entrance line. Electra's mother is presented by Sophocles as a hard, unpleasant woman, frightened of Electra. She speaks first in the formal debate, justifying the murder of Agamemnon by reference to Iphigenia's sacrifice. In her reply Electra attempts to whitewash her father's action by giving a different version of the story from that in Aeschylus: Artemis was angry with Agamemnon for accidentally killing a stag in her grove and then boasting about it. More telling as a debating point is Electra's turning the "blood for blood" argument against her mother. Her very long rhesis builds up to a passionate climax of denunciation, and we must be conscious of the retaliation motif operating at the level of words as well as actions and also of two powerful personalities engaged in dramatic conflict. When Electra's strictures provoke an angry expostulation from Clytemnestra, the daughter rather movingly assures her that she *is* ashamed of her behavior, even if (once again) she is forced into it by her mother's example (621).

At last, Clytemnestra calls an end to the argument by demanding quiet while she offers sacrifice and prayers to Apollo. At an onstage altar she asks the god, almost blasphemously, to grant her continued enjoyment of the fruits of adultery and murder.

False Messenger Scene (660–822)

The Pedagogue's narrative is a tour de force. Sophocles uses the Messenger speech convention with brilliant originality to convince Clytemnestra – and Electra too – that Orestes is dead and so to prepare for the admission of her murderers into the palace. There is an extraordinary double effect: the narrative of the disastrous chariot race is so thrilling in its own right that the audience's imagination can respond to it as if it were true to the last compelling detail; at the same time it can be relished in the knowledge that it is all a colossal fiction. Sophocles' original audience would also have appreciated the echoes of Homer's chariot race in the funeral games of Patroclus in *Iliad* 23 <TRACK G6, lines 734–48> 🔊

The poet's treatment of Clytemnestra's reaction to the news is another masterstroke of subtlety. Her feelings are mixed, and she is allowed a momentary qualm: "Giving birth is a strange thing. No wrong can make you hate the child you have borne" (770–1). But her sense of relief triumphs. She can now sleep at night, free from the fear of her son's vengeful return and from her daughter's constant threats. She ushers the Pedagogue into the palace after a final gloat of triumph over the devastated Electra.

The episode concludes with one of the most movingly eloquent passages in Greek tragedy (804–22) as Electra, left alone with the Chorus, expresses her grief and total despair: she will waste away in front of the palace door and die. <TRACK G7, lines 804–22> ⊚

Lament for Electra and Chorus (823–70)

Electra's grief, though, demands musical expression. In a further intensification of emotion Sophocles gives her a formal *kommos* with the Chorus, involving song and doubtless some kind of choreographed movement and gesture. In two strophic pairs Electra utters her cries of lamentation, while the Women try to calm and comfort her. The substance of the words is less important than the musical effect of the antiphony, largely in short phrases, with frequent use of the untranslatable Greek cries of woe. The speech and intensity of the exchange is evident in the splitting of some cola between Electra and the Chorus.

The first pair of strophes is composed in 3/4 time with some syllables protracted to sound for two. <TRACK G8, lines 823–36> ⊚ In the second pair a steadier 2/4 pulse prevails as the song winds down in a diminuendo, while Electra deplores that she will be unable to pay her brother the appropriate funeral rites.

This impassioned movement, striking in itself, also depends on the audience's awareness that Electra has been as deceived by the Pedagogue's narrative as Clytemnestra. For the next 350 lines the drama hinges on Electra's continued certainty that her brother is dead, when he is alive.

Third Episode (871–1057)

Enter, bursting with joy, Chrysothemis! On her visit to Agamemnon's tomb she has found offerings, including a lock of hair (of course, as in Aeschylus and Euripides); these *must* come from Orestes, no one else could have left them. Sophocles twists the knife further in Electra's wound by giving her excited sister a longish narration of her discovery (892–919). In the subsequent, largely stichomythic, dialogue Electra "disabuses" her sister: Orestes is dead and the offerings must be from an unknown sympathizer. The irony here is perfect, as is the little speech (934–7) in which Chrysothemis expresses her deflated hopes.

At 938 the scene acquires a new impetus as Electra slowly broaches a new plan in which she wants her sister's cooperation: will she join her in killing Aegisthus? In a long rhesis (947–89) Electra argues her case: she and Chrysothemis are now on their own and can only expect to grow old unmarried. In an unexpected shift of moral ground and a splendid flight of rhetoric Electra fantasizes about their future glory. The Coryphaeus' comment (990–1) that "forethought" is required by both sisters is a mild statement for the reaction that a normal Greek would have to Electra's reckless and unwomanly proposal. So Chrysothemis argues in her rhesis of reply (992–1014): such an attempt can only result in failure and an inglorious death. Her position is very reminiscent of Ismene's in the Prologue to *Antigone*, as is Electra's declaration that she will go it alone (1017–20).

The scene reaches its climax and conclusion in a passionate stichomythic exchange which renews the conflict between practicalities and absolutist principles. Once again Sophocles makes moral philosophy intensely dramatic; and as Chrysothemis retires indoors, we may well identify with her parting shot of warning to Electra in her uncompromising stance. Could Electra have been so unhinged by her extremity of grief for Orestes as to be starting to lose her sanity and self-knowledge?

Second Stasimon (1058–97)

During the preceding episode the Coryphaeus has sided with Chrysothemis in urging fore-thought (1015–16). This beautiful song, however, comes down firmly in Electra's favor.

In the first pair of strophes the Women commend the wisdom of the birds (storks?) who tend their parents – as also exhibited by Electra in the piety she has shown towards the dead Agamemnon. At 1063 they switch abruptly to the punishment of the sinners (presumably Clytemnestra and Aegisthus) and deploy "reproaches," like those of the Libation Bearers in Aeschylus, to rouse the dead sons of Atreus to vengeance. They challenge them with the division between the sisters which has left Electra to fight on her own. In the second strophic pair they commend Electra for choosing the path of wisdom and goodness and for championing the highest laws. Here again there seems to be a deliberate recall of Antigone and her moral stance – a point of importance for what is to come in the drama's dénouement.

The rhythms of this ode are as fine as its imagery. Strophe/Antistrophe A reflects the transition of thought at 1063, containing two runs of "anacreontic" phrases in 3/4 time (see Appendix C), separated in 1063–5 (=1075–7) by three four-square choriambic cola. Strophe/Antistrophe B emphasizes Electra's nobility and steadfastness in a steadier, largely iambic pulse with powerful syncopation in the final verses. <TRACK G9, lines 1058–69 and 1090–7> ◉

Fourth Episode (1098–383), Including *Amoibaion* for Electra and Orestes (1232–87)

The Chorus's "voice of reproach" to the dead evidently results in the entrance of Orestes and Pylades, with an attendant or two (1123), bearing the urn supposedly containing Orestes' ashes. At last the audience can anticipate a scene of recognition between brother and sister, though Sophocles maintains suspense for the best part of ten minutes.

To start with, though, Orestes is not thinking about Electra who has not featured in his plan. His concern is to gain admission to the palace in the Pedagogue's wake. The episode begins slowly and quietly as he establishes from the Coryphaeus that he has come to Aegisthus' house and asks for someone to announce his arrival. Electra is introduced as "nearest of kin" and directed by Orestes to go indoors. But not yet. Electra is dismayed by the sight of the urn and asks the stranger to let her hold it in her hands so that she can lament. "Take it across," says Orestes. "She can't be an enemy – a friend, maybe, or one of the family." Even now Sophocles will not allow him to infer that he could be talking to his sister.

Electra's speech with the urn (1126–70) is rightly celebrated for its emotional power and speaks for itself. The salient points are Electra's profound attachment to the brother she originally rescued as a child, her devastating sense of loss and also of *annihilation*. "Let me come into this little house of yours, nothingness into nothing, and live with you in the earth" (1165–7). We may be reminded of Creon's sense of nothingness at the end of *Antigone* (1325) – another significant intertextual detail. <TRACK G10, lines 1126–42 and 1165–70> ◉

Through all this overwhelming pathos, Orestes has stood by in silence. Now at last (1174) he has to speak, though he is at first careful to confirm that it *is* Electra he sees before him. Through a long passage of stichomythia (1176–226), the audience is kept waiting in unbearable suspense while Electra, still believing that she is talking to a stranger, expresses her puzzlement that he should be concerned for her and, in reply to his questions, enlarges on her unhappy predicament in the palace. Before revealing himself, Orestes still has to establish the loyalty of the Chorus before asking Electra to let go of the urn to which she is so passionately clinging. There is an agonizing moment as she begs him not to remove it and he forces it from her hand to prompt further tears of distress. Slowly, slowly he lets on that the ashes are not those of Orestes – who is alive. The dialogue breaks into half-lines as the revelation reaches its ultimate climax and the two speakers fall into each other's arms. <TRACK G11, lines 1205–29> ◉

Electra then expresses her joy to the Chorus (1227–9), but this is far from enough. Musical expression in lyric meters is indispensable and an *amoibaion* between brother and sister follows in the form of a strophic triad. Electra loudly expresses her hysterical rapture in a mixture of sung dochmiacs and iambics, while Orestes is made to respond in spoken iambic trimeters with words of cold caution. But Electra is having none of it; silence is impossible. <TRACK G12, lines 1232–52> ◉

We are ready for the dénouement, but the episode has still another hundred lines to run. When Orestes tells Electra that she is looking too happy and must be weeping when they go indoors, she continues in full flow (1301–21): Orestes need not worry; her unrestrained tears of joy will look like tears of grief! There is a flurry of danger at 1322 when steps are heard and the Pedagogue bursts out of the house to scold the two for dangerous talking and then to give Orestes an update on the situation indoors. When Electra learns that this new arrival is the slave whom she got to smuggle Orestes away to Phocis, she again indulges in crazily extravagant utterance (1354–63): it is almost as if the Pedagogue were Agamemnon himself returned!

Throughout this long episode, though Orestes is on the point of murdering his mother, Electra has been the prime focus of attention. Sophocles has wanted to show his heroine swinging from an extremity of grief to an extremity of joy. In her proposal to murder Aegisthus earlier on, there have been signs of madness. What must be her mental condition now?

At 1364 the Pedagogue calls Orestes to immediate action while Clytemnestra is alone at home and Aegisthus still away. Quickly Orestes takes his party into the palace, while Electra remains outside for a prayer to Apollo to aid the plot and "show mankind what recompense the gods bestow on impiety." She cannot be thinking of the impious act which Orestes is about to perform, but the audience can. She then makes her own exit.

Fourth Stasimon (1384–97)

The tension mounts in a very short but exciting song as the women envisage the god of war in inexorable advance and Orestes stealthily pacing through the palace hall, sword in hand, shrouded in darkness by Hermes, the god of deception. The two men are "inescapable dogs who hunt down wicked crimes" (1387–8), that is Furies themselves (see p. 125). The striking imagery is matched by the rhythms: two 5/8 bars to start with, followed by taut dochmiacs contrasting with longer phrases of steady iambic pulse. <TRACK G13, lines 1384–97> ◉

Exodos (1398–510)

The physical action, so long suspended, now follows thick and fast. The murders of Clytemnestra and Aegisthus are executed in rapid, businesslike succession (for the order see p. 125) and the play is brought to a peculiarly disturbing conclusion. Some have seen this final scene as melodrama, but Electra's reactions to the two killings make it genuinely tragic.

The first section (1398–441, prior to Aegisthus' entry) takes the form of a strophic pair, with soloists in iambic trimeters (including some half-lines) and the Chorus's interjections in lyric meters. Though four lines of the antistrophe are lost, the formal symmetry is peculiarly striking at the horrendous moment of the mother-murder. The poetic stylization is part of the effect.

(Strophe) – Suddenly (1398), Electra re-emerges from indoors to keep watch in case Aegisthus returns unseen. Sophocles still wants us to concentrate on *her* reactions to the situation. Very soon we hear three fearful cries of anguish from Clytemnestra offstage and then the fourth shriek, "Ah me! I am struck!" – the identical death-cry that Aeschylus gives Agamemnon (*Agam.*1343). "Strike her a *second* blow if you have the strength!" (1416) yells out Electra at the door. The queen's final cry indicates that the second blow has fallen, but Electra's savagely vindictive words have been even more blood-chilling.[13] They are reinforced by the Chorus's ensuing lines (1418–21): "The curses are now at work. The former dead are draining their killers' blood in retribution." Here is the overall tragic situation of the *Oresteia* newly expressed in blood-sucking Furies (see p. 125) who do not visibly appear but are incarnated in both Orestes and his sister.

(Antistrophe) – Now Orestes and Pylades come from the house. "How goes it?" asks Electra. "In the *house* [as opposed to outside it?]," replies Orestes, "all is well if Apollo prophesied well" (1424–5). On Orestes' lips "if" must mean "as surely as;" he has no qualms, as the Coryphaeus evidently has none at this point (1423), though the audience may feel uncomfortable. We are allowed no time to speculate as Aegisthus is sighted and the men withdraw once more to face their ultimate test.

Enter Aegisthus at 1442, along an *eisodos*, in excitement at the report of Orestes' death. Sighting Electra, he questions her in unpleasantly bullying mode and we relish the ironies of Electra's answers. He then orders the doors to be opened, so that the people can see Orestes' corpse. Here we can only guess at the staging, but I imagine that Electra herself does Aegisthus' bidding (1464) and stands to the side. Out glides the *ekklêma*, with Orestes and Pylades standing in a tableau behind Clytemnestra's covered body, now represented by a dummy.[14] When the trolley halts, the two young men step down to either side of it. Aegisthus would like to gloat but "piously" forbears and calls for the shroud to be lifted. "Lift it yourself," says Orestes; and the nasty king raises the cover to find the corpse of his wife lying there and himself threatened by two drawn swords. Realizing what has happened and who Orestes is, he pleads for mercy. Then – dramatically cutting into the middle of a line – we hear a loud voice:

"No, brother, for god's sake, don't give him the chance to argue with you. Kill him at once and throw out his corpse to the buriers it is appropriate for him to obtain, far from our sight! No other payment for all I have suffered can suffice for me."

These are Electra's final words. The "appropriate buriers" can be none other than the dogs and vultures. She is demanding what Nestor in Homer (*Odyssey* 3.255–61) claims Menelaus would have done had he returned from Troy to find Aegisthus still alive. But this echo of Sophocles' own *Antigone* is even more disturbing. If Electra was portrayed by the Chorus as like Antigone in 1095–7, the Fury of vengeance whom she now embodies has turned her into

Creon and she has ended up no less morally annihilated. More even than that, these terrible words suggest that she has lost the self-knowledge that she showed at the start of the play (p. 127).

A brief altercation between the men follows before Aegisthus is driven indoors (we may assume that the *ekkyklêma* is withdrawn at 1491 ff. to leave the doorway clear). Orestes' brutal parting shot is: "I want you to die in agony. All who presume to defy the law ought to be punished like this – kill them!" (1503–7). These final words typify the cold ruthlessness with which Sophocles has invested him from the Prologue on.

The play ends with three short lines for the Chorus in anapaests, perhaps delivered solo by the Coryphaeus. They have often been treated as a signing off which supports the view of a happy, uncomplicated ending. My own view is that "the seed of Atreus," to whom the lines are addressed is Electra herself, rather than the house generally, and that she is still onstage to make this clear. There are ironical overtones in the very last line (1510);[15] but that apart, the run of the sentence clearly puts the emphasis on the *suffering* which Electra has had to endure before "only just emerging in freedom." Electra may be no longer a slave, but what her release has cost!

With this reading, the focus of the play remains on Electra at the end. After the lines are spoken, she can slowly make her exit into the *skênê*, as the Chorus files out along the *eisodos* by which they entered.

Conclusion

"Matricide without tears?" Surely not. As a study of what revenge does to its perpetrators, it is a profoundly disturbing and human play, packed with intense emotion and striking characterization. Though the ending appears to leave the traditional story in mid-air, the poet's point has been powerfully made. As in *Antigone*, there is a fascinating exploration of the ethical principles that govern human decisions. At all times the drama is shaped and controlled within its generic form by the hand of a master.

Notes

1 See Cropp (2013, 31–2); March (2001, 20–2).
2 Associated with Jebb (1894) and endorsed by March (2001).
3 *Odyssey* books 1, 3, 4 and 11.
4 Notably Winnington-Ingram (1980).
5 Lines 112, 276, 491, 1387–8. Blood-sucking Furies are also implied at 785–6, 1420–1.
6 The point is raised only in 1410–11 when Clytemnestra cries out "My child, pity the woman who bore you!" but she does not expose her breasts as at *Cho.* 896–8 or Eur. *El.* 1206–7.
7 Pylades is a mute character, the son of Strophius, king of Crisa in Phocis and Agamemnon's brother-in-law, who had given Orestes refuge and brought him up. He comes on here with Orestes as in Aeschylus' *Chorephori* and other Greek tragedies. The closeness between the cousins was seen as a prototype of male friendship.
8 I have no doubt that all of 78–81 should be allocated to the Pedagogue and 82–5 to Orestes. Some editions (including the Loeb text) have Orestes raising the question of waiting to listen

and then being recalled to his duty by the Pedagogue. But the Pedagogue is not Orestes' evil genius. The decision that the cry issuing from the house should be ignored is far more telling on the lips of the businesslike Orestes who has just given the old Slave his orders.

9 Sophocles here could well be imitating Euripides' *Electra*, which follows the same pattern.

10 There is a similar exchange in the Parodos of Euripides' *Electra*, though the women there are unmarried and more of the heroine's age.

11 An "isometric" translation of this lyric movement (and others in this play) can be studied in Raeburn (2008).

12 Sophocles' audience would have been familiar with the myth of Pelops who competed in a chariot race with Oenomaus, the king of Pisa, in order to marry his daughter Hippodamia. In one version of the story, Pelops won by bribing the king's charioteer, Myrtilus, to sabotage his master's vehicle. For his reward Myrtilus demanded a night with Hippodamia, but was thrown into the sea from his chariot, cursing Pelops and his descendants as he fell.

13 I cannot believe that Sophocles intended his audience to see the second blow merely as the logical and expected correlation to the multiple blows which Aeschylus made Clytemnestra deal to her husband (there are three anyway, cf. *Agam.* 1386). The line is intended to shock.

14 The actor who played Clytemnestra will now have come on as Aegisthus.

15 "Made perfect by this present impulse" could also suggest "finished off by this assault."

References

Text: *Sophocles Electra* (Loeb edition, Vol. 2). 2004. Cambridge, MA: Harvard University Press, edited and translated by Hugh Lloyd-Jones.

Cropp, M. 2013. *Euripides Electra*, 2nd edn. Warminster: Aris and Phillips.

Gellie, G.H. 1972. *Sophocles: a Reading*. Melbourne University Press.

Raeburn, D. 2008. *Sophocles' Electra and Other Plays*. London: Penguin Books.

Winnington-Ingram, R.P. 1980. *Sophocles, an Interpretation*. Cambridge: Cambridge University Press.

Commentaries

Finglass, P. 2007. *Sophocles Electra*. Cambridge: Cambridge University Press.

Jebb, R.C. 1989. *The Electra of Sophocles*, republished by Bristol University Press in 2012.

Kells, J.H. 1973. *Sophocles: Electra*. Cambridge: Cambridge University Press.

March, Jenny. 2001. *Sophocles: Electra*. Warminster: Aris & Phillips.

Further Reading

Lloyd, Michael. 2005. *Sophocles: Electra*. London: Duckworth. A useful guide to the play, modern criticism and reception.

9

Euripides

The Plays

Euripides composed some 90 plays, of which eighteen survive more or less complete.[1] These bear witness to a varied output which includes plays that can hardly be called "tragic" in the usual sense, as they have happy endings. They are grouped here under various headings.[2]

Most commonly read and performed in modern times are: *Medea* (431), *Hippolytus* (428), *Electra* (about 420?), *Trojan Women* (415) and *Bacchae* (405). Other predominantly serious plays include: *Hecuba* (425?), *Hercules Mad* (414?), *Orestes* (408) and *Iphigenia in Aulis* (406?). In lighter vein, sometimes called tragicomedies are: *Ion* (413?), *Iphigenia among the Taurians* (413?) and *Helen* (412). *Alcestis* (438) also has a happy ending and *Cyclops* (about 408) is the one full surviving example of a satyr-play (p. 3). Less well known are *Children of Heracles* (about 430), *Andromache* (about 428), *Suppliants* (423) and *Phoenician Women* (409).

Life and Times

Euripides was probably born in the 480s. Although his life coincided roughly with that of Sophocles, he came to the fore as a dramatist rather later and had far fewer victories to his credit in the City Dionysia. He was a controversial playwright, mocked in Aristophanes' *Frogs* (405) for his unconventional writing, but much admired outside Greece.[3] Most of the information handed down to us about his life was evidently based on references to him in comedy and cannot be taken seriously. It is generally supposed that he left Athens at the end of his life and died about 406 in Macedonia at the court of King Archelaus. In the fourth century his plays were revived both in Athens and in other cities of mainland Greece or southern Italy.

Dramatic Achievement

Sophocles had developed the basic form of Greek tragedy as far as it could go. Euripides' achievement consists rather in the way he used and played with the genre to express his original ideas and distinctive approach. It is doubtless the maverick character of his oeuvre which inspired Aristophanes' caricatures. Generalization is difficult as there is such a variety in both the content and tone of the surviving plays, which are better considered individually in their own terms than forced into a single pattern. What does emerge, though, is a focus on human

Greek Tragedies as Plays for Performance, First Edition. David Raeburn.
© 2017 John Wiley & Sons, Inc. Published 2017 by John Wiley & Sons, Inc.
Companion website: www.wiley.com/go/raeburn

personality which would have accorded with the growing art of the solo actor (p. 83) no less than Euripides' own mindset.

What follows attempts briefly to suggest what is "different" about Euripides' work in his approach to the mythical material of his tragedies, the part played in them by the gods, his deployment of the tragic genre per se, the characterization of dramatis personae and his linguistic style. Apart from their powerful emotional impact, the plays have a strongly intellectual content.

Thought and Outlook

What is very evident from Euripides' plays is the influence of the Sophists (p. 82), not only in his rhetorical style but also in his skeptical, down-to-earth approach to the stories he dramatized. "Realistic" and "un-heroic" are descriptions often applied to this, but they need qualifying. Realistic details are still confined within a formalized poetic framework and some of Euripides' characters, especially women, do act heroically (Barlow 1986, 18–19). The three plays explored in this volume, however, may all be considered "provocative," which may explain why the poet seems to have been less honored as a prophet in his own country than elsewhere during his lifetime. Certainly, he liked to consider his characters' attitudes and points of view in ways which could run counter to contemporary Athenian stereotypes.

Where the gods are concerned, Aristophanes represented Euripides as subversive (e.g. at *Frogs* 889–91); but they are a constant in the plays and several times brought onstage as characters. The rituals of prayer, supplication, sacrifice and so on remain embedded in the dramatic texture. For Euripides, though, the gods are not a "given," never to be questioned as they were for Aeschylus and Sophocles. He is prepared to bring them into his plays as it suits him best in each one. In *Medea* the deities Earth and Sun have a special significance (see p. 145). In *Hippolytus* Aphrodite is a spiteful goddess who resents the young prince's neglect but also represents the sexual instinct with its generative force in human life; her rival Artemis, who enshrines the chastity to which Hippolytus is committed, cannot be understood in such broad terms as Aphrodite. Similarly, Dionysus in *Bacchae* is given his simple function as a god of wine and revelry but his worship is also made to embody something like our "herd instinct."

Apollo is the god of the Delphic oracle, who emerges rather badly from *Electra* and *Ion*. This could have something to do with the fact that Delphi backed Sparta against Athens in the Peloponnesian War; but Euripides clearly lacks the reverence for oracles that is evidenced in *Oedipus Tyrannus*. Even Zeus can be attacked by Amphitryon in *Heracles Mad* (339–47). Indeed, the gods of myth can be presented as *excessively* malign, as Cadmus complains of Dionysus (*Bacchae*, 1348). For Euripides, therefore, while the gods offer a framework of reference, they do not imply an order in the universe (see Grube 1941, 41–62).

Where Euripides stood politically is not easy to divine. In *Medea*, dated 431, Athens is extolled as the home of culture and the arts, appropriately enough as it offers the setting in which he can examine his gifts as a poet. The city also emerges well from *Supplices* (423?), less so in the *Trojan Women* if the behavior of the Greeks relates to that of the Athenians towards the island of Melos in 416. If the poet left Athens at the end of his life because he was fed up with it, there is no strong evidence to support this.

Dramatic Technique

Euripides does not seem to have introduced a great deal of technical innovation in the actual presentation of tragedy. He might perhaps have gone in for unusual spectacular effects, as in Medea's sun-chariot or the palace miracle in *Bacchae*. Costumes might also have been more realistic, if Electra's rags are anything to go by. He was evidently a skilled composer and towards the end of his career was experimenting with a kind of new music which was coming into vogue. Features commonly noted in his dramaturgy include the use of monologues to put the audience in the picture at the start of his plays and of the *deus ex machina* in his closing scenes. Another development was the sung monody which he liked to compose for his solo actors, to allow characters to reflect their own preoccupations or emotional state at a heightened level.

Euripides' focus on human personality and conflict was bound to affect his deployment of the medium. The solo actor's long speech becomes even more important, particularly in the presentation of introductory material in his prologues, the rhetorical expression of alternative points of view in formal debate and in the vividly detailed descriptions that are the hallmark of his Messenger narratives. In stichomythia he can risk very long exchanges as another means of argument or conflict at a human level.

This means that the chorus features less prominently than in Aeschylus or Sophocles. That said, it is always there and an integral part of each play's design. Like Sophocles, Euripides uses it flexibly to suit his needs at any given time. Although transitions between episodes and stasima may be more abrupt, the odes can clearly be seen and analyzed as part of the dramatic continuum. The imagery is often extremely beautiful and the use of meter consummate.

Though much in Euripides' plays is very grim, there is also a sense in which he wants his plays to be "fun." For him tragedy need not exclude satire or even downright laughter. He is prepared to be naughty and to entertain by playing tricks with the conventions of the genre or surprising his audience by novel, often paradoxical treatments that depend for their effect on the public's familiarity with the work of other poets. He likes to tease by building up suspense and then falsifying expectations. The abrupt transitions can go with sudden shifts of sympathy or a sharp discontinuity of tone, which can still work very successfully in modern performance.

Characterization

Many readers will be familiar with Sophocles' remark, quoted in Aristotle (*Poetics*, 1460b) that where he presented his characters "as they ought to be," Euripides portrayed them "as they are". Euripides' creations are arrestingly convincing, often in surprising ways (Jason, Orestes and Pentheus are good examples); they are sometimes, as in the case of his Electra, treated with a sophistication and complexity which take account of human inconsistency and irrationality. The prominence in many plays of female characters and the poet's sympathetic insight into their emotional responses to events suggest an interest that goes beyond theatrical potential. While it would be a mistake, I think, to look for subtexts or for characters with an "inner life" outside the drama's limits, there is a sharpness to be detected in the human observation which make Euripides' plays seem very "real" to us. Some scholars are reluctant to import the word "psychological" into their discussions of Greek tragedy, but this poet appears to have been very familiar with phenomena which we might use the language of modern psychology to describe.

Language and Style

As befitted the more realistic human treatment of his myths, Euripides' style is much nearer to the colloquial than in Aeschylus or Sophocles. The vocabulary is less highly poetic and metaphor less frequent during the episodes. His language, however, still is subject to the formal discipline of the iambic trimeter, even if this becomes more relaxed through the greater use of "resolution" as his oeuvre progresses. Indeed, it is the tension between the more natural vocabulary in which his characters express their emotions and the formalizations of the genre that gives his works the sharp explosive quality which makes them very strong in performance. A further contrast can be seen between the more spontaneous iambic sections and the elaborately wrought composition of the lyric movements.

Moreover, the structure and argumentation of the debating and some other speeches clearly owe a great deal to the techniques of sophistic rhetoric. Word power, which operated as a kind of magical control on the action in Aeschylus and can be strongly felt in the verbal ironies of Sophocles, is now much more weakly embodied in the persuasive effects of oratory. In the long speeches which Euripides gives his characters to deliver in the *agon* scenes, and sometimes elsewhere, the arguments often amount to no more than adventitious debating points, what is sometimes referred to as "the rhetoric of the situation." Examples of that in the plays explored here are Jason's speech of self-justification (*Med.* 522–75), Electra's abusive address to Aegisthus' corpse (*El.* 907–56) and Tiresias' defense of Dionysus (*Bacch.* 266–327).

Summary

Euripides emerges as a strikingly original artist both in his thinking and as a dramatist. Like Aeschylus and Sophocles he possessed an unerring instinct for the theater and for the genre in which he composed. He seems to have taken Attic tragedy to a limit after which it would continue to exist for posterity either in the revival of popular works or as it eventually evolved into the situational drama of Menander's New Comedy. All of his surviving plays are interesting and many are richly entertaining, universal in their vision and lasting in their impact.

Notes

1 A nineteenth, *Rhesus*, is attributed to Euripides but is generally considered inauthentic today.
2 Most of the dates given are conjectural and based on Euripides' metrical practice in the iambic trimeter. The plays are listed in a possible chronological order in each group.
3 Plutarch's *Life of Nicias* records that some of the Athenian captive survivors of the Sicilian expedition won their freedom by chanting choruses from Euripides that they happened to remember.

References

Barlow, Shirley A. 1986. *Euripides Trojan Women*. Warminster: Aris & Phillips.
Grube, G.M.A. 1941. *The Drama of Euripides*. London: Methuen.

Further Reading

Grube, G.M.A. 1941. *The Drama of Euripides*. London: Methuen. A substantial detailed account of Euripides' work and its characteristics.

Knox, B.M.W. 1989. *Cambridge History of Classical Literature*, Vol. 1, Part 2, Chapter 1.5. A useful introduction.

Morwood, J. 2002. *The Plays of Euripides*. Bristol: Bristol Classical Press. Includes a short account of each play, with an agreeable personal slant, for students.

10

Medea

Introduction

Medea is one of the most frequently performed Greek tragedies today and it is not hard to understand why. It is an excellently constructed, very theatrical piece; and it touches on human emotions that are eminently recognizable, even if it derives from a society in which there was a great deal less equality between the sexes than readers of this book are familiar with. The title role is one which, like Sophocles' Electra, particularly attracts modern actors.

Euripides was well advanced in his middle life when he composed the play for performance in 431 BC, just before the start of the Peloponnesian War. For the Athenians of the time, the atmosphere would not have been one of special anticipation or foreboding, as most Greeks at that time lived under the shadow of war. Although Athens gets an important mention in the drama, *Medea* is not a political play but one essentially concerned with relationships between men and women. What matters more is the previous development of the myth in poetry.

It is interesting that Euripides was only awarded the third prize in the competition of 431. Since *Medea* was just one of the four plays that he mounted for the occasion, it would be wrong to infer that this particular play was adversely received. Nonetheless, it portrays an injured woman scoring heavily against a man and getting away with it. The famous hero Jason is presented in a far from glamorous light and emerges from the story extremely badly. The statement is a bold one.

The Myth

Euripides' audience would have been very familiar with the story of Jason and the Argonauts in their quest for the golden fleece in the distant land of Colchis at the east of the Black Sea. Medea was the daughter of the Colchian king Aeêtes and the granddaughter of the sun god Helios. She fell passionately in love with Jason and used her magic arts to help him obtain the fleece before returning with him to Greece. To assist their escape she murdered her brother and scattered pieces of his body over the sea to delay her father's pursuit. Back in her lover's hereditary kingdom of Iolcos, she disposed of Jason's usurping uncle Pelias by persuading his daughters to dismember the old man in expectation of rejuvenating him (the subject of one of Euripides' earliest plays, performed in 455). This, however, only won exile for Jason, Medea and their children to Corinth. Here Jason decided to put Medea aside and to form a marriage alliance with the daughter of the Corinthian king, traditionally known as Glauce, though unnamed in Euripides' play.

Greek Tragedies as Plays for Performance, First Edition. David Raeburn.
© 2017 John Wiley & Sons, Inc. Published 2017 by John Wiley & Sons, Inc.
Companion website: www.wiley.com/go/raeburn

The fullest account of this story before Euripides was given in Pindar's fourth Pythian ode, dated to 462; but this does not explore the breakup of the relationship between Jason and Medea. The connection of Medea with Corinth seems to go back to an earlier Corinthian poet, Eumelus, of whom very little is known. There was also a tradition which linked Medea with Athens, where she became the wife of King Aegeus and tried to poison his son Theseus, whom she saw as a threat. However, there is no earlier source which makes Medea kill her children and it is highly probable that this was Euripides' own innovation. It is possible that an earlier version had the children killed by the Corinthians in revenge for the death of Glauce, though this is not certain (Mossman 2011, 7–8).

Synopsis

Euripides' play is set in Corinth where Jason has just formed his new alliance. The focus is on Medea's sense of betrayal and rejection and on the revenge she takes on Jason and the Corinthian royal family. The initial situation is the impending banishment of Medea and her children from Corinthian soil because she has been uttering angry threats. She persuades King Creon to allow her one more day, supposedly to prepare for her journey, but in reality to wreak her terrible revenge. She goes on to secure the promise of sanctuary after her crime from Aegeus, the king of Athens. Jason's new wife, together with her father, is destroyed through the sending of a poisoned robe; and she deals her ultimate blow at Jason himself by killing the children she has borne him, before escaping to Athens through the sky in the chariot of the sun god Helios.

Interpretation

This story in the theater could well have resulted in nothing better than a bloodthirsty melodrama. Euripides lends it tragic depth by exploring the clash between male and female points of view. The essential confrontation is between Jason's insensitive chauvinism and Medea's passionate fury at his rejection of her. The conflict is between two personalities but, as children are involved, it is also a family issue.

Though much here appears very modern, the play needs to be understood through the lens of its original performance and public. It was acted by men before an audience that consisted entirely, or very predominantly, of men. Athenian women belonged indoors and their role was essentially domestic while men engaged in outdoor activities and political life. Everything that occurs in *Medea* should be related to this.

Medea is before all else a woman whose feelings have been deeply hurt and whose resentment knows no practical limits. She is a barbarian, but that is not so much an aspect of her character as of her situation: her alienness emphasizes her loneliness and the enormity of her abandonment. Her magical powers likewise are more a factor in the plot, not emphasized by Euripides to make her character more sinister. It comes, in fact, as a surprise that in parts of the play she is presented more like a normal Greek woman. At times Euripides invests her with a kind of heroic stature more associated in the Greek mind with men, but her essential womanhood is paramount. Heroic associations serve chiefly to lend her dignity and authority as a woman in her situation and in the action that she takes.

Appalling as Medea's murder of her children to spite Jason may appear, it is not inexplicable. No incidences of such a crime are recorded from ancient times but in our own day newspapers and criminologists quote cases of child murder, often with the motive of hurting the marriage partner (Easterling 1977). Psychology apart, Euripides makes the crime convincing *dramatically* by showing Medea's powerful mind and will wavering over this part of her revenge.

If Medea's characterization was more subtle than might have been expected, Jason's would have come as a real surprise. In the popular imagination, the famous Argonaut was a glamorous hero with plenty of *aretê*, masculine valor. In Euripides he comes across as possibly the most unattractive character in the whole of surviving Greek tragedy. His besetting quality is *amathia*, human insensitivity, which makes him both intolerably patronizing towards Medea and uncomprehending to the point of exasperation when her outraged feelings lead her to object to behavior which he regards as sensible and even considerate. The conclusion of this conflict between Medea's irrational, though justified, feelings and Jason's totally different masculine mentality is an unequivocal victory for Medea. If the men who composed Euripides' audience recognized anything of themselves in Jason, the play could have touched them on a very raw nerve.

The main images of the play are first drawn from the animal kingdom, reflecting Medea's savage anger and irrationality. This is complemented by metaphors derived from sea and traveling, which evoke the voyage of the Argonauts, the turbulence and varying currents in Medea's mind and the transitions to which she has exposed herself. There are also passages referring to music and song, which may serve to highlight the dramatic form in which Medea's story is being told and so to lend it a kind of universal objectivity. Finally, the gods most frequently invoked in the text are Earth, Zeus and the sun, which may recall the chthonian/Olympian dichotomy of the *Oresteia* (p. 34) and can thus be seen as symbolizing the female and male domains.

Dramaturgy

Medea shows Euripides to have been a master of suspense, like Sophocles, and also of surprise. He also demonstrates his skill in manipulating his audience's sympathy: for most of the time we are invited to identify with Medea, while realizing how formidable she is, but at the end even with the appalling Jason.

The poet used his medium to tell his story in a tight and convincing structure: first expounding his situation and its themes in a striking way, going on to Medea's confrontation with three men, during which her plans are seen evolving, then followed by the execution of those plans in two different ways, with a very powerful closing scene which hammers home Euripides' main point. At various stages in the sequence Medea is allowed long speeches in which she articulates or debates her plans, so that the audience can watch her carrying them out.

The Chorus of Corinthian women is well integrated into this scheme with lyric songs that are not particularly long but pertinent to the mood and situation. The odes are used first to establish sympathy for Medea, and later to emphasize the horror of her revenge. Among the minor characters, two slaves in the persons of the Nurse and the Pedagogue help to establish the domestic character of the drama; while the two children, mute until their death-cries are heard, are used to powerful effect when they are onstage.

The principal mode of utterance in this play is the long iambic rhesis. Medea is not allowed a lyric monody in which to air her resentment with Jason or grieve over her children. Mossman

(2011, 49–53), observes that rational calculation predominates in her characterization, so that the iambic trimeter suits her best. There is less stichomythia in this play than in the other Euripides pieces explored in this volume; it seems to have been saved up chiefly for the final slanging match between Medea and Jason. Anapaests, though, play a powerful part in the early scenes and at certain points (especially 1081–115) they are used by contrast to lower the temperature and offer the audience a little respite.

The *skênê* is the place which houses Medea and her children. Jason has abandoned it and always enters by an *eisodos*. The use of the roof and the crane in the closing scene is one of the surprises that the poet contrived in this play.

Dramatic Analysis

Line numbers refer to the Greek text in the Loeb edition (see end of this chapter), which has a parallel English translation. For the terminology of the discrete movements, see Appendix A; for the lyric structure and meters, see Appendix B or TRACK 0. ◉

Prologue (1–130)

The play's opening section offers a powerful and a varied introduction in three parts.

The Nurse's Rhesis (1–48)

Euripides begins his drama, as he usually does, with a monologue in which a character states the background to the action that is to be unfolded and may also anticipate what is to come. The speaker here is an old slave-woman, retainer of Medea's household (49), called Nurse in the manuscripts, who has presumably looked after Medea's children and perhaps Medea herself. She herself is passionately involved in the situation, as is evidenced by the strong rhetorical beginning: "How I wish the ship Argo had never winged its way to the land of Colchis through the dark-blue Clashing Rocks!" This sets the tone for what is to be a gutsy play which does not pull its punches. We can also regard the Symplegades, the clashing rocks which destroyed ships at the entrance to the Black Sea, not just as a mythological allusion to the voyage of the Argonauts but as an image for the clashes of viewpoint and personality that will dominate the play's action.[1] <TRACK H1, lines 1–15> ◉

The themes emphasized during the Nurse's exposition are: love turned to hatred (16) and Medea's formidable nature (44–5), which she fears will erupt in violence. The speech ends, though, in rather homely way as the arrival of the children is announced; they have finished their game of hoops[2] and their mother's troubles are not on their young minds. Interestingly the Pedagogue who accompanies them is *not* included in the entrance announcement but only introduced by the Nurse at 53.

Dialogue for Pedagogue and Nurse (49–95)

Two slaves talking together are unique in tragedy and point to the play's down-to-earth tone, even though the style of their language is not colloquial as it would be in a comedy. We can enjoy their exchange of information while the little boys, now established as part of the drama (though we do not yet know why), presumably sit apart, playing some innocent game. There is an engaging quality in the Pedagogue's description of how he had eavesdropped on gossip over a game of draughts that Creon is shortly to expel Medea and the children, unopposed by Jason. At the end the Nurse dispatches the children indoors with a warning not to go near their mother in her gloomy and threatening mood.

Anapaests for Medea (offstage) and Nurse (96–130)

The boys are halted in their tracks by a loud cry of despairing lament from within the house – the first shocking surprise of the play. The lines are in a new meter, anapaests, and, what is more, they are *sung*.[3] The sound comes as a sudden jolt, though there can be no doubt of its source. "There it is!" says the Nurse, catching the more exciting mode of utterance, though in *spoken* anapaests which contrast effectively with Medea's sung exclamations. Once again she instructs the children to go indoors quickly. The clouds are gathering, she says, and the lightning is about to flash – as it does at 111, when another terrifying offstage wail indicates that the poor children have not succeeded in keeping out of their mother's way and Medea is heard violently cursing them, their father and the whole house. The Nurse's anapaests continue in protest, but the emotional temperature drops as she generalizes (119–30) on the extreme feelings of princes and reflects on the advantages of a lowly situation.[4]

Parodos (131–212)

Enter the Chorus of Corinthian Women. They have arrived in response to the unhappy cries of Medea who is their established friend (138). During the following sequence, Medea continues to lament loudly and pray for death, the Chorus tries to reassure her and the Nurse expresses her despair. At 180–3 the Women send her indoors to fetch Medea outside as they want to see and comfort her. The Nurse agrees but only exits after a disproportionately long, seemingly irrelevant and very strange discourse (190–203) on the uselessness of music therapy for sick minds.[5] While she is gone, the Chorus briefly recapitulates the reason for their presence in an attractive lyric (205–12).

Formally speaking, the dramaturgy here is most unusual. There are three participants in the movement: Medea (offstage) with two passages in sung ("lyric" or "melic") anapaests, the Nurse in three passages of spoken anapaests, and the Chorus in four rather beautiful stanzas in a mixture of lyric meters (dactylic, aeolic and iambic).[6] Of these only the middle two are in strophic correspondence, the two outer ones are free-standing; moreover the first three *begin* in anapaests, which has a dovetailing effect with the utterances of the two soloists. Indeed, it seems probable that the Chorus's physical entrance was made along one of the *eisodoi* during the Nurse's final anapaests in the Prologue,[7] so that there was no break at all in the flow of speech at a major and normal dividing point (after 130). <TRACK H2, lines 132–58> ⊙

I suspect that we here have a deliberately contrived effect which serves three purposes. First, the anapaestic dovetailing establishes the Chorus less as a detached body, but more as a group of sympathetic women *involved* as community representatives in Medea's plight – an important signal to the male audience. Second, the alternation of the Chorus with two soloists (one offstage, the other on) is in itself unsettling and maintains the emotional temperature at a high level until 189, after which it drops with the Nurse's curious digression (190–203) on music's uselessness.[8] Finally, the seamless continuity of Prologue and Parodos makes Medea's entry all the more striking as her actual appearance at the *skênê* doors *could* be followed by a long pause, while the audience waits to hear what she will say after her offstage buildup, when the pipe has ceased its accompaniment.

First Episode (214–409)

This movement, like the Prologue, falls into three sections. Medea's confrontation with Creon is central and framed by two long speeches for the protagonist.

Medea's Rhesis to the Chorus (214–66)

After Medea's buildup through her offstage cries and the Nurse's description of her savage temper, Euripides gives us a further surprise with the cool and calm formality of this address to the women of Corinth. It is a carefully constructed rhesis, the object of which is to persuade Medea's audience to keep silent if she can find a means of punishing Jason for his wrong to her. This is, of course, essential to the plot. Euripides wants Medea to reveal her machinations to his own audience and the Chorus cannot be allowed to interfere with their execution. He ensures this complicity by making Medea appeal for their sympathy as women.

Rhetorical technique is evident from the outset in Medea's conciliatory introduction: she has come out of doors, because she does not want to appear "stuck up" and knows she must conform to people's prejudices. <TRACK H3, lines 214–29> ⓞ Particularly interesting are her detailed description of women's position in society, that is the society of contemporary Athens, and her famous counter to the argument that women live safely at home, while men fight in war: "I would rather stand three times in the battle line than give birth once" (250–1). Then the peroration: "In other ways a woman is full of fear, not brave like a soldier, but when she is wronged in the matter of *bed*, no mind is more murderous (lit. blood-polluted)." Euripides has used this important speech to emphasize – to his male audience – that women have their own point of view and their own ways of reacting to injury in love.

Medea's Confrontation with Creon (271–356)[9]

At this point Medea is shown in the first of her encounters with men. The king of Corinth is evidently frightened of her, as he betrays in the peremptory tone in which he orders her and the children – to go into exile *immediately*. We watch with fascination as Medea skillfully prevails with ease, weaving disingenuous arguments to counter Creon's suspicions, falling at his feet in ritual supplication and wearing him down in one of the play's four passages of stichomythia. She implores him for one day's grace for the children's sake. This resonates with him (see 329) and he gives way, though he sees that he is making a mistake (350)! By her force of personality, Medea has manipulated her adversary to her own will.

Medea's Declaration of Intent (358–409)

In a few transitional anapaests the Coryphaeus asks where she can turn in her desperate plight. Her grand rhesis in response establishes her as a figure of almost demonic stature. She announces that the extra day will allow her to make three corpses, father, daughter and husband – no mention of the children yet, and Jason's death is included. <TRACK H4, lines 364–75> ⓞ Carefully she debates the best method and settles on poison; then she considers the need for sanctuary after her crime. The climax to the speech (395–405) is deeply sinister, like Lady Macbeth's invocation of the powers of darkness. The resonances in her earlier speech of women expected to be submissive, domestic creatures are totally belied. "Though most helpless in good deeds, of every evil they are the cleverest *tektones*, craftsmen." In her aggressive plan for revenge and refusal to be mocked by her enemies, Medea is claiming to be as powerful as a man and makes her exit on that note.

First Stasimon (410–45)

The pipe starts up again and the Chorus now comes into its own for its first independent song, in two pairs of strophes. The first catches the mood of Medea's menacing triumph: rivers are turning back in their course, men are proved crafty perjurers and honor is now coming to the race of women! The dactylo-epitrite meter associated with Pindar's victory odes perfectly expresses the feeling of women on the march. <TRACK H5, lines 411–20> ◉ The subject matter changes in the second pair, moving from the general to the particular. The themes are Medea's dishonored exile in a foreign country with no refuge to turn to and Jason's broken oaths. The meter soon shifts to the lilting aeolic phrases heard earlier in the Parodos and which evoke a degree of pathos.[10] <TRACK H6, lines 439–45> ◉ Sympathy with Medea is maintained, but the song's emphasis on broken oaths proves the context for the central scene of the play which follows.

Second Episode (446–626)

The confrontation between Jason and Medea is a great movement, though not one in which the plot is advanced. It takes the form of an *agôn* or debate in three long set speeches which express the two characters' clashing viewpoints. Here we have Euripides' take on the battle of the sexes and the episode is particularly interesting for its presentation of Jason, the next of the poet's surprises.

In his opening speech (446–64), the glamorous hero turns out to be unbearably self-righteous and patronizing as he commends his own tolerance of Medea's anger and generosity in his practical concern for his family's arrangements in exile. No wonder that Medea explodes with "You lowest of the low!" in the first words of her long reply (465–519), in which she attacks him for his shamelessness, ingratitude for her help in winning the golden fleece, and after that his broken oaths and betrayal in taking a new wife when she herself had borne him children. <TRACK H7, lines 465–91> ◉ Jason's unfazed reply at equal length (522–75) is as self-revealing as his first speech. He only owes gratitude to Aphrodite who *forced* Medea to fall in love with him; Medea now enjoys all the advantages of Greek civilization and is consequently more famous than she would have been, at the back of beyond, in Colchis. <TRACK H8, lines 522–44> ◉

He goes on to argue that his new marriage, in the difficult circumstances, is a blessing to them all – "now keep your cool!" (550). (A rare moment in Greek tragedy where the text specifically indicates a reaction in the middle of a rhesis; Medea is obviously about to fly at Jason.) "You women," he concludes, "are so dependent on your sex-life for your happiness. Things would be so much easier if children could be born some other way!" (569–75). In all this

Jason's predominating quality, his insensitivity, is apparent and the speech can be seen as a powerful satire on male chauvinism.

After the heavier fire of the long speeches, Medea and Jason continue to snipe at one another in shorter ones of varying length. The scene ends with Jason insisting that he is doing his best to be helpful and Medea sending him packing. She probably remains onstage for the ode that follows.

Second Stasimon (629–62)

The second choral song follows a similar pattern to the first. Strophic pair A looks back and is more of a general reflection: pair B particularizes Medea's predicament and looks forward. Looking back is the prayer to Aphrodite that she will bestow love in moderation and preserve the women from the infidelity and quarrelling which ruin marriage. In the second pair a return to the theme of Medea's loneliness prepares for the entrance of Aegeus, king of Athens, who will offer her the sanctuary she needs after she has carried out her murderous designs.

The respective meters of A and B again involve a contrast between dactylo-epitrites and aeolics. The sensuous musical measures come as something of a relief after the bitter wrangling of the *agôn*. <TRACK H9, lines 629–35 and 645–53> ⓞ

Third Episode (663–823)

In her encounter with Aegeus, as in the scene with Creon, Medea uses her wits and personality to manipulate a man in authority – though where Creon was suspicious, Aegeus is trusting. The scenes mirror each other in including visual acts of ritual supplication.

In a long passage of stichomythia Aegeus reveals that he has come to Corinth on a journey from Delphi, where he has consulted the oracle about a remedy for childlessness but received an obscure reply. Medea in her turn informs Aegeus of her own impending exile and then supplicates him for protection in Athens in return for a promise that by her medicines she can give him the children he wants. Aegeus agrees, and Medea makes him swear an oath by Earth and Sun which guarantees her a home in Athens.

This scene falls at the play's halfway mark and is in rather a lower key than what has come earlier, though the supplication and solemn oath-taking lend it some dramatic impressiveness. After Aegeus' departure (763) Medea breaks into another burst of terrifying triumph and, from now on, the audience is given little opportunity to relax. She outlines what she now proposes: She will pretend to make up her quarrel with Jason and ask him to get the sentence of exile on the children remitted, by using them to deliver the present of a poisoned robe and crown to his new bride.

At this point (790–3) Euripides drops his bombshell. Medea announces that she will kill her children, to complete her destruction of Jason's house before she leaves the land. This is the main dramatic surprise which the poet has carefully saved up, though he has prepared for it by bringing on the children in the Prologue. Furthermore, the significance of children generally as an aspect of male status has been foreshadowed in all of the scenes with Creon, Jason and Aegeus. This ultimate horror is to be the climax of Euripides' tragedy in showing the extreme limits to which injured love can go. As Medea points out to the protesting Coryphaeus, this is how she can most hurt Jason (817).

The scene ends with an instruction to an attendant to fetch Jason and a timely reminder to the Chorus to keep their promised silence. Medea, once again, probably remains onstage.[11]

Third Stasimon (824–65)

While the audience awaits Jason's arrival, Euripides treats it to a peculiar beautiful choral song, once more in two pairs of strophes, each of which takes up a theme from the preceding episode. The first offers a certain relief from tension and takes its cue from Aegeus in a sensuously lovely hymn to Athens, which must surely have appealed to Euripides' public. The city is praised in language drawn from mythology and nature for its wisdom and culture. The *Erôtes*, Loves, are companions to Wisdom and work together for all kinds of excellence. This appears to suggest that at Athens there exists a constructive harmony between passion and understanding, in which human sexuality is sublimated in the pursuits of the arts and philosophy. We have certainly seen sexual love (a major theme of the preceding stasimon) and wisdom (in the sense of cleverness or skill) working together in Medea – but for thoroughly evil ends. There is thus a disturbing mismatch between what Athens represents and Medea's admission there for sanctuary. The meter is again dactylo-epitrite. <TRACK H10, lines 824–32>

It therefore makes sense for the Chorus to ask in the second pair of strophes, now in shorter and more urgent aeolic phrases, how Athens will receive her, the child-murderess, and then turning upstage to plead with her not to go through with her appalling intention. Euripides is no longer using his chorus to establish sympathy for Medea but to emphasize the horror of the dreadful revenge that Jason's betrayal has provoked her to. <TRACK H11, lines 846–55>

Fourth Episode (866–975)

The ensuing scene is a brilliant piece of theatrical writing and merits a full account.

Jason enters in response to Medea's summons and the tone of his speech is, as at his earlier entrance, self-righteously obliging. Medea is now at her most beguiling as she pretends to apologize for her earlier behavior and agrees to cooperate in Jason's new marriage. She acts her part to perfection, while the audience who knows the game she is playing watches in fascination. At 894 she calls the children out of doors to embrace their father and to join in the feigned reconciliation. They run across to take Jason's hand and, at this touching domestic reunion, Euripides makes Medea's own nerve crack. She bursts into tears at the thought of the crime she is going to commit and explains it away as emotion inspired by the ending of her quarrel with Jason (899–905) – a wonderful human touch which prepares for Medea's anguished debate with herself in the following scene.

Jason is completely taken in and reacts in a kindly, if still patronizing, way. He becomes almost attractive as he talks to his boys and prays that they will grow up to be sturdy young men, superior to his enemies (he sees his children as extensions of himself, but this is very Greek and very real). The passage (914–21) in turn anticipates the sympathy which Euripides will want to bring to Jason in the closing scene. Once again, at 922, Medea turns away in tears and explains this to Jason as pity for the children's uncertain future. This leads her to suggest that he should ask Creon to allow the boys to stay when she goes into exile. He must coax his new wife into appealing to her father on their behalf, and she herself will help by sending Glauce some specially beautiful presents.

An attendant is sent quickly to fetch the robe out of the house, and Medea gives the boys their instructions for delivering "these bridal gifts" (956), presumably contained in some kind of casket. There is a moment of delightful suspense when Jason, in a nice touch of vanity, protests: "This is quite unnecessary; I'm sure she'll listen to *me*." But Medea prevails with a deliciously arch rejoinder: "No, dear, please!"[12] Gold is better than innumerable words. *Hers* is the luck." There is a glorious kind of nervous exhilaration in the ironies and short phrases of Medea's speech which brings this enthralling scene to its climax and the exit of all but the Women of Corinth and Medea herself, who again remains in the background.

Fourth Stasimon (976–1001)

The Chorus advances for their next song, again in two strophic pairs but rather shorter ones. The first words are of the children going to their death. This could be playing on a traditional expectation that the Corinthians rather than Medea would kill the boys (see p. 144) and that they may not be seen again (Mossman 2011, 310). Tension is certainly mounting high as Glauce is pictured delightedly putting on the poisoned robe and crown.

In the second pair of strophes the pace is maintained, but the mood shifts, first towards compassion for Jason who has procured the death of his children and new bride, and come to such an unheroic ending (995), and then for Medea herself in the grief she will feel for murdering her children because Jason has betrayed her in love. The rhythm is, I believe, rapid-moving to express agitation, mostly in dactylo-epitrites but with some other metrical units in pair B.[13] <TRACK H12, lines 976–81 and 991–5> ◉

Fifth Episode (1002–250)

This movement can be broken down into four sections:

Medea and the Pedagogue (1002–20)

The choral song leads at once into an excited entrance as the Pedagogue returns – with the children. Medea's gifts have been accepted and the children reprieved! But then he sights Medea who is standing unresponsive to his good news (1005), with face downcast and tears in her eyes (1012). The mood suddenly changes as uncomprehendingly he tries to comfort her[14] before she send him back indoors (1019–20).

Medea's Monologue (1021–80)

Now for the first time Medea is alone with the children (we forget the Chorus for the time being) and there follows the famous speech which shows her torn between two powerful conflicting emotions: her love for her children and her desire to spite Jason. Though the latter eventually wins, Euripides allows her to give full expression to the gentler maternal feelings which she has so far controlled, with difficulty. The trials of bearing and rearing the children were all in vain. She movingly articulates the family rituals she will no longer be involved in; and there is almost unbearable poignancy at the end when she takes their hands to kiss them and feel the softness of their cheeks (1071–2, 1074–5). All this contrasts strongly with the quasi-heroic hardening of heart at 1049–50 in the thought that her enemies must not go unpunished to laugh at her. After her final words of tenderness to her children, she sends them emotionally indoors, saying, "I cannot look at them but am overcome by anguish!" (1076–7). <TRACK H13, lines 1064–77> ◉ The speech could end there with Medea sinking to the ground in despair. If so, Euripides is maintaining suspense by ending the rhesis on a note of uncertainty: could the children *still* be spared?[15]

Anapaests for Coryphaeus (1081–115)

Some dividing material is needed here to separate Medea's monologue from the Messenger scene, but the final choral buildup to the children's murder is yet to come. Respite is required before the next assault on the audience's emotion. Hence an anapaestic passage in a much lower key, probably delivered by the Chorus Leader.

The argument and its dry tone, though, are distinctly puzzling: it is better not to have children at all, because of all the trouble and disappointment they can give to parents – this in a drama which has stressed the emotional and social importance of children, above all in the moving monologue that has just been performed! There may be a clue to this in the strangely long preamble (1081–9), which asserts that *some* women, one among many maybe, are not totally uncultured. This might be understood as subverting the conventional stereotype of women in contemporary male society at Athens. Similarly, the suggestion that children are not worth parents' effort could be seen as a challenge to the male chauvinism which perceives children as essentially there to do their father's credit. It is nonetheless easy to find the change of tone in this satirical "filler" unsatisfactory, even in Euripides.

The Messenger Scene (1116–250)

Medea, whom we may imagine as collapsed on the ground during the Coryphaeus' homily, now rises to her feet: she has long been awaiting news and now can hail the arrival, in hot haste, of one of Jason's servants as the inevitable Messenger. "Flee, Medea!" he urges dramatically, "by any means of sea or land transport that you can." The following lines return in tone to the malevolent, vindictive Medea who requires the Messenger to take his time in describing the deaths of Glauce and Creon – the more agonizing, the better!

Medea's hopes and, doubtless, the audience's expectations are not confounded by the brilliant narrative that follows. The graphic and gruesome detail speaks for itself. No punches are pulled and our withers cannot but be wrung by this great speech for a powerful actor. The recording gives the picture of Glauce delightedly putting on the poisoned robe, with the appalling consequence. <TRACK H14, lines 1156–80> ◉ No less horrific is the description of the bride's father with his flesh being torn away by contact with the robe (1211–17). After the speaker has made his exit with the conventional comments on the shadowiness of human existence, Medea finally confirms her resolve to kill the children and leave the land as soon as possible – she does not say how. She steels herself to perform her frightful deed, to stifle her love for her children and lament them later. But Euripides gives her a sympathetic exit line, "I (am an) unhappy *woman*!"

Fourth Stasimon, Incorporating the Death of Medea's Children (1251–91)

The Chorus sweeps forward for their final song, which is an impassioned plea to Earth and Sun to regard Medea and restrain her from killing Helios' descendants. The meter is now the agitated dochmiac (see Appendix B), which Euripides likes to use at moments of high excitement, particularly to precede a murder at the climax of a play.[16] Antistrophe A challenges Medea herself: "Your birth pangs were in vain, you who left the mouth of the Clashing Rocks [cf. 2]. Why has your anger led you to incur such pollution?" <TRACK H15, lines 1251–60> ◉

Strophe B incorporates the children's offstage iambic death cries within the metrical structure, as the Chorus reacts in further dochmiacs. The stylization here calls for careful treatment in performance, but the moment should be a terrible one. In the antistrophe the Chorus reinforces their sense of horror by quoting the only parallel they know, Ino, another mother who killed her children and was related to Jason.[17] The final sentence deplores the trouble caused by "women's bed" in further emphasis of this major theme.

Exodos (1293–419)

The closing scene has a strong beginning with Jason tearing on to rescue his children from the angry Corinthians after the death of Glauce and Creon, only to be told that Medea has killed them too. He calls on the servants to let him into the house to see his little boys' bodies, and all eyes in the ancient theater will have been focused at this point on the doors of the *skênê*, in the expectation of the *ekkyklêma* emerging with the children's corpses displayed and, probably, Medea standing over them, sword in hand. Instead, Euripides offers his final surprise, as we hear a voice – from on high. The poet has used his other available piece of stage machinery, the *mêchanê*, to suspend Medea, as though she were a god, on the *skênê* roof. She appears aloft in the chariot drawn by winged serpents that belongs to her grandfather Helios, the sun god, and the dead bodies of her children are there beside her. Her escape to Athens is not to be by sea or land, as suggested by the Messenger (1122–3), but through the air, and all Jason can do is to revile her from below.

This is an astonishing coup de théâtre, but it has been well prepared for by the previous references to Helios (406, 746, 752, 764, 954, 1252). Euripides has also associated the Sun with Earth among the chief deities invoked during the play (148, 746, 752, 1251–2). These are the elemental powers in the universe which correspond to the two strands of deities in Greek religion, the Olympian and the chthonian, the former essentially male-oriented, the latter female-based (p. 34). The association is entirely appropriate to a play about elemental forces in human nature which relate to the polarity of the sexes. If the sky can be regarded as the masculine domain, then Medea on the roof in the sun's chariot has triumphantly usurped it. Moreover, though she herself remains human and not a god, we can view the use of the *deus ex machina* convention as an apotheosis of the *thumos*, the angry energy, which Medea has exemplified in her demonstration of the destructive, uncontrollable nature of human passion when released in the story that the audience has witnessed.

Anger, indeed, dominates the rest of the play. Visually, Jason and Medea are inexorably separated, he below and she on top in more than physical superiority. Jason's long speech reviling her (1323–50) is of no avail. Medea's answer (1351–60) is that Zeus, the god of the sky, is on her side. The argument continues powerfully in a stichomythic slanging-match (1361–77), at the end of which Jason implores to be allowed to bury his sons' bodies and lament them. Once again he loses. Medea will take the corpses to the shrine of Hera in Corinth and bury them there, to protect their graves. Future rituals involving a solemn procession at Corinth will serve to atone for this impious murder.[18] After that she will go on to live with Aegeus at Athens, while Jason will die an unhappy death, struck on the head by a fragment of the Argo.

At 1389 the tension is heightened for the final exchange as the adversaries launch into ana-paests. Jason asks to kiss his children's lips and touch their soft skin (we remember Medea's monologue, 1071 and 1075), but Medea's final riposte is that words are wasted. As Jason calls the gods to witness his sufferings at the hands of "this lioness," we may at least feel a little sym-pathy for the man whose insensitivity to a woman's feelings has cost him everything which give his life either status or emotional meaning. <TRACK H16, lines 1389–414> ◉ The feeling will be intensified at the dialogue's end when Medea, with the children's bodies, is hoisted away through the air and Jason makes his lonely, humiliated, earthbound exit down one of the *eisodoi*.

To round off the play the Chorus, or its Leader, comments on the unexpectedness of human life in lines which also occur at the end of four other Euripidean tragedies.[19] Scholars have tended to reject this conventional tailpiece as unsuitable in *Medea*; but the lines are certainly consistent with what would have struck Euripides' male audience as a disturbingly, if not shockingly, paradoxical conclusion to his play.

Conclusion

The play well illustrates Euripides' subversive approach to conventional thinking. If Thomas Middleton wrote a play called *Women, Beware Women*, *Medea* might well be subtitled "Men, Beware Women." It certainly is the perfect "gender studies" text in the Greek tragic corpus. From a dramatic angle, Euripides shows remarkable skill in manipulating his audience's sym-pathy: Medea, for all her terrifying vindictiveness, has a valid point of view; while Jason's punishment for his dreadful insensitivity is allowed a degree of pathos at the end. At the same time, the poet uses the tragic medium to produce a drama that is very tightly structured, packed with surprises and riveting throughout, except in a few curious passages where he judged that his audience needed a rest.

Notes

1 The Symplegades are mentioned later on at 211–12 (by implication), then at 434–5 and 1263–4.
2 Pace Mastronarde (2002). I should be sorry if the Greek word simply meant "running around."
3 This is indicated by the Doric forms (see Appendix B and p. 2).
4 See note 8.
5 The passage is strange because in other sources the power of music to heal *is* acknowledged. For a possible dramatic explanation see note 8.
6 Particularly attractive is the repetition of the lilting 'hagesichorean' plus rest at 151–3 (=176–8) and again at 156–7 (=181–2).
7 See note 8.

8 A deliberate drop in tension is the only way in which I can make sense of 190–203, but see Mossman (2011) and Mastronarde (2002) ad loc. (A modern director would probably wish to cut the passage.) I am tempted to give a similar reason for the flatness of 119–30: the lines can safely be "killed" by the movement of the entering Chorus.

9 Lines 355–6 may well be spurious (see Mossman 2011).

10 The recording follows the alternative metrical analysis given in Mastronarde (2012, 240). Hagesichoreans with rests are greatly to be preferred to repeated line divisions in mid-word that are both suspect in themselves and musically very dull.

11 For opposing views on the staging here see Mastronarde (2002) and Mossman (2011). On balance I think it more effective for Medea to be actually present in the background for the Chorus to turn upstage and plead with her.

12 Line 964, *me moi su.* The little colloquialism is perfect.

13 The final line (995 = 1001) is a syncopated iambic trimeter, which may in Aeschylean fashion reflect the implication of the words that Jason has got his comeuppance.

14 Students who know ancient Greek will appreciate the ironies of 1015–16.

15 I think that Mossman (2011) is right to athetize 1056–63 and 1078–80 as actors' interpolations. Both passages present real problems of language and sense. Two advantages follow from the excisions: the first is that the children's fate remains uncertain; the second that Medea now hardens her heart only once rather than twice (as she would if 1056–63 were retained as genuine), and this makes the speech more compellingly real, less artificially rhetorical, like Ovid's several imitations of it in his *Metamorphoses.*

16 The meter is similarly used in both of the other Euripides plays examined in this book (*El.* 1147–62, *Ba.* 977–1023).

17 See Mossman (2011, 351–2) for the choice of Ino rather than Procne who would have offered a closer mythological parallel.

18 In establishing a cult, Medea is behaving more like a goddess than a human being. Euripides is also offering a novel aetiology for a cult associated with Medea's children which certainly existed at Corinth until 146 BC. It seems originally to have been an atonement ritual based on a tradition that Medea's children were killed by the Corinthians, which would explain why Euripides has played with that possibility in the drama (see Mossman 2011, 365).

19 *Alcestis, Andromache, Helen* and *Bacchae.*

References

Text: *Euripides Medea* (Loeb edition, Vol. 1). Cambridge, MA: Harvard University Press, edited and translated by David Kovacs.

Easterling, P.E. 1977. "The Infanticide in Euripides' *Medea*." *Yale Classical Studies* 25, 177–91, reprinted in J. Mossman (ed.) 2003. *Oxford Readings in Euripides*. Oxford: Oxford University Press.

Mastronarde, Donald, J. 2002. *Euripides: Medea*. Cambridge: Cambridge University Press.

Mossman, J. 2011. *Euripides: Medea*. Warminster: Aris & Phillips.

Commentaries

Mastronarde, Donald, J. 2002. *Euripides: Medea*. Cambridge: Cambridge University Press.

Mossman, J. 2011. *Euripides: Medea*. Warminster: Aris & Phillips.

11

Electra (Euripides)

Introduction

As we have seen, both Antigone and Sophocles treated the story of Orestes' revenge on his mother for the murder of his father as exemplifying the tragic situation of a justice which depends on self-help and calls for further retribution in turn. Aeschylus conceived the continuing chain of crime and punishment as resolvable in the juridical systems of organized society; Sophocles in his *Electra* explored the tragically destructive effect on the personalities of individuals involved in the process.

Euripides' *Electra* is also concerned with individuals but focuses less on revenge in general as on matricide as such. He evidently could not accept the Aeschylean paradox that a crime of such enormity could also be a duty ordained by a god. The play's marked intertextuality with the *Oresteia* makes it clear that he was establishing his own independent line on the myth; he used the tragic medium to express an unqualified horror of matricide and to explore the sort of people who could be brought to commit such an atrocity. In doing this he appears to have assumed some acquaintance with the *Oresteia* in the Athenian audience, such as might have been afforded by a fairly recent revival of Aeschylus' Trilogy at the festival.[1]

Euripides' down-to-earth treatment of his myth makes this play very unusual in terms of tragic norms. The first part of it, at least, has a domestic atmosphere which contrasts sharply with the heroic world of most Greek tragedies. The drama involves strong contrasts in tone: the poet is happy to introduce a good deal of comedy into his presentation and to play tricks with the conventions of tragedy, while contriving a climax and closing scene that are filled with pathos.

The play's date is uncertain, but metrical features suggest one between 422 and 417, with 420 or 419 statistically the most likely (see Cropp 2013, 31–3 for an exhaustive discussion). The play has no obvious political overtones which could suggest otherwise. If this is correct, Euripides' *Electra* probably predates Sophocles'. For the main outlines of the myth see on the *Oresteia* (p. 33).

Synopsis

The play is set in the mountain countryside outside the city of Argos and the *skênê* represents the humble dwelling of the peasant farmer to whom Electra has been married off by Aegisthus. Orestes, accompanied by Pylades, returns incognito to meet his sister before carrying out

Greek Tragedies as Plays for Performance, First Edition. David Raeburn.
© 2017 John Wiley & Sons, Inc. Published 2017 by John Wiley & Sons, Inc.
Companion website: www.wiley.com/go/raeburn

Apollo's command. Hesitation over his matricidal mission makes the recognition between brother and sister slow to come about. Murders are eventually plotted and executed: Aegisthus is killed while performing a sacrifice, Clytemnestra is lured by a trick to Electra's house. After their mother's murder, Orestes and Electra are united in their shared remorse but immediately forced to separate by their different destinies as revealed by the god Castor.

Interpretation

Like Sophocles' *Electra*, Euripides' play has attracted conflicting interpretations.[2] twentieth-century scholars (notably Knox 1979) have tended to emphasize the poet's critical approach to received myth and remarked on the play's realism and satirical tone. They see Euripides treating Clytemnestra's murder as unequivocally nasty and even presenting Aegisthus' demise as discreditable; moreover, both of Agamemnon's assassins are invested with redeeming features. Fundamental to this view is the characterization of Orestes and Electra: the former is a reluctant hero who wishes to postpone the execution of his matricidal mission for as long as possible and is only driven to it by his forcefully vindictive sister. Electra herself is morbidly embittered by her degraded circumstances and presented unsympathetically until the closing scene when she is shown shattered by remorse. Such, says Euripides, are the sort of people who would kill their mothers in real life and that is how they would feel afterwards. This interpretation accords well not only with the domestic atmosphere but also with Euripides' delight in surprise and paradox; it is outlined in the analysis that follows.

Some modern scholars (e.g. Lloyd 1986, and to some extent Cropp 2013) have been unhappy with an interpretation which is felt to savor too much of modern psychology. Electra's self-pitying postures are to be explained in terms of Greek conventions of lament; while Orestes is seen as cautious rather than indecisive, and his long delay in revealing himself to Electra is a device to increase dramatic tension. Dramatic analysis, however, suggests that this is a play of exceptional sophistication and subtlety. The characterization is elaborate but not deployed for its own sake, as in a modern play. It is integral to Euripides' treatment of his myth.

Dramaturgy

Structurally, the play falls, like *Choephori*, into the three phases of preparation, murder and aftermath. The first of these is very largely directed to the exposition of Electra's and Orestes' character; the second draws its power not from fast-moving action, as in Aeschylus and Sophocles, but more from narrative description and rhetorical rhesis; the final phase, absent in Sophocles, does refer to Orestes' pursuit by the Furies but makes much more of the human revulsion which vengeful murder can inspire in its perpetrators after the event.

The list of dramatis personae is illuminating. Electra's peasant farmer husband is a peculiarly delightful creation, as is the old shepherd who was Agamemnon's pedagogue, introduced to effect the long-delayed recognition between Orestes and Electra. Clytemnestra is far from the formidably masculine character the audience could have remembered from Aeschylus' *Agamemnon*; she is presented almost sympathetically. (Aegisthus is not brought onstage but described quite favorably in the Messenger speech which portrays his sacrilegious murder.) For his *deux ex machina*, Euripides chooses Castor (accompanied by Polydeuces/Pollux), one of Clytemnestra's brothers in the myth, to voice a thinly veiled criticism of Apollo, whose oracle instructed Orestes to kill his mother. For all these roles Euripides used his third actor to remarkably varied and lively effect.

The Chorus of young Mycenaean women, who represent Electra's local community in the mountains, is used first to highlight Electra's attitude and behavior, rather as in Sophocles. In their two central songs, by contrast, they take the audience into a world of romanticized mythology which throws the dominant earthiness of the play's tone into high relief. This is a particularly good example of the tragic poets' flexibility in their use of the chorus.

Tragedy's formal characteristics of rhesis and stichomythia are used with the mastery of a mature artist. The long dialogue between Orestes and Electra in the first episode can be singled out as a peculiarly brilliant use of the stichomythic form to articulate the characterization of Clytemnestra's murderers; while the rhetorical techniques of the Sophists feature importantly in Electra's vitriolic address to Aegisthus' corpse and in the *agôn* between herself and Clytemnestra.

The stage-building in this play does not represent the usual palace frontage but Electra's humble house in the wilds (168). How this was indicated we can only guess; Cropp (2013) suggests some painting or draping of the *skênê* to suggest a cottage. This does not preclude the use of the *mêchanê* for the divine appearance at the play's end.

One other feature of Euripides' dramaturgy needs highlighting: his use of stage properties not so much as adventitious touches for the sake of realism but as emphasizing the various themes which underlie his basic treatment of the story in his drama.[3]

Dramatic Analysis

Line numbers refer to the Greek text in the Loeb edition (see end of this chapter), which has a parallel English translation. For the terminology of the discrete movements, see Appendix A; for the lyric structure and meters, see Appendix B or hear TRACK 0. 🔘

Prologue (1–111)

The opening scene falls, as in *Medea*, into three distinct sections. These merit a rather full and detailed description as they offer the clues to Euripides' highly original approach and well illustrate the drama's unusual tone.

Opening Rhesis (1–53)

The play opens, as normal in Euripides, with a monologue from a character who does not immediately introduce himself. Line 1 tells us that we are in Argos, from where Agamemnon sailed to Troy and returned after sacking the city, only to be murdered by Clytemnestra and Aegisthus, who is now king. So far, so familiar. Agamemnon's children come next. Orestes was stolen away to be reared in Phocis by his father's old tutor. If Euripides' *Electra* precedes Sophocles', this may be a new detail in the story; it is important as this tutor is to feature later on. Electra's background is more elaborately delineated: when she reached puberty, her hand in marriage was sought by the leading princes in Greece, but Aegisthus was afraid she would bear a noble son to avenge Agamemnon, so he plotted to kill her; but her mother, "cruel though she was," rescued her daughter from a fate which, unlike her husband's murder, could not be publicly justified.

All this is new stuff. Who *is* this speaker? And how will he continue? Aegisthus now put a price on Orestes' head and gave Electra to *himself* to have as his wife. He, we are told at last, is Electra's impoverished husband, chosen so that his feeble social standing would weaken Aegisthus' fears of revenge. What is more, he has respected Electra's virginity, as his own lowly position and respect for Orestes require. "If anyone calls me stupid for that, his moral standards are rotten and he is just as stupid as I!" (50–3)

Electra's situation is now clear: she has been married off to a social inferior, who may be thoroughly decent but whose means are severely constrained. Deprived of her royal status, she is living in a humiliating marriage which has left her childless and condemned her to a life of poverty. Moreover, the final lines of the Peasant's monologue have been expressed in a tone that engages the audience in an intimate way, more comic than tragic, and helps to establish the world of this play and the down-to-earth treatment of the story.

Electra's Entry and Exchange with the Peasant (54–81)

The Peasant fades into the background as Electra emerges from the central entrance, dressed in a ragged costume (185, 304) and carrying a water-pitcher on her head like a slave or peasant woman. "O black night, nurse of golden stars!" she begins in a grandiose invocation which, apart from indicating the time, is a conventional prelude to some kind of indignant outpouring and characterizes the stagey posturing with which Euripides wants to associate his heroine. Almost at once she undercuts herself: she does not really *need* to fetch water from the river herself, but she wants the gods to be aware of Aegisthus' *hubris* and Clytemnestra's monstrous behavior in expelling her and Orestes from their house (57–63). Is Electra's demonstration with her waterpot perhaps a little contrived? <TRACK J1, lines 54–63> ◉

Her husband advances to remonstrate: this drudgery on his behalf is beneath her and unnecessary. But Electra's reply makes it clear that she is determined to go ahead with her demonstration and is quite capable of finding an excellent alternative reason for doing so: her husband has been so kind to her, and she must do her bit to help! His response, though, shows that he has her measure: "Well, go if you like! It's not far to the stream" (77–8). Electra departs in silence and her husband goes off to begin the sowing.

Orestes' Opening Rhesis (82–111)

Enter Orestes, accompanied as usual by Pylades, and probably, a couple of attendants carrying baggage who are needed later (360). This entrance contrasts strongly with that of the Sophoclean Orestes who walks confidently into the city, all ready to engage in the deception which will lead on to his nasty work. This one is timid and furtive: Euripides' Orestes is hanging round the borders of the country so that he can slip quickly across the frontier if he is recognized (95–7). The syntax of 86–7 betrays his deep uneasiness over his matricidal mission.[4] He explains to Pylades that he needs to meet Electra, as in Aeschylus (though not in Sophocles), and get her help in the plan. Then, as dawn starts to break, he sights a woman with shorn hair whom he takes to be a slave as she is carrying a water-pitcher. The two men crouch down at one side.

Electra's Monody (112–66) and Parodos (167–212)

The entrance of the Chorus is preceded, as in Sophocles, by a monody for Electra, which takes the form of a self-pitying lament. It involves the ritual gesture of cheek-tearing and head-beating with her hands, so she carefully plants her water-pot – the symbol of her self-martyrdom – on the ground to make this possible (140). She prays for Orestes' return, but more to rescue herself from her miserable existence (130–6) than to avenge his father's murder (137–8). Two lines (125–6) oddly inserted into the strophic structure are particularly revealing:

> Come awaken the *same* lament,
> Lift up the *pleasure* of many tears.

"The same," no doubt, because it is being constantly renewed. The notion that tears are a pleasure, that is a relief, could be a conventional oxymoron but I have no doubt that Electra positively *enjoys* her tears.[5] There is a balancing insert (150–6) into the second strophic pair: this has Electra posturing as a swan moaning for her trapped father, which is similarly artificial and self-regarding.

Metrically the monody consists largely of four-pulse cola, with insistent anapaestic or dactylic units to introduce each one of the four strophic stanzas. (In the second pair I think that 140–9 is balanced by 157–66, rather than as printed in the Loeb text.) The rhythms suggest a spacious regularity and relentlessness behind the dirge being chanted. <TRACK J2, lines 112–26>

The choral entrance movement takes the form of an *amoibaion* (lyric exchange) of two strophes containing nine cola for the Chorus and fifteen for Electra. It is metrically similar to the monody and can be treated as an extension of it.

The Chorus consists of local unmarried girls who are excitedly on their way to join in the rituals of the temple of Hera, the goddess of marriage, and want Electra to join them. The situation points up the irony of Electra's awkward position as a married woman who is still a virgin, but she does not reject her peers' invitation because she is married. The tears that govern her life and her ragged clothes, so inappropriate to the daughter of Troy's conqueror, preclude her involvement. <TRACK J3, lines 167–89> "Borrow a dress and some jewelry from *me*," say the girls; but Electra will have none of that. She prefers her grievance to its solution – and the water-pot is still onstage to remind the audience of that.[6] The Chorus's remonstration that she will get further by honoring the gods rather than weeping is of no avail.

First Episode (213–431)

This long scene portrays the meeting of Orestes with Electra, during which her readiness to kill her mother is established (278–81) and he might then be fairly expected to reveal his identity. He does not do so and it takes another 300 lines, some fifteen to twenty minutes of stage-time, for the truth to emerge. The scene simply ends with the Peasant inviting the strangers indoors and being sent off by Electra to get food to entertain them. In this episode, Euripides uses stichomythia and rhesis with remarkable skill to illuminate and develop his portraiture of Orestes and Electra.

The opening lines show Electra in a preposterously melodramatic light. As Orestes and Pylades emerge from hiding, she at once supposes them to be violent criminals, out to murder and rape her. Euripides teases his audience by requiring the Chorus, who would normally remain in the *orchêstra* to the end of the play, to start running off in panic. When Orestes reassuringly explains that he has come to Electra with a message from her brother, her assumed terror is instantly transformed to exaggerated rapture (229, 231). <TRACK J4, lines 215–32>

This introduction sets the tone for the dialogue that follows (233–89). In a long passage of adversarial stichomythia, Electra and Orestes are subtly made to air their own egocentric preoccupations, she with her degraded plight and he with the miseries of exile and social embarrassment that his sister has been married off to a mere laborer. Of special note are the lines in which Electra refers scornfully to Orestes' continued absence (245, 263, 275). These serve as punctuation marks in the dialogue and require a pause before Orestes changes the subject. They also make it clear that this point is crucial in Electra's list of grievances.

At 276 Orestes tentatively raises the question of killing Agamemnon's murderers and Electra's attitude is unequivocal: she would happily slit her mother's throat – and die. The complicity of the Chorus has been established (272–3), so Orestes now has no reason to maintain his incognito. The only person, it emerges, who could recognize him is Agamemnon's old tutor who smuggled him away (285–7) – a clear sign to the audience that the recognition between Orestes and Electra will not be spontaneous but through a third party. Orestes' reluctance to kill his mother, coupled with Electra's bloodthirsty vindictiveness, will cause him to stall for as long as he can.

He therefore asks Electra to describe her sufferings so that he can relay them to Orestes. A long rhetorical rhesis follows (300–38), in which she catalogues her woes, among which Euripides makes her highlight her need to fetch water from the river and (in juxtaposition) her exclusion from festival rites *in successive lines* (309–10). <TRACK J5, lines 300–12> ◎ Among other things, she describes Aegisthus drunkenly jumping on Agamemnon's neglected grave, "as they say" (327), and so probably her own invention, then bitterly comes back to the theme of her brother's failure to return.

The Peasant's re-entrance at 339 provides a delightful return to domestic comedy. Electra has to explain the presence of strange young men at her door to her husband, who at once insists on offering them hospitality and ordering their attendants to take the baggage indoors.[7] But Euripides delays Orestes' exit by giving him a sententious rhesis (367–400) in which, inspired by the paradox of a humble peasant behaving so nobly, he discourses in sophistic mode on "How can you tell a good man?" Dramatically, this shows Orestes continuing to stall over revealing himself. It also ironically raises the question whether Orestes himself is a "good man" in the sense of a conventional hero who will not shirk the task of revenge on his foes.

At last, though, Orestes and Pylades go indoors with their luggage (see note 7) and the scene concludes with another amusing domestic exchange, in which Electra scolds her husband for inviting strangers in when they are so poor. She sends him off to fetch food from her father's old tutor and he makes his exit with a charming reflection (426–31) on the usefulness of money if one wants to entertain guests or pay the doctor's bill; otherwise, so long as one's belly's full, it does not count for much! On this very homely note, the long scene ends. With the Old Man's arrival the audience can look forward to the long-delayed recognition, but first the Chorus must have its turn.

First Stasimon (432–86)[8]

In an extraordinary contrast of tone, the Chorus in song and dance transports the audience into a totally different world. Kitchen sink yields to romanticized epic. The address is to the "famous ships" which once went to Troy, escorting the dancing sea-nymphs as dolphins leapt and swirled about the prows, and carrying the swift-footed Achilles on his way with

Agamemnon. Rhythm is beautifully employed in this song, with stately aeolics predominating in the first strophic pair. <TRACK J6, lines 432–41>

In Antistrophe A the subject changes to the Nereids who carried arms for Achilles from the fire-god Hephaestus over the mountains of Greece to Thessaly where the hero was being raised by Chiron the centaur. In the second pair of strophes the depictions embossed on the various arms are described – not the peaceful scenes from daily life that Homer contrives for Achilles' shield in the *Iliad* but Perseus flying over the sea with the Gorgon's head in his hand, then other monstrous images which mark a progression from the tranquillity of Nereids and dolphins to something more sinister and horrible. Here the meter includes some running dactyls and launches very delightfully into triple-time ionics for the flying Perseus image (460–2 = 473–5). <TRACK J7, lines 452–62>

Suddenly (479), the audience is jerked back in the epode from mythical fantasy to the play's realities: "It was a king of warriors such as this (Achilles) that you killed, Clytemnestra, and for whose death your own throat will soon be dripping with blood." This abrupt transition is powerfully marked by the entry of sharply insistent iambics. <TRACK J8, lines 477–86> The connection of thought may be tenuous but it is forceful enough. The ode is not after all a purely decorative insertion. The switch to high poetry has thrown the realistic, non-heroic tone into high relief and so emphasized Euripides' novel approach to the myth he is dramatizing.

Second Episode (487–698) The Recognition Scene[9]

Enter the Old Man whose arrival the audience has been awaiting in the expectation that this will lead to the long-delayed recognition of Orestes and Electra. He has stumbled up the mountain with bent back and tottering knee (489–92), carrying the food he has been asked to bring for the strangers: a newborn lamb, garlands, cheeses and a little vintage wine (494–9). With this remarkable entrance, we are back to the kitchen sink, and the props are Aristophanic in number. Given the rarity of props in Greek tragedy and their frequency in comedy (see note 3), this is a signal that the scene to come will be in deliberately comic vein.

After Electra has come out to meet the Old Man, a passage follows (508–46), on which much scholarship has been focused. The Old Man has visited Agamemnon's tomb, where he has sighted a lock of blonde hair which suggests that Orestes has returned and laid an offering. A footprint and a woven garment are also mentioned as possible recognition tokens – as indeed they are in Aeschylus' *Choephori*, with which this passage must be connected. Instead of welcoming these three tokens as evidence of Orestes' return, Electra is made to deride them with a mixture of valid and captious arguments. Some scholars, with varying degrees of tolerance, have treated this passage as essentially a gratuitous parody of Aeschylus, without necessarily observing that Electra's contemptuous rejection of the tokens is consistent with her characterization. She is resisting the conclusion that Orestes has returned because there is a real, though paradoxical, sense in which *she does not want him back*. His continued absence has been prominent in the list of grievances that have become her life, and we have twice (over the water-pot and the festival dress) seen her rejecting a solution to her grievances.[10]

At the end of a highly entertaining argument, at 548 the Old Man abruptly cuts it short and asks to *see* the strangers. Orestes and Pylades emerge on cue from the house and an extremely funny piece of stage business follows as the Old Man, to Orestes' obvious embarrassment, circles round him in scrutiny of his person. When he exultantly tells Electra to pray to the gods, she plays absurdly dumb, still resisting the obvious conclusion, while Orestes remains unhelpfully silent. She only yields when the Old Man has actually named Orestes and identified him by a scar on the forehead.[11] She has no choice now but to fling herself dramatically into Orestes' arms. The inevitable exchange in half-lines (*antilabê*) follows, though the lameness of the expression suggests modified rapture.

The scene is an outstanding example of Euripides' naughty subversion of tragedy's conventions (see Winnington-Ingram 1969). A recognition scene (*anagnorisis*) is a common feature of Greek tragedy, already seen in Aeschylus *Cho.* and in Sophocles *OT* and *El.* Here we have an "anti-recognition" between a character who does not want to be recognized and another who, for established psychological reasons, does not wish to recognize. It has taken a comic old figure to *force* them into it. As brother and sister at last embrace, the Chorus perhaps dances round them as they sing a short, almost perfunctory, hymn of joy (585–95) – in dochmiacs, naturally – to celebrate the day which has brought Orestes home. Orestes breaks away from Electra as soon as it is over (596–7).

The rest of the episode (598–698) is largely devoted to the planning of the separate murders of Aegisthus and Clytemnestra. In a long passage of stichomythia Orestes first consults the Old Man on how he can get access to kill Aegisthus; he himself is hopelessly lacking in ideas and it is left to the Old Man to suggest the details of a plan which will allow him to join the usurping king at a sacrifice outside the city where Clytemnestra will not be present. After 34 lines Orestes asks how he can kill both his targets together, and Electra suddenly breaks in with the blood-chilling "*I* shall arrange our mother's murder" (647). She now fills her brother's place in the stichomythic sequence while Orestes retreats. Electra, by contrast, knows exactly what is needed and gives the orders from now on: Clytemnestra must be lured to her house by a message that her daughter has produced a male child and needs her help with the postpartum rituals. First, though, the Old Man must put Orestes on his way. She turns to her brother (668): "The lots are drawn. Your turn comes first!" "I'll go", he replies, "if someone will show me the way" – an intriguing touch. Has he *heard* what has just been said, or been reflecting nervously on the heroic task ahead?

Now a sequence (671–84) which serves as the counterpart to Aeschylus' long lyric *kommos* in *Choephori* (301–478), designed to raise Agamemnon's ghost and the powers of the underworld to aid Orestes in his violent revenge. Euripides does it all in a brief stichomythic trio, with the Old Man serving in place of Aeschylus' Chorus. The episode ends with Electra giving Orestes a final exhortation: "Aegisthus is to die! I'll kill myself, if you fail" (685–7). The Old Man takes Orestes and Pylades on their way, and Electra exits into the *skênê* with instructions to the Chorus to signal her the result of the fight, while she waits, sword at the ready.

Second Stasimon (699–746)

This ode is like the First Stasimon in providing a contrast in tone and atmosphere which points up the difference between myth and reality. It follows a similar technique in telling a story only remotely connected with the play's action and linked tenuously with Clytemnestra at the end. The aeolic meter prevails throughout.

The opening picture is beguilingly pastoral, of a lamb with a golden fleece brought down from the mountains by Pan, to become a bone of contention between the brothers Atreus and

Thyestes in their dispute over the sovereignty of Argos. <TRACK J9, lines 699–712> ◉ Anger at Thyestes for seducing Atreus' wife and stealing the ominous lamb caused Zeus to reverse the course of the sun and the order of the seasons. <TRACK J10, lines 727–36> ◉ The tone of the poem is charmingly tranquil and detached, until the final stanza (737–46) when the Chorus expresses their skepticism at the idea that a mortal dispute could have such consequences; but frightening stories, they say, may encourage worship of the gods – "stories which you, Clytemnestra, forgot when you killed your husband!" Skepticism over myth hardly fits young peasant women. This feels more like the voice of the poet asking, for example: could Apollo *really* tell a man to kill his mother?

Third Episode (747–858)

At the beginning of the Messenger scene, Euripides plays naughty again. A distant cry is heard and the Coryphaeus calls Electra out, but she is not sure whether the shouting bodes victory or defeat. Electra melodramatically assumes defeat and starts to rush off. "Hold on," says the Leader, "until you know!" "Impossible!" comes the reply. "We're lost! Where are *messengers*?" "They'll come. It's no *light matter* to kill a king" (757–60).The poet cannot resist a joke at this point about the messenger convention, and he is still happy to make his heroine ridiculous. At once the Messenger bursts in with his joyful news of victory over Aegisthus. "Who are *you*?" asks Electra. "How can I know you are telling the truth?" "Your brother's servant! Don't you know me on sight?" (765–6).

   Electra can now hail the gods and justice, then request the story of Aegisthus' death in full detail. The Messenger speech (774–858) which follows is in Euripides' best narrative manner. The murder is given a splendid buildup in the courteously hospitable invitation the king offers the strangers to take part in his sacrifice (a far cry from his drunken behavior at Agamemnon's grave, as dubiously stated by Electra in 326–31), then in the graphic description of the preliminaries to the sacrifice and the sinister omens indicated when Aegisthus examines the victim's entrails. The actual murder, pace some scholars, is thoroughly discreditable: it is performed at a sacrifice by someone formally offered hospitality and from behind on the neck while the sacrificer is stooping over the entrails on the altar. Despite the enormity of this, the Messenger reports that Aegisthus' slaves have quickly transferred their allegiance to Orestes, who is now on his way to show Electra a head, "not a Gorgon's head,[12] but the man you detest, Aegisthus!" (855–7). The ironical implication must be that Orestes is hardly a hero like Perseus who was described holding the Gorgon's head on Achilles' shield in the First Stasimon (459–60).

Choral Victory Song with Electra (860–79)

This silly little dividing movement between episodes can hardly be called a stasimon. It consists of a pair of short strophes split by a seven-line iambic speech of joy for Electra (866–72). The maidens call on Electra to joy them in a dance of celebration for Orestes' victory which transcends the winning of a crown in the Olympic Games! The irony is compounded by the dactylo-epitrite meter used by Pindar in his epinician odes. <TRACK J12, lines 859–63> ◉

Fourth Episode (880–1146)

Irony continues when Electra, who has briefly gone indoors to fetch garlands, makes a grand entrance to offer the returning Orestes and Pylades a eulogistic greeting before she crowns their heads, as though they really were Olympic victors. In his response (890–9) Orestes is cock-a-hoop over his squalid achievement and piously thanks the gods for leading him. He then invites Electra to treat Aegisthus' corpse,[13] which has been brought out by attendants, as she will, whether by throwing it to the dogs or impaling it for the birds to devour – gruesome treatment which it hardly does Orestes credit to suggest.

Euripides gives Electra a sinisterly hesitant buildup to her next long speech in which she reviles Aegisthus' dead body. With a little encouragement from Orestes, she weighs in with a very frigid and formal opening which is a pointer to what follows. The rhesis consists largely of scandalous innuendos about the dead man's relationship with Clytemnestra and their mutual infidelities. These we may well regard (like 326–31) as nothing more than the products of Electra's malicious imagination. Indeed, the whole "cacology," for all its promised vitriol and rhetorical opening, can be seen by the discerning more as an example of empty invective and something of an anticlimax.[14] Although a powerful actress can make it all sound poisonously effective, I would see this speech as another example of Euripides' subtle originality in the dramaturgy of this play. Here are words that *lack* genuine power.

At the end of Electra's speech, the body is removed, supervised perhaps by Pylades, as Orestes and Electra are best left on their own with the Chorus to play the following scene. From now on the drama is genuinely tragic in tone; humor and falsified expectations are abandoned. Electra sights Clytemnestra approaching in a wagon and Orestes at last has to face the horror of killing his mother. In impassioned stichomythia he questions the wisdom of Apollo's oracle (871, 873), while Electra savagely insists on his duty of revenge and calls him a coward. (We may be reminded in this powerful passage of Lady Macbeth goading her uncertain husband to kill his royal guest.) In this crucial exchange we can sympathize strongly with Orestes in his agonized hesitation, while his twisted sister exerts her terrifying pressure. Finally, he yields and makes his deeply unhappy exit indoors (985–7). The atmosphere is now one of grim reality.

First of all Clytemnestra must be lured into the cottage. Euripides takes the opportunity, as Sophocles did, for an *agôn* between Electra and her mother; but he also models his scene on the *Agamemnon*, when the king is persuaded to enter his palace walking on purple garments. This is signaled at once by the entrance of Clytemnestra in a wagon, followed by a second one (see 1135) containing beautiful handmaidens who are, like Cassandra, Trojan captives (see p. 76 n. 7). Clytemnestra's instructions to them at 998 mirror *Agamemnon* 906 and 1039; and there is a further imitation of the Argive elders in the Coryphaeus' anapaestic greeting to the queen (988–97), though here the "watery friendship" against which Agamemnon is warned (*Agam.* 798) is more on the side of Euripides' Coryphaeus.

The arguments used in the *agôn* accord with Euripides' down-to-earth treatment of his story in concentrating predominantly on sexual relationships. The retribution theme is not absent, but the need for Iphigenia's sacrifice is attributed by Clytemnestra to Helen's immoral character and elopement with Paris; and her own adultery is very disingenuously said to have been prompted by Agamemnon's importation of Cassandra. Electra's blistering rhesis in reply includes an attack on Clytemnestra for dressing up to attract lovers as soon as the expedition had left for Troy (1069–74).

The mother's response to her daughter's indictment (1102–10) is another surprise and strangely touching: "You always were more your father's daughter; I will forgive you." In an

Figure 11.1 Euripides *Electra*, Cambridge Greek Play 1980. Source: Reproduced by permission of the Archive of Performances of Greek & Roman Drama.

emotional moment she expresses regret for what she did; she was too angry with her husband! Euripides is deliberately, and rather surprisingly, making Clytemnestra sympathetic to emphasize the horror of her impending murder.

The debate over, Electra reverts to "temptation scene" mode, as she role-plays her mother's part in *Agamemnon* to invite her indoors to perform the fictitious postpartum rites. At one suspenseful point (1107–8) Clytemnestra almost smells a rat: Electra's filthy appearance is hardly consistent with a newly delivered mother. But she agrees, and Electra exultantly ushers her in. "Please take care," she says with mock concern, "not to soil your dress on the smoky walls. You will pay the gods the sacrifice which you owe" (1139–41). After Clytemnestra has been swallowed up indoors, Electra is given her own set of lines on which to make a separate gloating exit (1142–6, cf. *Agam.* 973–4).

Third Stasimon (1147–64) and Murder Scene (1165–76)

As we wait in suspense for Clytemnestra's death-cries, the Chorus is used to build up the tension. As before the murder of Medea's children (*Medea* 1251–70), the taut irregular dochmiac rhythm prevails, punctuated by steadying iambics, syncopated in the final line of the stanza. In *Medea*, though, the Chorus deplores what the heroine is about to do and envisages the human consequences. Here, adopting the conventional philosophy of tit-for-tat, the Chorus replays the return and murder of Agamemnon for which Clytemnestra is paying the price.

Euripides wants to save up his interpretation of the murder's aftermath as a surprise. The musical impact of the passage is paramount.

The song's imagery is compelling in its own right: the palace echoing with Agamemnon's cries and his horror at his welcome home after ten years away (1151–3). Clytemnestra's adultery gets another mention (1156) and she has an axe to do the deed; the syncopation of 1162 suggests the heavy blows which killed her husband.[15]

Then (1165) the terrible cry from within: "My children, in the gods' name, don't kill your mother!"<TRACK J13, lines 1147–54 and 1165> ⦿ This is the play's climax, and the appeal is followed almost at once by a long shriek of anguish. In 1172–6 the Coryphaeus introduces Orestes and Electra staggering out of the house, befouled by their mother's blood. They are followed through the *skênê* door by the *ekkyklêma*, bearing the corpses of Clytemnestra and Aegisthus.

Kommos (1177–232) for Orestes, Electra and Chorus

Lyric mode is perfect for this deeply emotional movement which turns a subversive drama into real tragedy, as we understand the word. Three short pairs of strophes follow, in which the steady iambic rhythm prevails but with frequent use of resolution (long syllables broken up into two shorts) and syncopation to heighten the effect of heartrending anguish.

Orestes is filled with horror for the pollution he has incurred (1179). Again he questions Apollo's oracle as he contemplates the social and religious exclusion that matricide must entail (1190–7). He relives the moment when his mother bared her breast to him and pleaded for mercy, while (here genuinely like Perseus with the Gorgon) he held his cloak before his eyes as he plunged his sword into her throat (1221–3).

Even more compelling is the effect of what she has done on Electra. She confesses that she urged her brother on, and placed her own hand on his sword as he dealt the fatal stroke (1224–6). <TRACK J14, lines 1206–26> ⦿ In a total volte face she blames herself and the fire of her relentless hatred for the mother who bore her (1182–4). She also deplores the social exclusion which will leave her husbandless (1198–200).

The Chorus, while admitting the justice of Clytemnestra's punishment, deplores the act of matricide (1185–8). They commend Electra's change of heart after doing terrible things to her reluctant brother (1201–5) and sympathize with Orestes in his terrible anguish (1210–12).

The movement concludes quietly in a touching act of ritual (1227–32), as brother and sister together, in remorseful contrition, lay garments to cover their mother's body. The first audience may have recalled the corresponding scene in *Choephori* (980–4), when Aeschylus makes Orestes triumphantly display the robe used by Clytemnestra to entrap Agamemnon in his bath – another point of powerful contrast between the two plays and so a poignantly meaningful use of prop.

Exodos (1233–359)

Euripides has made his point. He has answered the questions of what sort of people would commit matricide and how they would feel at the end. But the play must be brought to a conclusion, and the tradition followed by Aeschylus went that Orestes was pursued by his mother's Furies to be tried and acquitted at Athens.

This is certainly a suitable moment, within the tragic convention, for the appearance of a *deus ex machina*. Announced by the Coryphaeus in anapaests (1233–7), two gods appear on the roof of the house, perhaps hoisted in by the crane. They are the Dioscuri (sons of Zeus), the heavenly twins, Castor and Polydeuces. They are appropriate here as the half-brothers of Clytemnestra and Helen, and their appearance has been foreshadowed by passing references earlier in the play.[16] They are benign deities who rescue sailors in distress and this is consistent with the bland tone of Castor's rhesis.[17]

The god first explains to Orestes that he and his brother have suspended their normal activity after sighting their sister's murder. "*She* has her just deserts," he says, "but *your* deed was wrong. And Apollo – well, he's my superior, so I'd better not say. He is wise, but his order to you was not" (1243–6). Euripides has used Castor to say, in the most discreet and diplomatic way, what he thinks of a story in which a god tells a man to kill his mother. After the moving *kommos*, the dry, subversive tone has re-emerged.

Castor then tells Orestes what the gods have decided for the future, and there follows a low-key summary (1250–75) of what happens in Aeschylus' *Eumenides.* The facts of Orestes' pursuit and trial are spelt out but even the Furies have little emotive value. In the end he will found a new city which will be named after himself. Clytemnestra will be interred by Menelaus who has just got back from Troy after recovering Helen from Egypt: "Zeus sent a phantom Helen to Troy to stir up war and carnage amongst mortals" (1282–3).[18] This casual remark maintains the flat tone and serves as another little dig at myths about the gods. Pylades will

Figure 11.2 Euripides *Electra*, Cambridge Greek Play 1980. Source: Reproduced by permission of the Archive of Performances of Greek & Roman Drama.

take Electra as his wife and Electra's admirable "husband" be set up in Phocis with "a load of wealth" (we may remember what the Peasant thought of riches at 426–31). Orestes himself can now be off to Athens; when he has played out his destined role in the murder story, he'll live happily ever after (1290–1).[19]

But Euripides will not end his play on a cozy undramatic note. The meter changes at 1292[20] to the stricter rhythm of anapaests and, from now on, speech is given an emotional lift by a musical accompaniment. Orestes and Electra ask permission to address the gods, who are asked why they did not protect their sister. "Fate and necessity led that way," they are told, "and the unwise utterances of Apollo's tongue" (1301–2) – one more tilt. But humanity now comes to the fore. The moment has come for brother and sister to part. United by their common guilt, the two have just discovered each other. For all Castor's pronouncements, their brighter future is no consolation. Euripides makes much of their parting embrace, which mirrors and contrasts profoundly with the enforced and hastily concluded embrace at the end of the recognition scene (546–7). The physical action here (1321–6) can indeed be seen as the *true* recognition between Orestes and Electra – who then are required to leave each other for ever. Electra, accompanied by Pylades, makes her slow exit weeping (1339), and we know that her tears are, at last, genuine. <TRACK J15, lines 1321–37> ◉

After that Orestes is forced into a hurried exit as Castor spies the Furies about to swoop. This happens so quickly (1342–6) as to be entirely unmemorable. It takes longer for Castor to announce his own and Polydeuces' departure to rescue more sailors, with a conventional statement advocating piety. The gods are whisked away leaving the Chorus to make their own exit with a fairly trite comment on life's uncertainty (1357–9).

Conclusion

This is a play of striking originality, probably the most sophisticated of surviving Greek tragedies in the elaborately contrived characterization which Euripides developed to make his main point: the impossibility of considering matricide a duty or anything but an affront to human sensibility. The changes of tone are remarkable, particularly in the two central choral stasima and in the shifts in sympathy towards Orestes and Electra in the later scenes. The dramaturgy is full of surprises, not least in the diverting mockery of tragic conventions and in the ingenious exploitation of the audience's very probable familiarity with the *Oresteia*. It is fascinating to compare this piece with Aeschylus' and Sophocles' treatment of the same myth; it throws Euripides' peculiar mindset and artistry into high relief.

Notes

1 After Aeschylus' death a decree was passed which permitted the revival of his plays in competition with those of living poets. There is no certain evidence for a revival of the *Oresteia* in the late fifth century but references in Aristophanes (*Acharnians* 9 ff., *Clouds* 534–6, and *Frogs* 868 ff., 1126 ff.) make one highly probable.
2 For a bibliography of the various approaches see Porter (1990, 255–81).
3 The use of props in this play is fully explored in Raeburn (2000). For the significance of props generally in Greek tragedy see Taplin (1978).

4 He has mentioned the wrongs done him by Aegisthus' "who killed my father – *and* (=as did) my accursed mother." The final words in the Greek read like an uncomfortably added appendage.

5 For the Homeric formula, cf. *Iliad* 24.313 and elsewhere. More pertinent here is Eur. *Andromache* 93–5, which speaks of a natural propensity in women to harp continually on their present troubles.

6 I do not think that a servant has come onstage to remove the pot. The imperative in 140 is addressed to Electra herself.

7 I see no reason to excise 360, as in the Loeb edition. As the water-pot symbolizes Electra's self-martyrdom, I have suggested (Raeburn 2000) that the luggage represents the heavy load that Orestes has to carry with him in Apollo's command to kill his mother.

8 For an excellent discussion of this and the Second Stasimon, Classics students are referred to Morwood (1981).

9 There is a fuller discussion of this scene in Raeburn (2000, 157–60).

10 Some have suggested that Electra rejects the tokens because the idea of Orestes' returning in secret (see 524–6) belies her imagined view of his coming as a conquering hero. But she is really resisting the suggestion that he has returned at all.

11 The scar as a recognition token would have been familiar from *Odyssey* 19 where Odysseus is recognized by the nurse Eurycleia through a scar on his thigh. The intertextual point here is that Eurycleia identifies the scar for herself, although Odysseus has deliberately turned away from the light, whereas Electra actually hesitates (575) to draw a conclusion that is staring her in the face.

12 "Not a Gorgon's head" was also a proverb for a sight that need not be feared, but the comparison with Perseus must be there, as it is in Aesch. *Cho.* 831–7.

13 The body, I think, rather than the severed head as suggested at the end of the Messenger speech (855). For a full discussion see Raeburn (2000, 161–3), in which I argue that this instance of falsified expectation anticipates the insubstantial rhetoric of Electra's cacology.

14 This interpretation is supported by the sententious tone of 940–4 and the mixed metaphors in 944.

15 Line 1162 gives a much stronger cue for Clytemnestra's cry at 1165. The simile of the mountain-lioness (1163–4) falls rather flat after it, and I suspect that, despite the Aeschylean association quoted by Cropp (2013, 226), these (formally odd) lines are interpolated.

16 Lines 312–13, 746, 990–3, 1064. Electra was betrothed to Castor before he became a god.

17 Cropp (2013, 11–12, 232) suggests that the divine perspective is broader and deeper.

18 The idea of the phantom Helen was taken from the lyric poet Stesichorus and became the basis for Euripides' later play *Helen*, which is very humorous.

19 Castor's concluding words "released from these toils" ironically recalls *Agam.* 1, 20 and *Eum.* 83.

20 This would have been a good cue for the *ekkyklêma* to be withdrawn.

References

Text: *Euripides Electra* (Loeb edition, Vol. 3). Cambridge, MA: Harvard University Press, edited and translated by David Kovacs.

Cropp, M. 2013. *Euripides: Electra*, 2nd edition, Warminster:, Aris and Phillips.

Knox, B.M.W. 1979. "Euripidean Comedy," in *Word and Action*, 250–4. Baltimore, MD: John Hopkins University Press.

Lloyd, M. 1986. "Realism and Character in Euripides' *Electra*," *Phoenix* 40, 1–19.

Morwood, J. 1981. "The Pattern of the Euripides *Electra*," *American Journal of Philology* 102, 362–70.

Porter, J.R. 1990. "Tiptoeing through the Corpses," *Greek Roman and Byzantine Studies* 31, 255–81.

Raeburn, D. 2000. "The Significance of Stage Properties in Euripides' *Electra*," *Greece and Rome* 47, 149–68.

Taplin, O. 1978. *Greek Tragedy in Action*. London: Methuen.

Winnington-Ingram, R.P. 1969. "Euripides, Poietes Sophos," *Arethusa* 2, 127–42, reprinted in Mossman, J. (ed.). 2003. *Oxford Readings in Euripides*, 47–63. Oxford: Oxford University Press.

Commentary

Cropp, M. 2013. *Euripides: Electra*, 2nd edn, Warminster: Aris & Phillips.

12

Bacchae

Bacchae (the Bacchants) was first performed at Athens after Euripides died in *.c.*406. The poet had left his home city for Macedonia where he spent his final days at the court of the king, Archelaus, and it is generally believed that he composed this play there.[1] It could indeed have had its first performance in the theater at Pella, but the allusions to contemporary theories and controversies make it likely that an eventual Athenian audience was also in mind (see Dodds 1960, xxxix–xl).

The tragedy concerns the myth of the god Dionysus, the son of Zeus by the mortal Semele, who arrives in Greece to manifest his disputed divinity and power in his native city of Thebes. Here he defeats the opposition of the young King Pentheus and subjects him to a peculiarly cruel death by way of punishment.

Dionysus was one among the pantheon of twelve Olympians at Athens but was unusual in having a mortal mother and a double birth. At a basic level he was perceived as a god of wine and ecstasy. One of his cult titles was Lyaeus, the one who "sets free" human beings, whether from worry or their inhibitions. In Attica local festivals, the Rural Dionysia, were occasions for country jollity or piously getting drunk; but the god was honored above all at Athens in the City Dionysia which celebrated the city's greatness in grand civic displays and in the cultural genres of dithyrambs (a type of choral hymn), tragedy and comedy. Dionysus was the god of the Attic theater and represented in cult-hymns by a mask attached to a tree.

The god was regularly portrayed in literature and vase paintings as attended by maenads or bacchae, women who danced to him in a state of ecstatic possession, wearing fawn skins and ivy crowns, and carrying a long wand tipped with clumps of ivy, knows as the *thyrsus*. Those women bonded together in groups called *thiasoi*. Euripides' play refers to a *trietêris* (133), a midwinter rite which was actually practiced by women's societies at Delphi in the mountains every other year. The culminating act of the dance was the *sparagmos*, the tearing to pieces of an animal victim, whose flesh would then be devoured raw in a kind of communion with the god.

Other details in the text of Euripides' play can be referred to various new cults from abroad which invaded Athens during the second half of the fifth century. One minor deity in particular, Sabazius, can be seen as a counterpart of Dionysus in promising identification with a deity (Dodds 1960, xxiii–v).

Greek Tragedies as Plays for Performance, First Edition. David Raeburn.
© 2017 John Wiley & Sons, Inc. Published 2017 by John Wiley & Sons, Inc.
Companion website: www.wiley.com/go/raeburn

Synopsis

The initial situation is unfolded in the Prologue: Dionysus has returned to his birthplace Thebes to manifest his divinity in Greece; he has assumed mortal guise as a beautiful young man leading a *thiasos* of maenads who have accompanied him from Asia. The sisters of his mother, Semele, who had denied his conception by Zeus, along with the other women of Thebes, have been driven to madness and have left their homes for Mount Cithaeron, where they are "sitting under the pines" in bacchic gear. The god is being opposed by the young king of Thebes, Pentheus, who has taken over the throne from his grandfather Cadmus.

The action of the play shows Dionysus gradually bringing Pentheus into his power. Arrested by the king, the god miraculously escapes from the stable where he is imprisoned and eventually tempts his adversary into going up to the mountain to spy on the maenads, himself dressed in bacchic costume. There Pentheus is sighted and torn to pieces by the demented women and his head is carried back to Thebes by his triumphant mother Agave in the belief that she is bearing the head of a lion. Her father Cadmus brings her back to her senses and she realizes what she has done.

Interpretation

What at first might appear a cruel and bloodthirsty story turns out to be a subtle and sophisticated study in human group behavior. The play has attracted a variety of interpretations. In modern times it has been treated as a glorification of sexual and other forms of liberation[2] and, as such, has appealed powerfully to directors who have championed the theater of the body. This runs counter to the text which indicates that the maenads, for all their strange behavior, are *not* engaging in sexual activity.

An influential view propounded by Seaford (1996) has seen the play as essentially an aetiology of contemporary initiation rites in Dionysiac cult. The difficulty here is that there is little evidence for mysteries of Dionysus in fifth-century Athens. Moreover, the scope of the piece, with its central imagery and ideas expressed, ranges well beyond cult rituals and practice. Seaford also sees Dionysus' triumph as the celebration of a new democracy at Thebes, after the royal family has been destroyed by the class-leveling god of wine. This could perhaps be seen as relevant to Athens during the years towards the end of the Peloponnesian war, when democracy seemed under threat; but it is very hard to view the play's ending, incomplete though it be, as entailing the establishment of a new political order. Such an interpretation appears to disregard the thrust of a deliberately constructed and particularly powerful drama which clearly ends on a note of sympathy for Dionysus' victims.

The excellent commentary of E.R. Dodds (1960) related the play to the new cults invading Athens during the period but also took the punishment of Pentheus to be a warning against repression of the human instinct to indulge in the "joyful vitality" of the Dionysiac experience. Is that, though, the warning which the drama as a whole amounts to?

I myself would concur with the interpretation of Winnington-Ingram (1948), which has the great merits, among others, of taking account of *all* the details of the text and of examining the play as a work of drama with a carefully contrived shape and direction. This view sees Euripides conceiving Dionysus not simply as a god whom the Greeks worshipped but as representing a force in human life, much as Aphrodite in *Hippolytus* evidently stands for the sexual instinct which both generates life and can also be relentlessly destructive. Similarly, in

Bacchae, Dionysus can signify the joyful liberation of group activity and thought-patterns but also the dangers of untrammeled emotionalism and of mindless identification with the crowd.

Winnington-Ingram draws particular attention to the collective attitudes expressed by the Chorus of Asian maenads during the course of their odes. These include the praise of an easy, relaxed, untroubled mode of existence (389–92); a preference for living for the day over long-term aspiration (397–9); a rejection of the intellectual (395) in favor of the values of the man in the street (430–1). "Wisdom" for the bacchanals is alarmingly declared, towards the play's climax, to be the satisfaction of "holding one's hand in triumph over one's foes" (877–80). These attitudes taken together add up to a philosophy for humanity in the herd.

A crucial theme that recurs again and again in the language of the text is that of "revelation." The play's action demonstrates Dionysus *manifesting* his divine identity and power. It can be said at the same time that Euripides is manifesting Dionysus for the force that he sees him representing in human nature – both beguiling and extremely dangerous (861). Dionysus can assume a smiling face in his mask (1021), but he can also reveal himself as an animal – a bull, a snake or a lion (1017–19). It is another crucial feature of the text that the images drawn from the animal world become increasingly prominent as the drama progresses and the action moves to its climax of horrific violence. The thrust of the play seems inescapable: the bacchic philosophy of "getting with it," of intimate association with the group, may be very attractive, but to follow that route to its limit is to be more like an animal than a human being. Our animal instincts are not to be denied, but we should not lay our critical faculties completely aside.

How far this "message" might have been inspired by dissatisfaction with the democratic politics of later fifth-century Athens with its susceptibility to demagogy and impulsive decision-making[3] must remain a matter of speculation. The theme, though, of the dangers implicit in crowd behavior is a universal one, and Euripides voiced it in a peculiarly trenchant way. A critical chord is undoubtedly struck early on in the satire of the scene with Cadmus and Tiresias.

Dramaturgy

From a formal point of view *Bacchae* may have come as a surprise in the light of Euripides' artistic innovation in his later plays (see p. 139). In the telling of this story, the poet established a renewed concentration on the two primary elements in the tragic genre. The Chorus plays a central and crucial role in the revelation of what Dionysus is made to represent; and the audience is treated to *two* Messenger speeches which describe the behavior of the gods' devotees in action. It is an essential part of Euripides' design to have two groups of bacchanals involved: the onstage Asian maenads who form the Chorus and the offstage Theban women whom Dionysus has driven mad and are the primary object of Pentheus' concern.

Conflict is at the heart of the plot and the characterization of the play's adversaries is achieved with extraordinary brilliance and subtlety. The god himself, with his smiling mask, is portrayed in his disguise as paradoxically cool and calm, though the menace of underlying cruelty is evident from the start. His easy, relaxed control, combined with an androgynous appearance, makes him compellingly fascinating. Pentheus himself is no less surprising. Euripides chooses not to confront dionysiac emotion with the voice of cold, calculating reason. The young king is excitable and irrational and thus in himself exhibits the dionysiac traits which allow him to entertain prurient suspicions about the Theban bacchanals and to be strangely captivated by Dionysus' appearance on their first encounter. It is the Dionysus in himself which makes it convincing for him to fall completely under the god's control and so to ensure his appalling demise. Pentheus' character and behavior are Euripides' "manifestation" of the god in the individual.

The Chorus in this piece does not consist of bystanders who can change tack to guide the audience's sympathy and response. The Bacchae are closely involved in the action as Dionysus' disguised band of followers, emotionally dependent on their leader and also used, as already indicated, to voice the mental attitudes which Euripides chooses to associate with the dionysiac. Their songs embrace the variety of moods that the god inspires, ranging from joyous rapture, sensuous tranquility and erotic escapism to righteous indignation and frenzied vindictiveness. All these are reflected not only in the thought and imagery of the poetry but no less in the music inherent in the rhythmical structure of the strophes. They reveal the poet at his most expressive, particularly in the exotic ionic meters of the Parodos and First Stasimon and the hectic, racing dochmiacs as the drama's climax approaches.

Stichomythia is employed extensively as the perfect medium for the three confrontational dialogues between the two main adversaries. Rhesis is mainly used for its expository function in the Prologue, Pentheus' opening speech and, most importantly for the two magnificent, complementary Messenger narratives. Apart from these, Tiresias' address to Pentheus is a highly intriguing piece of rhetoric in its deployment of sophistic argument; while Cadmus' beautiful speech of lament for his cruelly destroyed grandson contributes to the pathos as the drama moves towards its conclusion. Lyric *kommos* (for soloist and chorus) is the perfect medium for Agave's agitated entrance bearing Pentheus' head and the terrible celebration of her imagined triumph in the hunt.

Euripides used his *skênê* to represent the royal house of Thebes where Pentheus and his retired grandfather live. The text at 6–12 suggests a supplementary structure, close to the stage building and presumably to one side of it, decked with vine-leaves (11–12), from which smoke is issuing at the play's beginning. It seems too that flames appeared from it during the Palace Miracle (596–9). Stage effects are not common in surviving tragedy, but smoke may well have been used at the start of *Trojan Women* (line 8) to produce the atmosphere of a fallen city.[4] One *eisodos* was probably reserved for entrances from and exits to the mountain, with the opposite one leading to other locations.

Dramatic Analysis

Line numbers refer to the Greek text in the Loeb edition (see end of this chapter), which has a parallel English translation. For the terminology of the discrete movements, see Appendix A; for the lyric structure and meters, see Appendix B or hear TRACK 0. ⓞ

Prologue (1–63)

The play opens, as in *Medea* and *Electra*, with a monologue, this time from the lead character, the god Dionysus himself, though disguised as a mortal (4). It is clear from 455–7 that his mask had long luxuriant hair attached to it and portrayed him as effeminate, probably with a smiling mouth (Seaford 1996, 186 on line 439). He could be costumed in the dressy saffron yellow robe normally worn by women (Seaford 1996, 180 on line 353) but associated with Dionysus in Aristophanes' *Frogs* (Sommerstein 1996, 160 on *Frogs* 46).

"I'm back, here on Theban soil, I, Dionysus, the son of Zeus, whom Semele once brought forth with the helping hand of the lightning flame." After this introduction he points to his mother's smoking memorial, the place where his mother died when Zeus' lightning struck, doubtless in anticipation of the later stage effect (596–9). The main theme of Dionysus manifesting his godhead as the son of Zeus, in his mother's defense, is stated three times (22, 42, 50) as he outlines where he has come from, what he has already done to the women of Thebes (see synopsis) and how he proposes to fight the opposition from Pentheus. The final lines of the speech (55–63) splendidly cue in the entry of the Chorus, the *thiasos* of Asian bacchanals whose *exarchos*, male leader, he purports to be. They are to beat their Phrygian drums in procession round Pentheus' palace, while he will join the Theban maenads on Mount Cithaeron.

Parodos (64–167)

Enter the Chorus along one of the *eisodoi*, doubtless costumed in long dresses with fawn skins and ivy wreaths on their heads. They also appear to be holding and beating instruments rather like tambourines.[5] Their processional entrance will be solemn rather than frenetic as they call on any in the street to make way and for all to maintain a reverent silence. This is the prelude to the ritual act which follows in two pairs of strophes and an extremely striking epode. It is delivered in the triple-time ionic meter which is associated with the east and exotic contexts generally. <TRACK K1, lines 64–72> ⊙

In the strophes that follow, ionics feature prominently in combination with common time choriambic or dactylic phrases. The choral song proper (72 ff.) seems to be modeled on an actual cult hymn (Dodds 1960, 71). The main emphasis is on the joy and beauty of the bacchic religion, though there are occasional hints of the cult's bestial and more frightening aspects (113, 139). Strophe A begins with a beatitude, promising blessing to those initiated in the rituals of the Asiatic goddess Cybele and of Dionysus, also titled Bromios, "booming god," a name suggestive of the drum among other things. <TRACK K2, lines 73–87> ⊙ The next three stanzas recount the myths that lie behind bacchic rituals with their characteristic trappings and musical instruments. The curious story of Dionysus' double birth (first prematurely to Semele, then from Zeus's thigh) is followed by addresses to the birthplaces of the god's two parents, Semele in Thebes and Zeus in Crete. <TRACK K3, lines 105–19> ⊙ The song rises to an astonishing climax in the epode, as the Chorus expresses the rapturous excitement of their mountain revels and describes the male celebrant who represents Dionysus himself falling to the ground in frenzy, then leaping over the mountain ridges in the hunt for the sacrificial victim, while women follow with ecstatic cries to the music of drum and pipe.

Metrically this passage is the most complex in all the tragedies explored in this book. At the climax a succession of 5/8 and 3/8 bars (160–1) culminates in a run of racing dactyls to capture the joy of the bacchanal "bounding high in the air, like a foal with its mother at pasture." <TRACK K4, lines 135–66> ⊙ How Euripides would have choreographed this extraordinary epode we can have no idea. It can be safely assumed, though, that he wanted his audience, at this point, to be swept away in identification with the communal excitement and sense of uninhibited liberation that Dionysus/Bromios affords – as in the joy and relentless boom of the modern pop festival at Woodstock or Glastonbury.

First Episode (170–369)

In an astonishing contrast, the audience is now confronted by the ridiculous spectacle of two old men dressed in bacchic gear, determined quite inappropriately to be "in the swim." Claiming to be rejuvenated, they are ready to dance in honor of Dionysus up in the mountains. They are the blind prophet Tiresias and the retired king Cadmus, grandfather of the "god-fighter" Pentheus. Both turn out to have ulterior motives: for Cadmus it is a good thing to have a god in the family (181, 335–6); while Tiresias resembles the modern ecclesiastic who wants conventional religion to be "in touch" with contemporary trends and fashions.

The comic tone is unmistakable, particularly in 191–2, when Cadmus asks, "Shall we go in the chariot up to the mountains?" ("Shall we take the Rolls?") and Tiresias replies "No! That would be less respectful to the god" ("We must make the pilgrimage on foot."). In these two characters there is a powerful vein of satire, which brings the joyous ecstasy of the bacchanals into an entirely new perspective and suggests that Dionysus and what he represents need to be looked at critically. The old men's departure for Mount Cithaeron is delayed by the arrival of Pentheus, described by Cadmus as hurrying to the palace "in fluttered condition" (212–14). The announcement is a crucial indication of how Euripides proposes to treat Dionysus' antagonist.

Most of Pentheus' opening speech (215–62) is addressed to no one else on stage; it is much more like the address to the audience which Euripides uses in his prologues. The young king's attitude to the bacchanals is clear from the outset: their revels are a bogus excuse for wine parties and sex with men in the bushes (221–5). Some, he tells us, have been arrested and are in jail, and he proposes to hunt down the rest (226–32). Then some revealing lines (233–6): "They tell me that some foreigner has got in, a Lydian fellow who's a fake magician, with long blond locks that reek of scent, cheeks flushed, and eyes exuding sexual desire." If Pentheus catches him, he'll *lop his head* from his neck (241). As for the story about Semele's affair with Zeus and Dionysus' double birth, "that deserves a *hanging*" (246). Clearly, Euripides is not making Pentheus oppose the god with the voice of cold reason, but on the basis of irrational prejudice and suspicion founded on hearsay.

At 248 he enters the play and rounds on his grandfather Cadmus for his absurd appearance and then, in typical tragic tyrant mode, accuses the prophet of supporting Dionysus' cause for money; an extra god on the scene will offer more in the way of paid work in augury and sacrifice (255–7).

After an indignant intervention by the Coryphaeus (263–5), Tiresias weighs in with a long rhesis packed with sophistry, although he has expressly disowned it at 200 (a line normally assigned in texts to Tiresias and not to Cadmus, as in the Loeb edition). It starts with the formal introduction to a debating speech: Pentheus is glib and what he has said shows little sense. His first argument (274–85) adopts the language of the early Greek philosophers who saw the Dry and the Wet as the primary elements required for human existence. The earth-mother Demeter stands for dry food, bread, while the Wet is Dionysus who stands for wine (not water, as we might expect), which offers forgetfulness of care and the gift of sleep. The second argument (286–97) explains away the curious myth of Dionysus' second birth from Zeus's thigh in terms of a verbal confusion that is no less bizarre than the story itself. And so the speech continues until the end when Tiresias tells Pentheus, that he is *mad* as a man can be and: "Drugs won't find you a cure, though they may be part of your sickness."[6]

The episode now moves to its conclusion (330–69) as Cadmus pleads with his grandson to *say* that Dionysus is a god and Semele's son, even if he is not, for the honor of the family. When he asks to wreathe Pentheus' head with ivy, the young man reacts with wild disgust,

"Don't wipe your stupidity off on *me*!" He orders his men to wreck Tiresias' seat of augury "up and down" (349), a phrase used twice again in the play (602, 741) to indicate the confusion of bacchic violence. Others are ordered to track down "the effeminate alien who is infecting our women with this new virus and fouling their beds" (352–4). In his parting shot Tiresias plays on the ominous link between Pentheus' name and the word *penthos*, mourning (367–8).

Euripides has thus used his first episode to establish the critical light in which he is inviting his audience to view Dionysus, as a counterweight to his immediate attractions; to establish the spurious nature of the god's senior advocates; and also to present Pentheus with the irrational dionysiac qualities which will make it easy for Dionysus to gain ascendency over him during the scenes that follow.

First Stasimon (370–431)

The ensuing choral song is very beautiful and also extremely revealing. It starts with an appeal to *Hosia*, the reverent piety which Pentheus has affronted by his *hubris* towards Dionysus. The god is then extolled as the lord of the wine festival who with music and dance brings relief from care in sleep; the theme is taken up from Tiresias' rhesis (280–3). The meter is again ionic, now employed to peculiarly sensuous effect, especially in the repeated phrases which end in a heavy syllable, with the final light one cut off. <TRACK K5, lines 368–85>

This ode, more than any other, reveals the attitudes with which Euripides chooses to associate the uncritical worship of Dionysus. The bacchanals praise the life of *hêsuchia*, the relaxed tranquility which allows life to wash over one (389–92). "Cleverness is not wisdom" (395), a maxim which appears to reject the intellect, though what the women believe true wisdom to consist in has still to emerge. Life is short and high aspiration may lead one to miss what is immediately there to be enjoyed (397–9).

In Strophe B (402–16) the Chorus sing an "escape prayer." They would like to be wafted to Cyprus, Aphrodite's island, where dwell the Graces and Desire and where they may lawfully celebrate their mysteries. Whatever the Theban bacchanals may or may not be up to on the mountains, the mood here is certainly one of erotic escapism. The meter here has changed to aeolic, more in lilting phrases ending in light syllables. <TRACK K6, lines 402–16> In the antistrophe (417–31), the god is extolled once again as the giver of wine, that social leveler; he *hates* the person who will not settle for an easy life and abhors men of excess (such as Pentheus). The final lines (430–2) are an acceptance of the values and behavior of the "ordinary multitude," the man in the street. As his play develops, Euripides will invite his audience to consider what "ruddy Bacchus" and the beguiling sentiments that he inspires can lead to in practice.

Second Episode (434–518)

We now witness the first direct confrontation between Dionysus and Pentheus. The god, in his alluring mortal guise, has now been arrested in accordance with Pentheus' instructions and is led before him, with his hands bound behind his back. The Servant who brings him on confesses to his embarrassment in the capture of such a "tame animal" (436), who just smiled and waited calmly for his captors to do their job. He then adds the disturbing report that the women whom Pentheus had imprisoned in the public jail have all miraculously escaped and joined the other maenads in the mountains.

But Pentheus evidently fails to take in this second piece of news.[7] His gaze has lighted on his prisoner and his fascination has made him deaf. He orders the removal of his bonds and then addresses Dionysus in very revealing terms (453–9):

> Well, stranger boy, you're rather sexy!
> The women you've come to seduce must fancy you
> With that long hair – I can see you're not a wrestler –
> All the way down your cheeks. Extremely sexy!
> Your skin's so white! – a deliberate choice, I suppose.
> You've kept well out of the sun and stayed in the shade,
> Chasing sex with that gorgeous body of yours.[8]

The tone of these lines clearly indicates that Dionysus answers to something deeply embedded in Pentheus' own nature. Dramatically, this is an electrifying moment.

The engagement now begins in a long passage of stichomythia (460–508), in which Pentheus interrogates his prisoner with detailed questions about where he has come from and what his mysterious rites consist in, while Dionysus parries, often with obscure or coolly impertinent replies – we need to remember the mask with the fixed smile. As the dialogue develops, Pentheus' prurient fascination changes to frustration as he threatens to cut off his victim's hair and to put him in prison. As he calls on his servant to bind the god once again, he is told, "You don't know what your life is, what you are doing, or who you are!" (506). Faced almost with an identity crisis, Pentheus furiously orders the prisoner to be locked up in the palace stable and, in an unusual sound effect, the Chorus gets further on his nerves by beating their drums (513) – another powerfully dramatic moment. The stranger is calmly led offstage, with a warning to Pentheus that the god whose existence he denies will punish him for his insulting treatment.

Second Stasimon (519–70)

The ionic meter pervades this ode, as in the first part of the previous one. The mood, however, has passed from tranquil philosophizing to one of rejection, and then of hatred for Pentheus. The Chorus appeals first to the Theban river Dirce, whose streams washed the infant Dionysus after his birth from Zeus's thigh. Thebes has sadly rejected the bacchanals, though it must come eventually to accept Bromios. To boost their confidence, they rehearse the god's various names. <TRACK K7, lines 519–36> ◉ In the antistrophe Pentheus is upbraided for his bestial treatment of the maenads' leader, the god's proclaimer, now a prisoner in oppressive bonds. Finally, in the epode, the god himself is invoked to intervene, in the formulaic manner of naming the various shrines from which he might come.[9] <TRACK K8, lines 556–69> ◉

Third Episode (576–861)

The Chorus' invocation is very excitingly followed by booming offstage cries, purporting to come from Dionysus himself. He is manifesting his divine power in an earthquake which causes the whole palace to shake, the lintels in the colonnade to fall and shatter, and fire to break out on Semele's tomb. Here one can suppose some kind of visible effect in the side building from which smoke was issuing at the start of the play (p. 176). Much, I think, would still have been left to the audience's imagination. More important in this "palace miracle" scene would have been the screams of the maenads and their agitated verse in a mixture of different metrical elements, culminating in their throwing themselves down to the earth in abject terror (600–3). Right at the climax of this frenetic passage, Dionysus re-enters the *skênê*, in his mortal guise as before, and cool as a cucumber.

The following section (604–41) is composed in the rapid-flowing trochaic tetrameters encountered earlier in this book at Aesch. *Agam.* 1649–73 and Soph. *OT* 1515–30. The movement of the verse is perfect for Dionysus' reassurance to his devotees and for his mocking tone as he describes Pentheus' wild behavior in the stable, trying to tie cords round the legs of a bull in the belief that he was binding his prisoner,[10] then charging with a sword at a phantom image until the palace collapsed and he himself was able to walk quietly outside to rejoin his companions. <TRACK K9, lines 616–28> ⊙

At 642 Pentheus re-enters in fury to find his adversary calmly in front of the palace. He shouts for the gate-towers of the city to be barred, but, before the conflict can be taken further, a new character arrives. It is a Herdsman who has arrived to report to Pentheus how the bacchanals on the mountainside have been conducting themselves. A long narrative of almost a hundred lines follows (677–774) – the first of two great speeches in the messenger convention which Euripides exploits to brilliant effect in his demonstration of how bacchic behavior, and by implication the bacchic philosophy he has been enunciating, can extend to a terrifying, mindless violence which confounds the civilized human with the brute animal and creates total havoc.

Figure 12.1 *Bacchae*, Cloisters, New College, Oxford 2013. Source: Reproduced by permission of the Archive of Performances of Greek & Roman Drama.

The Herdsman's story begins with a picture of the Theban bacchanals peacefully sleeping – not, as Pentheus has suggested and the speaker specifically contradicts (686–8), drunk or indulging in covert sexual activity with men. They awake and set about their strange tasks in orderly fashion and harmonious relationship with the natural surroundings. As they begin a ritual dance, they are disturbed by a group of herdsmen and suddenly all hell breaks loose. They set on cattle in the belief that they are attacking their human assailants and tear the animals to pieces, then race down to the villages below, where they ransack everything "up and down" (see p. 179) before returning up the mountain to their starting point. At the finish of an astonishing narrative, the speaker appeals to Pentheus: "Accept this god who gave us the pain-killing vine. Without wine we would have no sex or any other pleasure" (773–4). The bathos here must be deliberate: Euripides is voicing the limited, naive view of the "ordinary person" (430–2), to point up the difference between that and the extremely dangerous force that he has shown Dionysus to represent in the narrative that his audience has just listened to.

At the end of the speech, Pentheus sends off the Herdsman with a message for his whole army to assemble in readiness for an attack on the Theban maenads. The confrontation between him and Dionysus is now resumed, the god urging quiet inaction and the king defying him in anger and frustration. At 809 Pentheus calls for his weapons – and the god responds with a long monosyllabic "Aaah!" before saying, "Do you want to *see* them, sitting there on the mountains?" to receive the reply, "Yes! I'd give a thousand fortunes to do it!" This is the turning point in the drama, whether the "aaah!" is played by an actor with a sinister quietness or (as I prefer) with a sudden animal-like roar. The sound serves to cast a spell on Pentheus, so that from now on he submits to the god, though not completely at this stage.

The switch from angry resistance to avid voyeurism is a strikingly dramatic moment and leads shortly to Dionysus' suggestion that, if Pentheus is to spy on the maenads in their wicked activities, he will need to go dressed up like one of them, in female garb (821). <TRACK K10, lines 800–16> For a few brief moments (822, 828) Pentheus protests at this transvestism,[11] but he is soon seduced by the prospect. At the end of an extraordinary run of stichomythia, in which Pentheus is shown wavering between fascinated consent and horrified revulsion, Dionysus sends him indoors to change, while he himself remains outside for a brief address to the Chorus. In gloating cruelty he announces his intention to drive the young man mad and make him a public laughing-stock before he departs to Hades – slaughtered by his mother. So he will acknowledge Dionysus, "a god most terrible in power, but most gentle in the sight of human beings" (861). In this closing line Euripides has encapsulated his god's ambivalent character as both beguilingly benign and terrifyingly dangerous.

Third Stasimon (862–912)

Dionysus' impending victory inspires a mood of intense excitement in the Asian maenads. In the strophe of this song they envisage dancing throughout the night in rapturous celebration of their freedom, like a fawn escaping a band of huntsmen. Animal images now predominate and aeolic rhythms feature to fine effect as the fawn leaps over the nets and bounds over the plain. This stanza is followed by a refrain (877–81), repeated after the antistrophe, which at last supplies the bacchic definition of "wisdom": "to hold one's hand in triumph over one's foes." Wisdom equals revenge. So that is what Dionysus stands for! <TRACK K11, lines 862–81>

The antistrophe consists of *gnômai*, generalizations, about the punishment of the sinner and the supremacy of the transcendent. The Greek of 895–6 is difficult but draws on the sophistic distinction between *nomos*, law and custom, and *phusis*, nature. The two are normally in conflict: laws and customs are needed to control our natural impulses. The perverse thought here ascribed to the bacchanals seems to be that laws and customs are grounded in natural instinct. The epode consists of further *gnômai* on the uncertainties of human life; happiness can only be measured in day-to-day terms. In this ode, then, Euripides makes his bacchanals express their sense of relief in the coming demise of Pentheus. As the climax of the drama draws nearer, he also adds to what he has suggested in the First Stasimon about the bacchic philosophy of life.

Fourth Episode (912–76)

Re-enter Dionysus from the palace to call Pentheus out with taunting words, in clever buildup to the separate entrance of his former opponent, now bizarrely dressed in full bacchic costume and clearly demented, as predicted towards the end of the preceding episode (850–1). He is now totally in Dionysus' power: he has the double vision of drunkenness and perceives the god as a bull (918–22). A macabre passage follows as Dionysus teasingly adjusts Pentheus' costume and appearance. His victim wants to be sure that his dress is hanging right and that he is holding his thyrsus in the correct hand. He pictures the maenads in the bushes "hugging

Figure 12.2 *Bacchae*, Cloisters, New College, Oxford 2013. Source: Reproduced by permission of the Archive of Performances of Greek & Roman Drama.

and mating like birds in the nets of love," before commanding Dionysus to conduct him through the middle of Thebes. The dialogue climaxes in half-lines, as the god prophesies the wretched man's public return in his mother's arms – perceived by Pentheus as the height of sensual luxury as he sweeps ecstatically offstage to his doom on the mountain (970). Dionysus is given a final gloat (971–6), as he calls on Agave and her sisters to "stretch out their hands," before he makes his own exit and follows.

Fourth Stasimon (977–1023)

The Chorus advance rapidly to carry the momentum forward. In sensationally violent dochmiac meter (often enhanced by the "resolution" of long syllables to two shorts) they call on the "running hounds of Madness to sting the bacchae on the mountains to rage against the frenzied man in woman's garb." The movement anticipates in song and dance what is to be described in the ensuing Messenger speech, that is the wild fury that will destroy Pentheus at the hands of his nearest kin and so reveal the dionysiac at its most extreme. Images of madness and irrationality are conjoined with others of the bestial and monstrous.

The structure of this ode parallels that of the previous one: strophe and antistrophe, each followed by a refrain, and then an epode. The strophe pictures the situation: Pentheus' mother Agave will sight him first and call out to the other bacchanals. The refrain (992–6), which adds jabbing iambics and bacchii to the dochmiacs, calls on Justice to drive her sword through the godless Pentheus' throat. <TRACK K12, lines 977–94> ◉ The antistrophe is more general in denouncing Pentheus' presumption and extolling the maenads' own piety. The climax is reached in the epode, as Dionysus is invoked to manifest himself in his animal forms, a bull, snake or lion, and "with smiling face" (1021) to entrap the hunter in his noose. The power and wild excitement of this poem can be appreciated by anyone who hears it delivered in the original Greek. <TRACK K13, lines 1017–23> ◉

Fifth Episode (1024–152)

In majestic grief for the house, the Messenger announces the death of Pentheus, news which the Chorus (still in dochmiacs) hails with cries of joy. The narrative proper (1043–152) relates how Dionysus miraculously raised Pentheus to watch the bacchanals from the top of a pine tree; a voice from the sky drew their attention to him; they then heaved the tree to the earth, set about tearing Pentheus to pieces and "played ball with his flesh." <TRACK K14, lines 1114–36> ◉ The vividness of the detail in this speech, together with the pulse of the iambic poetry, makes this an incomparable piece of dramatic composition, a gift to an actor, which can only be fully appreciated in performance.

From a structural point of view, we may observe the parallelism with the earlier messenger speech of the Herdsman. The women are again orderly and tranquil to start with, until they are disturbed and suddenly run wild. There is a similar confusion between human and animal: earlier the maenads had attacked cattle in the belief that their victims were men; now they destroy a man whom they think is a beast. Both speeches include the *sparagmos* of dionysiac ritual, and both are rounded off by a conclusion from the speaker which does little justice to the reality of the horror. Together they can be seen as two pillars of the drama which practically exemplify the dangers inherent in what Euripides sees as "Dionysus:" untrammeled emotionalism, following the crowd, rejection of critical faculties and so on. The two narratives illustrate how these things can lead to behavior which reduces human beings to the status of mere animals. The drama's climax and main conclusion have now been reached, though there is more to come by way of "pity and fear."

Fifth Stasimon (1153–64) and Entrance of Agave (1165–7)

In a brief astrophic song (mainly dochmiac and iambic) the Chorus express their triumph. The outcome of the victory may be tears and lamentation (1162), but "noble the fight which makes a mother steep her hands red in her own child's blood." They might show a touch of awareness in the reference to tears, but to hail Agave's achievement as a "fine contest" is chilling. The line (1163) naturally cues in the entrance of Agave herself with distorted eyes and bearing Pentheus' head, which she thinks has belonged to a mountain lion.

Exodus (1168–392), Including *Amoibaion* (1168–99)

This is the moment for Euripides to introduce a lyric movement for soloist and chorus – not a lament, however, but more a song of triumph in which Agave proclaims her horrifying achievement. A grisly exchange is formalized in strophic structure, with metrical units (mainly dochmiac and iambic, as in the two previous choral movements) broken up in the agitated antiphon. <TRACK K15, lines 1168–84> ◉ When Agave invites the women to "share her feast" (1184), the Chorus welcomes her, but there could be a touch of horrified compassion in the reaction, "What should I share, *poor woman*?" (1184, later echoed at 1200). The poet seems here to be using his otherwise vindictive Chorus to guide the audience's sympathy towards Agave in the ensuing scene.

The horror continues when, at 1200, the Coryphaeus invites Agave to display her hunting prize to her fellow citizens. Perhaps the actor here faces the audience proudly with Pentheus' head (in the form of a mask?), as she boasts of her (and her sisters') prowess. Her ironic call for her son Pentheus to nail the head to the palace frontage leads at 1216 to the entry of Cadmus with some attendants, presumably carrying the retrieved remains of Pentheus' body on a bier. Agave is still crazed enough to congratulate her father on his peerless daughters and ask him to receive her "prize of valor" into his hands (1239–40).

Stichomythia is now used to extraordinary effect as Cadmus brings Agave slowly back to her senses, until the appalling moment (1284) when she realizes that she is holding her own son's head in her arms. The sequence appears to follow modern psychotherapeutic practice[12] and is extremely compelling. Agave has now forgotten what she did in her frenzied condition and Cadmus has to explain how that was caused by the women's initial rejection of Dionysus.

At 1300 the subject turns to the orderly reassembling of Pentheus' limbs; but here there is an unfortunate gap in the transmitted text and some kind of conjectural restoration is required.[13] Perhaps Agave lays Pentheus' head with the rest of his body on the bier with some appropriate lines of lamentation. If so, ritual could here be employed to restore a kind of order out of the havoc that has been wreaked. What does survive is a beautiful speech of mourning for Cadmus (1302–26) which creates sympathy not only for him but also for Pentheus who, he says, was revered in his city and touchingly protective of his aged grandfather. Horror is yielding to pathos in the emotional sequence as the drama moves towards its conclusion.

Another major lacuna occurs in our text, which only restarts at what appears to be the tail end of a rhesis by Dionysus in which he must have explained what is going to happen to the various characters (much as Castor does in Euripides' *Electra*). Dionysus therefore must have made an epiphany, on some appropriate cue, as a *deus ex machina*, presumably in divine form with a fresh costume and mask. He might have begun his speech by reasserting his divinity, before going on to proclaim the expulsion of the polluted Agave and her sisters from Thebes, as implied by 1366. The text resumes with the weird prophecy that Cadmus and Harmonia will be transformed into snakes, go into exile and lead a barbarian horde to attack various Greek cities, though they will eventually land up on the Isles of the Blessed![14] The drama recovers at 1348 when Cadmus complains to Dionysus that "gods should not be like mortals when they are angry," to receive the dusty answer that it was all the will of Zeus. We may assume that the god disappears from view after 1351, leaving Agave and Cadmus to end the play.

Both characters can only deplore what is yet to come. The final section (1368–92), as in *Electra*, is in anapaests, as father and daughter bid each other a fond farewell. Agave never wants to see Cithaeron or a thyrsus again; they can be left to *other* Bacchae (1385–7). We can imagine them sadly making their exits in different directions.

The final lines assigned to the Chorus (1388–92) to see them off are the same, or almost the same, as in four other Euripides plays. They may be spurious but the theme, that the gods can show their power in unexpected ways, is not inapposite. Dionysus, the engagingly benign god of wine and revelry, can prove surprisingly devastating in his operation.

Conclusion

Euripides in retirement from Athens in Macedonia seems to have taken a detached view of Dionysus, the god of the Attic theatre. *Bacchae* is arguably the finest of all his extant tragedies. He uses his interpretation of the god to explore the phenomena of crowd behavior and human irrationality in a work that is universally relevant and abidingly forceful as drama. Much of the play's strength derives from the deployment of the tragic medium in its classic form, with primary dependence on the Chorus, the Messenger convention and the conflict of two solo antagonists. The thrust, progression and conclusion of the drama, with its emphasis on "revelation" and the gradual ascendancy of the brutal over the human in the imagery strongly support an overall interpretation which raises challenging questions about Dionysus as a force in life.

Notes

1   This fits the references at 565–70 to the region of Pieria and the river Axios. It may also be suggested by the special feeling for nature which characterizes the play and could have been inspired by the mountains and forests of the region.

2   See Hall, Macintosh and Wrigley (2004).

3   Eur. *Supplices* 412–14 can be quoted in this connection. Similarly, Thucydides 6.24.3 and 8.1.4.

4   The ancient equivalent of the modern "dry ice" cliché?

5 See Dodds (1944, notes on lines 59 and 124). The instruments are certainly deployed later at 513, though they can hardly be in the choreuts' hands throughout the play.

6 If this is a correct translation of the transmitted text, the sting in the speech's tail resonates interestingly with the association of drugs with the modern dionysiac activity of the pop festival.

7 At 499 he speaks of Dionysus in prison, "made to stand among the bacchanals" – but they are no longer there! For a similar effect in Eur. *Electra 669*, see p. 164.

8 This rather free translation comes from my own (unpublished) acting version.

9 The place names include Pieria and the River Axios in Macedonia, where Euripides almost certainly composed *Bacchae* – a compliment, doubtless, to his royal host. Lines 571–5, however, which refer to the River Ludias, strike me as an unhappy addition after the vibrant ending at 570, which provides an excellent cue, musically speaking, to Dionysus' offstage cries at 576. The lines are in an alien meter to the rest of the ode and import words which Euripides had used in *Hecuba* 451 ff. to describe the River Apidanos in Thessaly. I strongly suspect their authenticity here.

10 Winnington-Ingram (1948) sees this as symbolic of Pentheus trying to constrain the animal Dionysus in himself.

11 This was apparently a feature of male worshippers in Dionysiac ritual (Seaford 1996, 222).

12 See Dodds (1960, 230): "Agave is like a subject coming out of deep hypnosis" and Seaford (1996, 247–9).

13 Scholars have made some use of lines from the *Christus Patiens*, a medieval text from the eleventh or twelfth century. This is a play evidently based on *Bacchae*, in which Christ's passion is, astonishingly to us, assimilated to the 'persecution' of Dionysus. Seaford (1996, 144–5), usefully prints the verses that may be relevant.

14 On this strange passage, Winnington-Ingram (1948, 145) comments: "It is a rigmarole of odd mythology," which could perhaps involve "a faint ridicule of the mythology itself" in the incongruity between the quaint details and the "human, prosaic" characterization of Cadmus in the play.

References

Text: *Euripides Bacchae* (Loeb edition, Vol. 6). 2002. Cambridge, MA: Harvard University Press, edited and translated by David Kovacs.

Dodds, E.R. 1960. *Euripides Bacchae*, 2nd edn, Oxford: Oxford Clarendon Press.

Hall, E., Macintosh, F. and Wrigley A. (eds). 2004. *Dionysus since '69*. Oxford: Oxford University Press.

Seaford, R. 1996. *Euripides Bacchae*. Warminster: Aris & Phillips.

Winnington-Ingram, R.P. 1948. *Euripides and Dionysus*. Cambridge: Cambridge University Press. Republished 2012 with a Foreword by P.E. Easterling. Bristol: Bristol Classical Press.

Commentaries

Dodds, E.R. 1960. *Euripides Bacchae*, 2nd edn. Oxford: Oxford Clarendon Press.

Seaford, R. 1996. *Euripides Bacchae*. Warminster: Aris & Phillips.

Further Reading

Mills, S. 2006. *Euripides and Bacchae*. London: Duckworth. A useful general guide to the play, its criticism and reception.

Winnington-Ingram, R.P. 1948. *Euripides and Dionysus*. Cambridge: Cambridge University Press. An exemplary monograph on a single Greek tragedy.

Appendix A

Glossary of Greek Tragic Terms

The Performance Area

eisodos	one of two entrance passages between the stage-building and the audience
ekkyklêma	a low trolley wheeled out of the doors of the stage building to reveal corpses, etc.
mêchanê	a crane device for hoisting a god (the *deus ex machina*) onto the stage building roof
orchêstra	("dancing floor") the acting area mostly surrounded by the audience
proskênion	the platform in front of the skênê
skênê	the stage building with an entrance of double doors
theatron	the tiered area in which the spectators sat

The Performers

aulete	the musician who played the aulos, a double-reed pipe
choros	the group of 12 or 15 performers (choreutae) who formed the tragic chorus
coryphaeus	the Chorus leader
hypocritês	one of three solo actors
protagonist	the first or leading actor

Organization

chorêgos	the wealthy citizen who sponsored and organized the four plays catered by one poet at the City Dionysia

Dramatic Structure

Basic Features

epeisodion	a scene for solo actors between choral songs
exodos	the closing scene
parodos	the choral entrance song

Greek Tragedies as Plays for Performance, First Edition. David Raeburn.
© 2017 John Wiley & Sons, Inc. Published 2017 by John Wiley & Sons, Inc.
Companion website: www.wiley.com/go/raeburn

prologos   the opening scene for one or more solo actors
stasimon   a choral song

Incidental Features

agon   an adversarial exchange of long speeches between actors
amoibaion   a sung exchange between chorus and solo actor(s)
antilabe   the division of single iambic lines between actors at a climax
ephymnion   a passage inserted in a strophic structure, possibly repeated
epirrhema   a sung and spoken exchange between actors and chorus
kommos   an amoibaion consisting essentially of a lament
monody   a sung solo for a single actor
rhesis   a formal long speech
stichomythia   dialogue between solo actors in single lines or pairs of lines

The Language of Poetics

anagnorisis   a recognition scene, usually between characters
catharsis   "cleansing" or "purgation," Aristotle's term for the emotional effect of tragedy
ethos   character
hamartia   an error, intellectual or moral (not a flaw of character)
muthos   plot, story
peripateia   reversal of fortune or expectation
tragoidia   (lit. 'goat-song') tragedy as a presentational art form

Appendix B

Rhythm and Meter

Where English verse is based on word-stress and composed of "heavy" and "light" syllables, Greek poetry is quantitative, based on various patterns of "long' (—) and "short" (u) syllables, the long being equivalent in time to two shorts. The basic rhythm or "pulse' of a single metrical unit or "line" will normally be defined by long syllables.

Lines can be analyzed in terms of "feet" corresponding in principle to a dance "step." The most common of these are:

u —	Iambus
— u	Trochee
— —	Spondee
— u u	Dactyl
uu —	Anapaest
— u —	Cretic
u — —	Bacchius
---uu---	Choriambus
uu -- --	Ionic

In some meters, a long syllable may be broken up or resolved into two shorts, conversely, the short syllables in a dactyl or an anapaest can be replaced by a long, to produce a spondee.

The term "metron" is also used in relation to iambi, trochees, anapaests and ionics to denote a *pair* of feet, to reflect the left–right movement of the dance or march.

Chapter 1 distinguished between three kinds of delivery or "modes of utterance" in tragedy:

1) declamation without music
2) declamation with musical accompaniment
3) singing with musical accompaniment.

The following offers a very basic account of the meters used in each. Students who wish to explore the subject in greater depth are refereed to D.S. Raven (1962), *Greek Metre.* For the rhythmic pulse of the different patterns the reader should listen to the oral presentation in TRACK 0 ◉.

Greek Tragedies as Plays for Performance, First Edition. David Raeburn.
© 2017 John Wiley & Sons, Inc. Published 2017 by John Wiley & Sons, Inc.
Companion website: www.wiley.com/go/raeburn

Iambic Trimeter

This was the normal medium for the *spoken* parts of the genre. It consisted of three metra in the form x — u — (x indicates that the syllable can be either long or short). The line normally has a "caesura" (a break between words) after the first or third syllable of the second metron, thus dividing a line into two phrases of unequal length (5 + 7 syllables or 7 + 5), as in:

x — u — | x ll — u — | x — u —

or

x — u — | x — u ll — | x — u —

This pattern of verse composition lends itself well to a flexible delivery, with syntactical unity often crossing line-boundaries in "enjambment."

Trochaic Tetrameter Catalectic

A much less common spoken line, constructed of four trochaic metra in the form — u — x , with a break between words after the second metron and the removal of the final syllable of the line (*catalexis*):

— u — x | — u — x | — u — x | — u —

This rhythm here calls for a more strongly defined delivery than the iambic trimeter.

Anapaests

This meter usually serves as a "halfway house" between the spoken iambic trimeter and the sung lyric meters. It commonly takes the form of a dimeter (= two metra):

u u — u u — | u u — u u —

with a cadence, after a run of lines, in the catalectic form

u u — u u — | u u — — ∧

(accents indicate the first syllable of the footfall or "beat")
  u u — u u — is sometimes replaced by — u u — —, which produces an interesting variation that runs counter to the main beat, as in

u u — u u — | — u u — —

Anapaests may also form part of lyric structures, in which case the words will contain some forms of Doric Greek. These are known as "melic" anapaests.

Lyric Meters

The primary unit of composition in the sung movements of tragedy was the stanza or *strophe* (literally "turn"), probably referring to a notional choreographic sequence in which the chorus moved round the altar in the *orchêstra*. A strophe consists of a succession of sub-units, printed in single lines in our texts, which may be "metra" or else "cola," limbs. A "colon" is a longer unit than a single metron and one drawn from a stock of metrical phrases, the most important of which are listed below. A strophe is normally balanced by a metrically corresponding antistrophe and the "strophic pair" thus formed can be complemented into a triad by an epode, a free-standing third stanza, usually but not necessarily in a similar meter.

The analysis of a stanza into its constituent sub-units (colometry) is a matter of scholarly interpretation, as line divisions were not shown in the earliest Greek texts. Where alternative colometries are possible, a decision needs to be taken on the basis of a subjective judgment as to which rhythmical pattern is the more musical in its dramatic context. Account here may need to be taken of single beat "rests," when the voice is silent, at the end of a colon. This frequently occurs at a cadence and also in the middle of a strophe where it must be posited if a regular rhythm is to be maintained in the sequence of cola.

In general, it may be observed that lyric meters in which long syllables are separated by *one* short syllable (iambic and trochaic) tend to be strong and steady in their movement. Meters that involve the separation of long syllables by *two* shorts (dactylic, anapaestic, ionic) tend towards greater fluidity and often a faster tempo.

Lyric Iambics

These are based on the metron u — u — and are often varied by "syncopation," which involves the suppression of a short syllable and its absorption in the preceding or following long syllable, as in the "syncopated iambic trimeter," for example:

u —.— | . — u — | u —.—

which features prominently in the *Oresteia*.

Lyric Trochees

Based on — u — u these are often formed into dimeters in a catalectic form known as the *lecythion*:

— u — u | — u —

Lyric Dactyls

Phrases may include up to 7 dactyls, with — uu sometimes replaced by — —. The dactylic hexameter (6 dactyls or spondees) is the meter for epic poetry, so that dactylic units in tragedy sometimes have a grand Homeric ring.

Dactylo-Epitrite

This meter combines dactylic (— u u) units with "epitrites," which are trochiaic in the form — u — —, as in, for example:

— u u — u u — — | — u — —

It features commonly in the victory odes (*epinicia*) of the lyric poet Pindar and may communicate triumphant associations in a tragic context.

Aeolic (or Aeolo-Choriambic)

These terms categorize a wide variety of phrases normally ranging from 5 to 12 syllables, but expandable further. All include at least one choriambus (— u u —). Many were given special labels by ancient metricians, notably:

$$— \text{x} \mid — \text{u u} — \mid \text{u} — \textit{Glyconic}$$

and its catalectic form

$$— \text{x} \mid — \text{u u} — \mid — {}_{\wedge} \textit{Pherecratean}$$

In these phrases (as in dactylo-epitrites), long syllables may be separated by either one or two short syllables. It is a point of scholarly debate whether rhythm was strictly maintained, so that — u could last as long as — u u, or more flexible, treating *all* long and short syllables as *equally* long or short. The recorded illustrations which form part of this publication are based on the former assumption, chiefly on the grounds that a constant variation in the underlying pulse would make for a distracting awkwardness in choreographed movement.

Ionics (Sometimes Called ionics a Minore)

This meter is in 3/4 time, normally in the form of a dimeter:

$$\text{u u} — — \mid \text{u u} — —$$

It may be varied in a so-called "anaclastic" form, in which the middle two syllables are interchanged to produce:

$$\text{u u} — \text{u} — \text{u} — —, \text{ known as } \textit{anacreontic.}$$

These patterns are often associated with eastern or other exotic contexts and feature particularly in Aeschylus' *Persae* and Euripides' *Bacchae*.

Dochmiacs

In these, by contrast with the other cola, we do have an irregular rhythm in the form u — — u —, delivered in the recordings with the main pulse falling on the third syllable and a lesser one on the fifth, viz.:

$$\text{u} — — \text{u} — \mid \text{u} — — \text{u} —$$

This interpretation reflects the meaning of the Greek word *dochmios*, slanting. The tragedians used this meter to very special effect in moments of agitation or pathos, where the irregularity is appropriate and eloquent.

Index

actor, 2, 3, 5, 83, 138
  acting style, 6
  2nd actor, 15–16
  3rd actor, 16, 35, 37, 50, 64, 82, 159
  mutes, 50, 65, 77n.16
  protagonist, 37
Aeschylus
  characterization, 18–19, 35, 55
  contribution to genre, 15–16
  design, musical, 23
  epic, debt to, 17
  life, 15
  plays, 15
    Prometheus Bound, 13, 15, 93–4, 102n.11
    Seven against Thebes, 105
  politics, 16
  spectacle, 20
  structure, 17
  style, 19–20
  tasks, different, 23
  technique, dramatic, 17–18
  thought, 16
agon, contest, debate, 85, 139, 140, 149, 166
aidos, sense of shame, 127
altar, 58, 68
amathia, insensitivity, 145, 150, 155
ambivalence, verbal, 24, 41, 46, 76n.3 *see also*
    irony; word power
amoibaion, exchange, 7, 112–13, 127, 132,
    161, 185
anagnorisis see recognition scenes
anapaests, 7, 17, 146, 147, 153, 170
antilabê, half-line exchanges, 85, 112, 116,
    132, 164, 184

Aphrodite, 138, 149, 150, 174, 179 *see also*
    Eros
Apollo
  in Aeschylus, 34, 50, 57, 68
  in Sophocles, 118, 125
  in Euripides, 138, 166, 168–70
Archelaus, 137, 173, 182n.9
Archilochus, 7
Areopagus, 34, 73
Argos, 34, 73
Aristophanes, 7, 11, 19, 81, 137, 138, 163
Aristotle, 7, 12, 86n.4, 105, 106, 139
  catharsis, 10
atê, infatuation, madness, ruin, 18, 24, 29,
    43, 46, 48, 54, 67, 97
Athena, 34, 68
Athens, 34, 73, 151, 175, 186n.3
  empire, 83, 88
audience, 4–5
  addresses to, 108, 110, 139, 178
  involvement, 39, 58, 73, 148, 160
  sympathy, 145, 155, 170, 185
aulete, 8
aulos, pipe, 7, 8

bacchanals
  cult, 173
  philosophy, 175, 179, 182–3
burial rites, 88, 90

causation, 16, 29, 34–5, 36, 83, 97, 106
characterization, 6 *see also* Aeschylus;
    Sophocles; Euripides
characters, minor, 145, 158

Greek Tragedies as Plays for Performance, First Edition. David Raeburn.
© 2017 John Wiley & Sons, Inc. Published 2017 by John Wiley & Sons, Inc.
Companion website: www.wiley.com/go/raeburn

children, 145, 150, 151, 153
choral performance, 2
choregia, 4
choreography, 9, 71, 82
chorus, 5, 83
    in Aeschylus, 16, 37, 39, 41, 57–8, 68
    in Sophocles, 83, 89, 110, 114–15, 126
    in Euripides, 139, 145, 159, 175, 176
    leader, 5
    number, 5, 82
    origin, 2
    reference, forward and back, 83, 97, 150
    role as voice of poet, 96–7, 114, 165
Christus Patiens, 187n.13
Cimon, 34
City Dionysia, 3, 82, 173
comedy, 3, 10
costumes, 5–6
    in Aeschylus, 21, 24, 27, 69, 72, 74, 75,
        77n.17
    in Sophocles, 100, 109, 127
    in Euripides, 139, 160, 176, 177, 183, 186
    rags, 26, 30, 160

dance *see* choreography
Delphic mottos, 82–3, 107, 125–6
determination, multiple *see* causation
deus ex machina, 139, 154, 168–9, 186
dikê, justice, 33, 50, 67 *see also* justice; law
Dionysus, 38, 173–5, 182
    animal forms, 184
dithyramb, 2, 3, 173
dochmiacs, 154, 164, 167–8, 184
dreams, 25, 61, 115, 128
drum, 11

effects, special, 176, 181
eisodos, 4
ekkyklema, 4
    in Aeschylus, 37, 53, 65, 69
    in Sophocles, 89, 101, 133
    in Euripides, 154, 168
Eleusis, mysteries, 15, 38, 75
epeisodion, 3, 12, 53
Ephialtes, 34
epinikion, 2

epirrhema, 7, 26, 53
Erinyes *see* Furies
Eros, 98, 151 *see also* Aphrodite
ethics, 83, 90, 128, 131
euphemia, 18, 24, 38, 41, 45, 51, 75 *see also*
        omens; word power
Euripides
    characterization, 139–40, 144, 158
    contribution to genre, 137–8
    discontinuity of tone, 139, 157, 162–3, 164
    life, 137
    myth, approach to, 138, 158, 165
    plays, 137
        Rhesus, 13n.I, 140n.1
    politics, 145
    style, 140
    technique, dramatic, 139
    thought, 139
eusebeia, piety, religious duty, 88, 99,
        127, 179
exodos, 12

falsified expectation, 100, 116, 139,
        171n.13
family curse *see* guilt, inherited
fate *see* Moira, destiny
flaw, tragic, 86n.4
Freud, S., 105, 120n.9
Furies
    in Aeschylus, 34, 51, 57, 66, 68, 69, 72
    in Sophocles, 100, 125, 134n.5
    in Euripides, 169, 170

gender *see also* women
    in Aeschylus, 35, 38, 42, 56
    in Euripides, 143, 144, 145, 148, 150
gnomai, moral maxims, 11, 21, 28, 39, 93, 114,
        154, 183
gods, 11 *see also* Aphrodite; Apollo; Athena;
        Dionysus; Furies; Zeus
    in Aeschylus, 16, 24, 34, 68, 76
    in Sophocles, 82, 94, 107, 114
    in Euripides, 139, 145, 154
    intervention of, 26, 93, 94
guilt, inherited, 35, 36, 47, 90, 99, 105, 129,
        135n.12

Herodotus, 31, 102n.13
Homer, 2, 6, 10, 17, 23, 36, 55, 124, 163
hubris
    in Aeschylus, 19, 22, 29, 36, 46
    in Sophocles, 95, 106, 108, 114
    in Euripides, 179
humor
    in Aeschylus, 63
    in Sophocles, 93, 102n.8
    in Euripides, 139, 157, 160, 162, 164,
        165, 178

iambic trimeter, 7, 140
imagery, 19, 62, 97, 146, 175, 182
infanticide, 145
interpolation, suspected, 102n.13, 156n.15,
        171n.15, 187n.9
intertextuality
    in Sophocles, 128, 130, 131–2, 133–4
    in Euripides, 157, 163, 164, 166, 167,
        171n.12, 171n.19
irony
    in Sophocles, 84, ch.8 passim, 130, 134
    in Euripides, 156n.14, 162, 163

justice, 16, 34, 50, 56, 62–3, 67, 76 *see also dikê*,
        justice; law
    poetic, 30, 101
    retributive, *lex talionis*, 36, 40, 73,
        125, 129

kommos, lament, 7, 30, 51, 60–1, 98, 101,
        117–18, 130, 168
    stylization of grief, 118, 130

lament *see kommos*, lament
law
    divine, 83, 94, 131
    human, 94
    versus nature, 183
    unwritten, 88, 94
lyric structure, 7

Macedonia, 137, 173, 187n.9
masks, 3, 6, 118, 175, 176, 180, 186
matricide, 33, 123, 124, 157, 160, 168

mêchanê, 4, 72, 154, 169
messenger narratives
    in Aeschylus, 26, 43
    in Sophocles, 101, 117–18, 129
    in Euripides, 139, 153, 165, 175, 181–2,
        184–5
metatheater, 120n.8
meter, 6–7 *see also* rhythm
mirror scenes, 65, 101, 150, 170
modes of utterance, 6–7
Moira, destiny, 34, 54, 76
monody, 127, 139, 160–1
monologue, 37, 69, 139, 146, 152–3, 159,
        176–7, 178
music, 7–8, 139, 145, 147
    instruments, 8, 177, 180, 187n.5

omens, 25, 39, 61, 100 *see also* word
        power
    names as, 45–6, 179
oracles, 29, 39, 82, 84, 105, 110, 114, 138
orchêstra, 4, 58, 73
Orestes myth, 34, 123, 157

Panathenaea, 75
Parthenon, 88
pathei mathos, learning from suffering, 36, 40,
        41, 75, 75n.2
pause, 116, 148, 162
peitho, persuasion, 16, 19, 43, 74
Peloponnesian War, 3, 81, 105, 120n.4, 138,
        143, 174
Pericles, 21, 81, 83, 88, 102n.7, 105
Persian Wars, 21–2, 81, 88
philia, friendship, kinship, 90, 95
Phrynichus, 21, 31n.1
piety *see eusebeia*, piety, religious duty
Pindar, 2, 27, 143, 149, 165
Pisistratus, 3
Plato, 10, 94
plots, 10, 23, 36
polis, city-state, 11, 14n.15, 73, 94
pollution, 65, 66, 98, 117, 118, 168
progress, 93–4 *see also pathei mathos*, learning
        from suffering
prologos, 12, 84, 90, 139

properties, 5
  in Aeschylus, 48, 60, 65, 68, 77n.11, 77n.13
  in Sophocles, 131–2
  in Euripides, 152, 159, 163, 168, 171n.7
Protagoras, 94
psychology, 106, 139, 158 *see also* Freud

reactions, implied, 149
recognition scenes, 60, 116, 131–2,
      163–4, 170
religion *see* gods
retaliation *see* justice
rhapsodes, 2
rhesis, 7
  in Sophocles, 85, 92, 98, 100, 110–11
  in Euripides, 140, 145, 148, 159, 161, 162,
      166, 176
rhetoric, 85, 140, 143, 148, 159, 176
rhythm, 6–7, 23, 94, 97
  rhythmic *leitmotif*, 35, 40, 43, 46, 54, 59, 75
ritual
  actions, 27, 28, 59, 71, 168
  gestures, 26, 59, 61, 160
  lamentation, 26, 27
  perverted, 59, 165, 167
  purpose in Aeschylean tragedy, 18, 22

satire, 178
satyr play, 3, 33, 81
self-knowledge, 82, 107, 127, 134
Semnai Theai, 67, 74, 75
sequence and continuity, 17, 83, 139, 147–8
silences, 50, 101
skênê, 4, 16, 23, 35, 36–7, 38, 58, 68, 102n2,
      159, 176
  platform, 4, 13n.6, 16
  scene painting, 82
  side doors, 64, 70, 77n.9
slaves, 146–7
Solon, 7, 22
Sophia see wisdom
sophistry, 178
Sophists, 82, 85, 88, 138, 159
Sophocles
  characterization, 84–5, 89, 90, 108, 125–6
  contribution to genre, 82–3
  life, 8

plays, 81
  Oedipus Coloneus, 86n.2, 120n.10
  Trachiniae, 86n.3
  politics, 88
  style, 85–6
  technique, dramatic, 83–4
  thought, 82–3
sound of Greek, 85
  tonic accent, 8, 13–14n.12, 85, 86n.6
spectacle
  in Aeschylus, 20, 47, 48, 65, 74, 75
  in Sophocles, 91, 108, 109, 125–6
  in Euripides, 139
Sphinx, 105, 106, 120n.2
staging problems, 24–5, 28, 56, 64, 70, 73,
      76n.7, 77n.14, 77n.20
stasimon, 12
Stesichorus, 36, 171n.18
stichomythia, 7
  in Aeschylus, 17, 48, 85
  in Sophocles, 85, 109
  in Euripides, 139, 146, 155, 159, 161, 164,
      166, 176, 183
structure, 12, 17, 89, 145
suffering, 10
  learning from (*see pathei mathos*, learning
      from suffering)
supplication, 108, 148, 150
suspense
  in Aeschylus, 37, 50, 60
  in Sophocles, 89, 107, 116, 125, 131
  in Euripides, 145, 152, 153, 167

theatrical space, 14, 16
  spatial focus, 58, 62, 68
theatron, spectators' seating, 4
Themistocles, 22, 26
Thespis, 3
Thucydides, 102n.7, 186n.3
thumos, rage, 154
tragedy, Greek, 1
  hybrid form, 1–3
  origins, 2
  tragoidia, 10
transvestitism, 182, 187n.11
trilogic form, 15, 17, 33
trochaic tetrameter, 25, 52, 56, 119

unity of place, 71, 73
unity of time, 43, 76n.5, 83–4

Wagner, R., 35
wagon entrances, 25, 47, 166
wisdom, 128, 151, 175, 179, 182
women, 89, 139, 149, 153 *see also* gender
    attendance in theatre, 4–5
    sex life, 148, 149, 154

word power *see also* ambivalence,
    verbal; irony; omens; oracles;
    rhetoric
  in Aeschylus, 17–18, 24, 30,
    ch.4 passim
  in Sophocles, 84, 111
  in Euripides, 140, 166

Zeus, 27, 34, 40, 76, 95, 97, 139